THE JUDGEMENT OF NUREMBERG, 1946

uncovered editions

Titles in the series

uncovered editions

THE JUDGEMENT
OF NUREMBERG, 1946

London: The Stationery Office

First published 1946 Cmd. 6964
© Crown Copyright

This abridged edition
© The Stationery Office 1999
Reprinted with permission.

ISBN 0 11 702406 6

A CIP catalogue record for this book is available from the
British Library.

Printed in the UK by Biddles Limited, Guildford, Surrey
J93473   C50   11/99

Uncovered Editions are historic official papers which have not previously been available in a popular form. The series has been created directly from the archive of The Stationery Office in London, and the books have been chosen for the quality of their story telling. Some subjects are familiar, but others are less well known. Each is a moment of history.

So atrocious were the discoveries of the armies that entered Germany at the end of World War II that the governments of the major powers conducted the largest war crimes trial ever undertaken. The tribunal sought to bring to justice all those who had knowingly and actively participated in such appalling crimes.

Europe 1920: Borders as established by the Treaty of Versailles

On the 8th August, 1945, the Government of the United Kingdom of Great Britain and Northern Ireland, the Government of the United States of America, the Provisional Government of the French Republic, and the Government of the Union of Soviet Socialist Republics entered into an Agreement establishing this Tribunal for the trial of War Criminals whose offences have no particular geographical location. The following Governments of the United Nations have expressed their adherence to the Agreement:

Greece, Denmark, Yugoslavia, the Netherlands,

Czechoslovakia, Poland, Belgium, Ethiopia, Australia, Honduras, Norway, Panama, Luxemburg, Haiti, New Zealand, India, Venezuela, Uruguay, and Paraguay.

This Tribunal was invested with power to try and punish persons who had committed crimes against peace, war crimes and crimes against humanity.

The Tribunal., also, may declare that the group or organisation of which the individual was a member was a criminal organisation.

In Berlin, on the 18th October, 1945, an Indictment was lodged against the defendants named, who had been designated by the Committee of the Chief Prosecutors of the signatory Powers as major war criminals.

A copy of the Indictment in the German language was served upon each defendant in custody at least thirty days before the Trial opened.

This Indictment charges the defendants with crimes against peace by the planning, preparation, initiation and waging of wars of aggression, which were also wars in violation of international treaties, agreements and assurances: with war crimes: and with crimes against humanity. The defendants are also charged with participating in the formulation or execution of a common plan or conspiracy to commit all these crimes. The Tribunal was further asked by the Prosecution to declare all the named groups or organisations to be criminal.

The defendant Robert Ley committed suicide in prison on the 25th October, 1945. On the 15th November, 1945, the Tribunal decided that the defendant Gustav Krupp von Bohlen und Halbach could not then be tried because of his physical and mental condition, but that the charges against him in the Indictment should be retained for trial thereafter, if the physical and mental condition of the defendant should permit. On the 17th November, 1945, the Tribunal decided to try the defendant Bormann in his absence. After argument, and consideration of full medical reports, and a statement from the defendant himself, the Tribunal decided on the 1st December, 1945, that no grounds existed for a postponement of the trial against the defendant Hess because of his mental condition. A similar decision was made in the case of the defendant Streicher.

Counsel were either chosen by the defendants in custody themselves, or at their request were appointed by the Tribunal. In his absence the Tribunal appointed Counsel for the defendant Bormann, and also assigned Counsel to represent the named groups or organisations.

The Trial which was conducted in four languages—English, Russian, French and German—began on the 20th November, 1945, and pleas of "Not Guilty" were made by all the defendants except Bormann.

The hearing of evidence and the speeches of Counsel concluded on 31st August, 1946.

Four hundred and three open sessions of the Tribunal have been held. Thirty-three witnesses gave evidence orally for the Prosecution against the individual defendants, and 61 witnesses, in addition to 19 of the defendants, gave evidence for the Defence.

A further 143 witnesses gave evidence for the Defence by means of written answers to interrogatories.

The Tribunal appointed Commissioners to hear evidence relating to the organisations, and 101 witnesses were heard for the Defence before the Commissioners, and 1,809 affidavits from other witnesses were submitted. Six reports were also submitted, summarising the contents of a great number of further affidavits.

Thirty-eight thousand affidavits, signed by 155,000 people, were submitted on behalf of the Political Leaders, 136,213 on behalf of the SS, 10,000 on behalf of the SA, 7,000 on behalf of the SD, 3,000 on behalf of the General Staff and OKW, and 2,000 on behalf of the Gestapo.

The Tribunal itself heard 22 witnesses for the organisations. The documents tendered in evidence for the prosecution of the individual defendants and the organisations numbered several thousands. A complete stenographic record of everything said in court has been made, as well as an electrical recording of all the proceedings.

Copies of all the documents put in evidence by the Prosecution have been supplied to the Defence in the German language. The applications made by the defendants for the production of witnesses and documents raised serious problems in some instances, on account of the unsettled state of the country. It was also necessary to limit the number of witnesses to be called, in order to have an expeditious hearing. The Tribunal, after examination, granted all those applications which in their opinion were relevant to the defence of any defendant or named group or organisation, and were not cumulative. Facilities were provided for obtaining those witnesses and documents granted through the office of the General Secretary established by the Tribunal.

Much of the evidence presented to the Tribunal on behalf of the Prosecution was documentary evidence, captured by the Allied armies in German army headquarters, Government buildings, and elsewhere. Some of the documents were found in salt mines, buried in the ground, hidden behind false walls and in other places thought to be secure from discovery. The case, therefore, against the defendants rests in a large measure on documents of their own making, the authenticity of which has not been challenged except in one or two cases.

The individual defendants are indicted under Article 6 of the Charter, which is as follows:

"Article 6. The Tribunal established for the trial and punishment of the major war criminals of the European Axis countries shall have the power to try and punish persons who, acting in the interests of the European Axis countries, whether as individuals or as members of organisations, committed any of the following crimes:

"The following acts, or any of them, are crimes, coming within the jurisdiction of the Tribunal for which there shall be individual responsibility:

"(*a*) Crimes against Peace: namely, planning, preparation, initiation or waging of a war of aggression, or a war in violation of international treaties, agreements or assurances, or participation in a common plan or conspiracy for the accomplishment of any of the foregoing:

"(*b*) War Crimes: namely, violations of the laws or customs of war. Such violations shall include, but not be limited to, murder, ill-treatment or deportation to slave labour or for any other purpose of civilian population of or in occupied territory, murder or ill-treatment of prisoners of war or persons on the seas, killing of hostages, plunder of public or private property, wanton destruction of cities, towns or villages, or devastation not justified by military necessity:

"(*c*) Crimes against Humanity: namely, murder, extermination, enslavement, deportation, and other inhumane acts committed against any civilian population, before or during the war, or persecutions on political, racial or religious grounds in execution of or in connection with any crime within the jurisdiction of the Tribunal, whether or not in violation of the domestic law of the country where perpetrated.

"Leaders, organisers, instigators and accomplices participating in the formulation or execution of a common plan or conspiracy to commit any of the foregoing crimes are responsible for all acts performed by any persons in execution of such plan."

∞◆◆◆∞

For the purpose of showing the background of the aggressive war and war crimes charged in the Indictment, the Tribunal will begin by reviewing some of the events that followed the first world war, and in particular, by tracing the growth of the Nazi Party under Hitler's leadership to a position of supreme power from which it controlled the destiny of the whole German people, and paved the way for the alleged commission of all the crimes charged against the defendants.

On 5th January, 1919, not two months after the conclusion of the Armistice which ended the first World War, and six months before the signing of the Peace Treaties at Versailles, there came into being in Germany a small political party called the German Labour Party. On the 12th September, 1919, Adolf Hitler became a member of this party, and at the first public meeting held in Munich, on 24th February, 1920, he announced the party's programme. That programme, which remained unaltered until the party was dissolved in 1945, consisted of twenty-five points, of which the following five are of particular interest on account of the light they throw on the matters with which the Tribunal is concerned:

"Point 1. We demand the unification of all Germans in the Greater Germany, on the basis of the right of a self-determination of peoples.

Point 2. We demand equality of rights for the German people in respect to the other nations; abrogation of the peace treaties of Versailles and Saint Germain.

Point 3. We demand land and territory for the sustenance of our people, and the colonisation of our surplus population.

Point 4. Only a member of the race can be a citizen. A member of the race can only be one who is of German blood, without consideration of creed. Consequently no Jew can be a member of the race . . . .

Point 22. We demand abolition of the mercenary troops and formation of a national army."

Of these aims, the one which seems to have been regarded as the most important, and which figured in almost every public speech, was the removal of the "disgrace" of the Armistice, and the restrictions of the peace treaties of Versailles and Saint Germain. In a typical speech at Munich on the 13th April, 1923, for example, Hitler said with regard to the Treaty of Versailles:

"The treaty was made in order to bring twenty million Germans to their deaths, and to ruin the German nation . . . At its foundation our movement formulated three demands.

"1. Setting aside of the Peace Treaty.

2. Unification of all Germans.

3. Land and soil to feed our nation."

The demand for the unification of all Germans in the Greater Germany was to play a large part in the events preceding the seizure of Austria and Czechoslovakia; the abrogation of the Treaty of Versailles was to become a decisive motive in attempting to justify the policy of the German Government; the demand for land was to be the justification for the acquisition of "living space" at the expense of other nations; the expulsion of the Jews from membership of the race of German blood was to lead to the atrocities against the Jewish people; and the demand for a national army was to result in measures of rearmament on the largest possible scale, and ultimately to war.

On the 29th July, 1921, the Party which had changed its name to National Sozialistische Deutsche Arbeiter Partei (NSDAP) was reorganised, Hitler becoming the first "Chairman". It was in this year that the Sturmabteilung or SA was founded, with Hitler at its head, as a private paramilitary force, which allegedly was to be used for the purpose of protecting NSDAP leaders from attack by rival political parties, and preserving order at NSDAP meetings, but in reality was used for fighting political opponents on the streets. In March, 1923, the defendant Goering was appointed head of the SA.

The procedure within the Party was governed in the most absolute way by the leadership principle (Fuehrerprinzip).

According to the principle, each Fuehrer has the right to govern, administer or decree, subject to no control of any kind and at his complete discretion, subject only to the orders he received from above.

This principle applied in the first instance to Hitler himself as the Leader of the Party, and in a lesser degree to all other party officials. All members of the Party swore an oath of "eternal allegiance" to the Leader.

There were only two ways in which Germany could achieve the three main aims above-mentioned, by negotiation, or by force. The twenty-five points of the NSDAP programme do not specifically mention the methods on which the leaders of the party proposed to rely, but the history of the Nazi régime shows that Hitler and his followers were only prepared to negotiate on the terms that their demands were conceded, and that force would be used if they were not.

On the night of the 8th November, 1923, an abortive putsch took place in Munich. Hitler and some of his followers burst into a meeting in the Bürger-bräu Cellar, which was being addressed by the Bavarian Prime Minister Kehr, with the intention of obtaining from him a decision to march forthwith on Berlin. On the morning of the 9th November, however, no Bavarian support was forthcoming, and Hitler's demonstration was met by the armed forces of the Reichswehr and the Police. Only a few volleys were fired; and after a dozen of his followers had been killed, Hitler fled for his life, and the demonstration was over. The defendants Streicher, Frick and Hess all took part in the attempted rising. Hitler was later tried for high treason, and was convicted and sentenced to imprisonment. The SA was outlawed. Hitler was released from prison in 1924 and in 1925 the Schutzstaffel, or SS, was created, nominally to act as his personal bodyguard, but in reality to terrorise political opponents. This was also the year of the publication of "Mein Kampf", containing the political views and aims of Hitler, which came to be regarded as the authentic source of Nazi doctrine.

In the eight years that followed the publication of "Mein Kampf", the NSDAP greatly extended its activities throughout Germany, paying particular attention to the training of youth in the ideas of National Socialism. The first Nazi youth organisation had come into existence in 1922, but it was in 1925 that the Hitler Jugend was officially recognised by the NSDAP. In 1931 Baldur von Schirach, who had joined the NSDAP in 1925, became Reich Youth Leader of the NSDAP.

The Party exerted every effort to win political support from the German people. Elections were contested both for the Reichstag and the Landtage. The NSDAP leaders did not make any serious attempt to hide the fact that their only purpose in entering German Political life was in order to destroy the democratic structure of the Weimar Republic, and to substitute for it a National Socialist totalitarian réime which would enable them to carry out their avowed policies without opposition. In preparation for the day when he would obtain power in Germany, Hitler in January, 1929, appointed Heinrich Himmler as Reichsfuehrer SS with the special task of building the SS into a strong but *elite* group which would be dependable in all circumstances.

On the 30th January, 1933, Hitler succeeded in being appointed Chancellor of the Reich by President von Hindenburg. The defendants Goering, Schacht and von

Papen were active in enlisting support to bring this about. Von Papen had been appointed Reich Chancellor on the 1st June, 1932. On the 14th June he rescinded the decree of the Bruening Cabinet of the 13th April, 1932, which had dissolved the Nazi para-military organisations, including the SA and the SS. This was done by agreement between Hitler and von Papen, although von Papen denies that it was agreed as early as the 28th May, as Dr. Hans Volz asserts in "Dates from the History of the NSDAP"; but that it was the result of an agreement was admitted in evidence by von Papen.

The Reichstag elections of the 31st July, 1932, resulted in a great accession of strength to the NSDAP, and von Papen offered Hitler the post of Vice-Chancellor, which he refused, insisting upon the Chancellorship itself. In November, 1932, a petition signed by leading industrialists and financiers was presented to President Hindenburg, calling upon him to entrust the Chancellorship to Hitler; and in the collection of signatures to the petition Schacht took a prominent part.

The election of the 6th November, which followed the defeat of the Government, reduced the number of NSDAP members, but von Papen made further efforts to gain Hitler's participation, without success. On the 12th November, Schacht wrote to Hitler:

"I have no doubt that the present development of things can only lead to your becoming Chancellor. It seems as if our attempt to collect a number of signatures from business circles for this purpose was not altogether in vain . . .".

After Hitler's refusal of the 16th November, von Papen resigned, and was succeeded by General von Schleicher; but von Papen still continued his activities. He met Hitler at the house of the Cologne banker von

Schroeder on the 4th January, 1933, and attended a meeting at the defendant Ribbentrop's house on the 22nd January, with the defendant Goering and others. He also had an interview with President Hindenburg on the 9th January, and from the 22nd January onwards he discussed officially with Hindenburg the formation of a Hitler Cabinet.

Hitler held his first Cabinet meeting on the day of his appointment as Chancellor, at which the defendants Goering, Frick, Funk, von Neurath and von Papen were present in their official capacities. On the 28th February, 1933, the Reichstag building in Berlin was set on fire. This fire was used by Hitler and his Cabinet as a pretext for passing on the same day a decree suspending the constitutional guarantees of freedom. The decree was signed by President Hindenburg and countersigned by Hitler and the defendant Frick, who then occupied the post of Reich Minister of the Interior. On the 5th March elections were held, in which the NSDAP obtained 288 seats of the total of 647. The Hitler Cabinet was anxious to pass an "Enabling Act" that would give them full legislative powers, including the power to deviate from the Constitution. They were without the necessary majority in the Reichstag to be able to do this constitutionally. They therefore made use of the decree suspending the guarantees of freedom and took into so-called "protective custody" a large number of Communist deputies and party officials. Having done this, Hitler introduced the "Enabling Act" into the Reichstag, and after he had made it clear that if it was not passed, further forceful measures would be taken, the Act was passed on the 24th March, 1933.

The PRESIDENT: I will now ask Mr. Justice Birkett to continue reading the judgment.

The NSDAP, having achieved power in this way, now proceeded to extend its hold on every phase of German life. Other political parties were persecuted, their property and assets confiscated, and many of their members placed in concentration camps. On 26th April, 1933, the defendant Goering founded in Prussia the Gestapo as a secret police, and confided to the deputy leader of the Gestapo that its main task was to eliminate political opponents of National Socialism and Hitler. On the 14th July, 1933, a law was passed declaring the NSDAP to be the only political party, and making it criminal to maintain or form any other political party.

In order to place the complete control of the machinery of Government in the hands of the Nazi leaders, a series of laws and decrees were passed which reduced the powers of regional and local governments throughout Germany, transforming them into subordinate divisions of the Government of the Reich. Representative assemblies in the Laender were abolished and with them all local elections. The Government then proceeded to secure control of the Civil Service. This was achieved by a process of centralisation, and by a careful sifting of the whole Civil Service administration. By a law of the 7th April it was provided that officials "who were of non-Aryan descent" should be retired; and it was also decreed that "officials who because of their previous political activity cannot be guaranteed to exert themselves for the national state without reservation shall be discharged." The law of the 11th April, 1933, provided for the discharge of "all Civil Servants who belong to the Communist Party." Similarly, the Judiciary was subjected to control. Judges were removed from the Bench for political or racial reasons. They were spied upon and made subject to the strongest pressure to join the Nazi Party as an alternative to being dismissed. When the Supreme Court acquitted three of the four defendants charged with complicity in the Reichstag fire, its jurisdiction in cases of treason was thereafter taken away and given to a newly established "People's Court", consisting of two judges and five officials of the Party. Special courts were set up to try political crimes and only party members were appointed as judges. Persons were arrested by the SS for political reasons, and detained in prisons and concentration camps; and the judges were without power to intervene in any way. Pardons were granted to members of the Party who had been sentenced by the judges for proved offences. In 1935 several officials of the Hohenstein concentration camp were convicted of inflicting brutal treatment upon the inmates. High Nazi officials tried to influence the Court, and after the officials had been convicted, Hitler pardoned them all. In 1942 "Judges' letters" were sent to all German judges by the Government, instructing them as to the "general lines" that they must follow.

In their determination to remove all sources of opposition, the NSDAP leaders turned their attention to the trade unions, the churches and the Jews. In April, 1933, Hitler ordered the late defendant Ley, who was then staff director of the political organisation of the NSDAP, "to take over the trade unions." Most of the trade unions of Germany were joined together in two large federations, the "Free Trade Unions" and the "Christian Trade Unions." Unions outside these two large federations contained only 15 per cent. of the total union membership. On the 21st April, 1933, Ley issued an NSDAP directive announcing a "co-ordination action" to be carried out on the 2nd May against the Free Trade Unions. The directive ordered that SA and SS men were to be employed in the planned "occupation of trade union properties and for the taking into protective custody of personalities who come into question." At the conclusion of the action the official

NSDAP press service reported that the National Socialist Factory Cells Organisation had "eliminated the old leadership of Free Trade Unions" and taken over the leadership themselves. Similarly, on the 3rd May, 1933, the NSDAP press service announced that the Christian trade unions "have unconditionally subordinated themselves to the leadership of Adolf Hitler." In place of the trade unions the Nazi Government set up a German Labour Front (DAF), controlled by the NSDAP, and which, in practice, all workers in Germany were compelled to join. The chairmen of the unions were taken into custody and were subjected to ill-treatment, ranging from assault and battery to murder.

In their effort to combat the influence of the Christian churches, whose doctrines were fundamentally at variance with National Socialist philosophy and practice, the Nazi Government proceeded more slowly. The extreme step of banning the practice of the Christian religion was not taken, but year by year efforts were made to limit the influence of Christianity on the German people, since, in the words used by the defendant Bormann to the defendant Rosenberg in an official letter, "the Christian religion and National Socialist doctrines are not compatible." In the month of June, 1941, the defendant Bormann issued a secret decree on the relation of Christianity and National Socialism. The decree stated that:

"For the first time in German history the Fuehrer consciously and completely has the leadership in his own hand. With the Party, its components and attached units, the Fuehrer has created for himself and thereby the German Reich Leadership, an instrument which makes him independent of the Treaty. . . . More and more the people must be separated from the churches and their organs, the Pastor . . . Never again must an influence on leadership of the people be yielded to the churches. This influence must be broken completely and finally. Only the Reich Government and by its direction the Party, its components and attached units, have a right to leadership of the people."

From the earliest days of the NSDAP, anti-Semitism had occupied a prominent place in National Socialist thought and propaganda. The Jews, who were considered to have no right to German citizenship, were held to have been largely responsible for the troubles with which the nation was afflicted following on the war of 1914–18. Furthermore, the antipathy to the Jews was intensified by the insistence which was laid upon the superiority of the Germanic race and blood. The second chapter of Book 1 of "Mein Kampf" is dedicated to what may be called the "Master Race" theory, the doctrine of Aryan superiority over all other races, and the right of Germans in virtue of this superiority to dominate and use other peoples for their own ends. With the coming of the Nazis into power in 1933, persecution of the Jews became official state policy. On the 1st April, 1933, a boycott of Jewish enterprises was approved by the Nazi Reich Cabinet, and during the following years a series of anti-Semitic laws were passed, restricting the activities of Jews in the Civil Service, in the legal profession, in journalism and in the armed forces. In September, 1935, the so-called Nuremberg Laws were passed, the most important effect of which was to deprive Jews of German citizenship. In this way the influence of Jewish elements on the affairs of Germany was extinguished, and one more potential source of opposition to Nazi policy was rendered powerless.

In any consideration of the crushing of opposition, the massacre of the 30th June, 1934, must not be forgotten. It has become known as the "Roehm Purge" or "the blood bath", and revealed the methods which Hitler and his immediate associates, including the defendant

Goering, were ready to employ to strike down all opposition and consolidate their power. On that day Roehm, the Chief of Staff of the SA since 1931, was murdered by Hitler's orders, and the "Old Guard" of the SA was massacred without trial and without warning. The opportunity was taken to murder a large number of people who at one time or another had opposed Hitler.

The ostensible ground for the murder of Roehm was that he was plotting to overthrow Hitler, and the defendant Goering gave evidence that knowledge of such a plot had come to his ears. Whether this was so or not it is not necessary to determine.

On July 3rd the Cabinet approved Hitler's action and described it as "legitimate self-defence by the State."

Shortly afterwards Hindenburg died, and Hitler became both Reich President and Chancellor. At the Nazi-dominated plebiscite, which followed, 38 million Germans expressed their approval, and with the Reichswehr taking the oath of allegiance to the Fuehrer, full power was now in Hitler's hands.

Germany had accepted the Dictatorship with all its methods of terror, and its cynical and open denial of the rule of law.

Apart from the policy of crushing the potential opponents of their régime, the Nazi Government took active steps to increase its power over the German population. In the field of education, everything was done to ensure that the youth of Germany was brought up in the atmosphere of National Socialism and accepted National Socialist teachings. As early as the 7th April, 1933, the law reorganising the Civil Service had made it possible for the Nazi Government to remove all "Subversive and unreliable teachers"; and this was followed by numerous other measures to make sure that the schools were staffed by teachers who could be trusted to teach their pupils the full meaning of National Socialist creed. Apart from the influence of National Socialist teaching in the schools, the Hitler Youth Organisation was also relied upon by the Nazi Leaders for obtaining fanatical support from the younger generation. The defendant von Schirach, who had been Reich Youth Leader of the NSDAP since 1931, was appointed Youth Leader of the German Reich in June, 1933. Soon all the youth organisation had been either dissolved or absorbed by the Hitler Youth, with the exception of the Catholic Youth. The Hitler Youth was organised on strict military lines, and as early as 1933 the Wehrmacht was cooperating in providing pre-military training for the Reich Youth.

The Nazi Government endeavoured to unite the nation in support of their policies through the extensive use of propaganda. A number of agencies were set up whose duty was to control and influence the press, radio, films, publishing firms, etc., in Germany, and to supervise entertainment and cultural and artistic activities. All these agencies came under Goebbels' Ministry of the People's Enlightenment and Propaganda, which together with a corresponding organisation in the NSDAP and the Reich Chamber of Culture, was ultimately responsible for exercising this supervision. The defendant Rosenberg played a leading part in disseminating the National Socialist doctrines on behalf of the Party, and the defendant Fritzsche, in conjunction with Goebbels, performed the same task for the State.

The greatest emphasis was laid on the supreme mission of the German people to lead and dominate by virtue of their Nordic blood and racial purity, and the ground was thus being prepared for the acceptance of the idea of German world supremacy.

Through the effective control of the radio and the press, the German people, during the years which followed 1933, were subjected to the most intensive propaganda in furtherance of the régime. Hostile criticism, indeed criticism of any kind, was forbidden, and the severest penalties were imposed on those who indulged in it.

Independent judgment, based on freedom of thought, was rendered quite impossible.

During the years immediately following Hitler's appointment as Chancellor, the Nazi Government set about reorganising the economic life of Germany, and in particular the armament industry. This was done on a vast scale and with extreme thoroughness.

It was necessary to lay a secure financial foundation for the building of armaments, and in April, 1936, the defendant Goering was appointed co-ordinator for raw materials and foreign exchange, and empowered to supervise all State and Party activities in these fields. In this capacity he brought together the War Minister, the Minister of Economics, the Reich Finance Minister, the President of the Reichsbank and the Prussian Finance Minister to discuss problems connected with war mobilisation, and on the 27th May, 1936, in addressing these men, Goering opposed any financial limitation of war production and added that "all measures are to be considered from the stand-point of an assured waging of war." At the Party Rally in Nuremberg in 1936. Hitler announced the establishment of the Four Year Plan and the appointment of Goering as the Plenipotentiary in charge. Goering was already engaged in building a strong air force and on the 8th July, 1938, he announced to a number of leading German aircraft manufacturers that the German Air Force was already superior in quality and quantity to the English. On the 14th October, 1938, at another conference, Goering announced that Hitler had instructed him to organise a gigantic armament programme, which would make insignificant all previous achievements. He said that he had been ordered to build as rapidly as possible an air force five times as large as originally planned, to increase the speed of the rearmament of the navy and army, and to concentrate on offensive weapons, principally heavy artillery and heavy tanks. He then laid down a specific programme designed to accomplish these ends. The extent to which rearmament had been accomplished was stated by Hitler in his memorandum of 9th October, 1939, after the campaign in Poland. He said:

"The military application of our people's strength has been carried through to such an extent that within a short time at any rate it cannot be markedly improved upon by any manner of effort . . .

"The warlike equipment of the German people is at present larger in quantity and better in quality for a greater number of German divisions than in the year 1914. The weapons themselves, taking a substantial cross-section, are more modern than in the case with any other country in the world at this time. They have just proved their supreme war worthiness in their victorious campaign . . . There is no evidence available to show that any country in the world disposes of a better total ammunition stock than the Reich . . . The A.A. artillery is not equalled by any country in the world."

In this reorganisation of the economic life of Germany for military purposes, the Nazi Government found the German armament industry quite willing to cooperate, and to play its part in the rearmament programme. In April, 1933, Gustav Krupp von Bohlen submitted to Hitler on behalf of the Reich Association of German Industry a plan for the reorganisation of German industry, which he stated was characterised by the desire to co-ordinate economic measures and political necessity. In the plan itself, Krupp stated that "the turn of political events is in line with the wishes which I myself and the board of directors have cherished for a long time." What Krupp meant by this statement is fully shown by the draft text of a speech which he planned to deliver in the University of Berlin in January, 1944, though the speech was in fact never delivered. Referring to the years 1919 to 1933, Krupp wrote: "It is the one great merit of the entire German war economy that it did not remain idle during those bad years, even though its activity could not be brought to light, for obvious reasons. Through years of secret work, scientific and basic groundwork was laid in order to be ready again to work for the German armed forces at the appointed hour, without loss of time or experience. . . . Only through the secret activity of German enterprise together with the experience gained meanwhile through production of peace time goods, was it possible after 1933 to fall into step with the new tasks arrived at, restoring Germany's military power."

In October, 1933, Germany withdrew from the International Disarmament Conference and League of Nations. In 1935, the Nazi Government decided to take the first open steps to free itself from its obligations under the Treaty of Versailles. On the 10th March, 1935, the defendant Goering announced that Germany was building a military air force. Six days later, on the 16th March, 1935, a law was passed bearing the signatures, among others, of the defendants Goering, Hess, Frank, Frick, Schacht and von Neurath, instituting compulsory military service and fixing the establishment of the German Army at a peace time strength of 500,000 men. In an endeavour to reassure public opinion in other countries, the Government announced on the 21st May, 1935, that Germany would, though renouncing the disarmament clauses, still respect the territorial limitations of the

Versailles Treaty, and would comply with the Locarno Pacts. Nevertheless, on the very day of this announcement, the secret Reich Defence Law was passed and its publication forbidden by Hitler. In this law, the powers and duties of the Chancellor and other Ministers were defined, should Germany become involved in war. It is clear from this law that by May of 1935 Hitler and his Government had arrived at the stage in the carrying out of their policies when it was necessary for them to have in existence the requisite machinery for the administration and government of Germany in the event of their policy leading to war.

At the same time that this preparation of the German economy for war was being carried out, the German armed forces themselves were preparing for a rebuilding of Germany's armed strength.

The Germany Navy was particularly active in this regard. The official German Naval historians, Assmann and Gladisch, admit that the Treaty of Versailles had only been in force for a few months before it was violated, particularly in the construction of a new submarine arm.

The publications of Captain Schuessler and Oberst Scherf, both of which were sponsored by the defendant Raeder, were designed to show the German people the nature of the Navy's effort to rearm in defiance of the Treaty of Versailles.

The full details of these publications have been given in evidence.

On the 12th May, 1934 the defendant Raeder issued the Top Secret armament plan for what was called the Third Armament Phase. This contained the sentence

"All theoretical and practical A-preparations are to be drawn up with a primary view to readiness for a war *without any alert period*."

One month later, in June 1934, the defendant Raeder had a conversation with Hitler in which Hitler instructed him to keep secret the construction of U-boats and of warships over the limit of 10,000 tons which was then being undertaken.

And on the 2nd November, 1934, the defendant Raeder had another conversation with Hitler and the defendant Goering, in which Hitler said that he considered it vital that the German Navy "should be increased as planned, as no war could be carried on if the Navy was not able to safeguard the ore imports from Scandinavia."

The large orders for building given in 1933 and 1934 are sought to be excused by the defendant Raeder on the ground that negotiations were in progress for an agreement between Germany and Great Britain permitting Germany to build ships in excess of the provisions of the Treaty of Versailles. This agreement, which was signed in 1935, restricted the German Navy to a tonnage equal to one-third of that of the British, except in respect of U-boats where 45 per cent. was agreed, subject always to the right to exceed this proportion after first informing the British Government and giving them an opportunity of discussion.

The Anglo-German Treaty followed in 1937, under which both Powers bound themselves to notify full details of their building programme at least four months before any action was taken.

It is admitted that these clauses were not adhered to by Germany.

In capital vessels, for example, the displacement details were falsified by 20 per cent., whilst in the case of U-boats, the German historians Assmann and Gladisch say:

"It is probably just in the sphere of submarine construction that Germany adhered the least to the restrictions of the German–British Treaty."

The importance of these breaches of the Treaty is seen when the motive for this re-armament is considered. In the year 1940 the defendant Raeder himself wrote:

"The Fuehrer hoped until the last moment to be able to put off the threatening conflict with England until 1944–5. At that time, the Navy would have had available a fleet with a powerful U-boat superiority, and a much more favourable ratio as regards strength in all other types of ships, particularly those designed for warfare on the High Seas."

The Nazi Government, as already stated, announced on the 21st May, 1935, their intention to respect the territorial limitations of the Treaty of Versailles. On the 7th March, 1936, in defiance of that Treaty, the demilitarised zone of the Rhineland was entered by German troops. In announcing this action to the German Reichstag, Hitler endeavoured to justify the re-entry by references to the recently concluded alliances between France and the Soviet Union, and between Czechoslovakia and the Soviet Union. He also tried to meet the hostile reaction which he no doubt expected to follow this violation of the Treaty by saying:

"We have no territorial claims to make in Europe."

The Tribunal now turns to the consideration of the Crimes against peace charged in the Indictment. Count One of the Indictment charges the defendants with conspiring or having a common plan to commit crimes against peace.

Count Two of the Indictment charges the defendants with committing specific crimes against peace by planning, preparing, initiating, and waging wars of aggression against a number of other States. It will be convenient to consider the question of the existence of a common plan and the question of aggressive war together, and to deal later in this Judgment with the question of the individual responsibility of the defendants.

The charges in the Indictment that the defendants planned and waged aggressive wars are charges of the utmost gravity. War is essentially an evil thing. Its consequences are not confined to the belligerent states alone, but affect the whole world.

To initiate a war of aggression, therefore, is not only an international crime; it is the supreme international crime differing only from other war crimes in that it contains within itself the accumulated evil of the whole.

The first acts of aggression referred to in the Indictment are the seizure of Austria and Czechoslovakia and the first war of aggression charged in the Indictment is the war against Poland begun on the 1st September, 1939.

Before examining that charge it is necessary to look more closely at some of the events which preceded these acts of aggression. The war against Poland did not come suddenly out of an otherwise clear sky; the evidence has made it plain that this war of aggression, as well as the seizure of Austria and Czechoslovakia, was pre-meditated and carefully prepared, and was not undertaken until the moment was thought opportune for it to be carried through as a definite part of the pre-ordained scheme and plan.

For the aggressive designs of the Nazi Government were not accidents arising out of the immediate political situation in Europe and the world; they were a deliberate and essential part of Nazi foreign policy.

From the beginning, the National Socialist movement claimed that its object was to unite the German people in the consciousness of their mission and destiny, based on inherent qualities of race, and under the guidance of the Fuehrer.

For its achievement, two things were deemed to be essential: the disruption of the European order as it had existed since the Treaty of Versailles, and the creation of a Greater Germany beyond the frontiers of 1914. This necessarily involved the seizure of foreign territories.

War was seen to be inevitable, or at the very least, highly probable, if these purposes were to be accomplished. The German people, therefore, with all their resources, were to be organised as a great political-military army, schooled to obey without question any policy decreed by the State.

In "Mein Kampf" Hitler had made this view quite plain. It must be remembered that "Mein Kampf" was no mere private diary in which the secret thoughts of Hitler were set down. Its contents were rather proclaimed from the house-tops. It was used in the schools and Universities and among the Hitler Youth, in the SS and the SA, and among the German people generally, even down to the presentation of an official copy to all newly-married people. By the year 1945 over 6fi million copies had been circulated. The general contents are well known. Over and over again Hitler asserted his belief in the necessity of force as the means of solving international problems, as in the following quotation:

"The soil on which we now live was not a gift bestowed by Heaven on our forefathers. They had to conquer it by risking their lives. So also in the future, our people will not obtain territory, and therewith the means of existence, as a favour from any other people, but will have to win it by the power of a triumphant sword."

"Mein Kampf" contains many such passages, and the

extolling of force as an instrument of foreign policy is openly proclaimed.

The precise objectives of this policy of force are also set forth in detail. The very first page of the book asserts that "German-Austria must be restored to the great German Motherland," not on economic grounds, but because "people of the same blood should be in the same Reich."

The restoration of the German frontiers of 1914 is declared to be wholly insufficient, and if Germany is to exist at all, it must be as a world power with the necessary territorial magnitude.

"Mein Kampf" is quite explicit in stating where the increased territory is to be found:

"Therefore we National Socialists have purposely drawn a line through the line of conduct followed by pre-war Germany in foreign policy. We put an end to the perpetual Germanic march towards the South and West of Europe, and turn our eyes towards the lands of the East. We finally put a stop to the colonial and trade policy of the pre-war times, and pass over to the territorial policy of the future.

But when we speak of new territory in Europe to-day, we must think principally of Russia and the border states subject to her."

"Mein Kampf" is not to be regarded as a mere literary exercise, nor as an inflexible policy or plan incapable of modification.

Its importance lies in the unmistakable attitude of aggression revealed throughout its pages.

Evidence from captured documents has revealed that Hitler held four secret meetings to which the Tribunal proposes to make special reference because of the light they shed upon the question of the common plan and aggressive war.

These meetings took place on the 5th of November, 1937, the 23rd of May, 1939, the 22nd of August, 1939, and the 23rd of November, 1939.

At these meetings important declarations were made by Hitler as to his purposes, which are quite unmistakable in their terms.

The documents which record what took place at these meetings have been subject to some criticism at the hands of defending Counsel.

Their essential authenticity is not denied, but it is said, for example, that they do not purpose to be verbatim transcripts of the speeches they record, that the document dealing with the meeting on the 5th November, 1937, was dated five days after the meeting had taken place, and that the two documents dealing with the meeting of August 22nd, 1939, differ form one another, and are unsigned.

Making the fullest allowance for criticism of this kind, the Tribunal is of the opinion that the documents are documents of the highest value, and that their authenticity and substantial truth are established.

They are obviously careful records of the events they describe, and they have been preserved as such in the archives of the German Government, from whose custody they were captured. Such documents could never be dismissed as inventions, nor even as inaccurate or distorted; they plainly record events which actually took place.

It will perhaps be useful to deal first of all with the meeting of the 23rd November, 1939, when Hitler called his Supreme Commanders together. A record was made of what was said, by one of those present. At the date of the meeting, Austria and Czechoslovakia had been incorporated into the German Reich, Poland had been conquered by the German armies, and the war with Great Britain and France was still in its static phase. The moment was opportune for a review of past events. Hitler informed the Commanders that the purpose of the Conference was to give them an idea of the world of his thoughts, and to tell them his decision. He thereupon reviewed his political task since 1919, and referred to the secession of Germany from the League of Nations, the denunciation of the Disarmament Conference, the order for re-armament, the introduction of compulsory armed service, the occupation of the Rhineland, the seizure of Austria, and the action against Czechoslovakia. He stated:

"One year later, Austria came; this step also was considered doubtful. It brought about a considerable reinforcement of the Reich. The next step was Bohemia, Moravia and Poland. This step also was not possible to accomplish in one campaign. First of all, the western fortification had to be finished. It was not possible to reach the goal in one effort. It was clear to me from the first moment that I could not be satisfied with the Sudeten German territory. That was only a partial solution. The decision to march into Bohemia was made. Then followed the erection of the Protectorate and with that the basis for the action against Poland was laid, but I wasn't quite clear at that time whether I should start first against the East and then in the West or vice versa . . . Basically I did not organise the armed forces in order not to strike. The decision to strike was always in me. Earlier or later I wanted to solve the problem. Under pressure it was decided that the East was to be attacked first."

This address, reviewing past events and re-affirming the aggressive intentions present from the beginning, puts beyond any question of doubt the character of the actions against Austria and Czechoslovakia, and the war against Poland.

For they had all been accomplished according to plan; and the nature of that plan must now be examined in a little more detail.

At the meeting of the 23rd November, 1939, Hitler was looking back to things accomplished; at the earlier meetings now to be considered, he was looking forward, and revealing his plans to his confederates. The comparison is instructive.

The meeting held at the Reich Chancellery in Berlin on the 5th November, 1937, was attended by Lieut.-Colonel Hoszbach, Hitler's personal adjutant, who compiled a long note of the proceedings, which he dated the 10th November, 1937, and signed.

The persons present were Hitler, and the defendants Goering, von Neurath and Raeder, in their capacities as Commander-in-Chief of the Luftwaffe, Reich Foreign Minister and Commander-in-Chief of the Navy respectively, General von Blomberg, Minister of War, and General von Fritsch, the Commander-in-Chief of the Army.

Hitler began by saying that the subject of the conference was of such high importance that in other States it would have taken place before the Cabinet. He went on to say that the subject matter of his speech was the result of his detailed deliberations, and of his experience during his four and a half years of Government. He requested that the statements he was about to make should be looked upon in the case of his death as his last will and testament. Hitler's main theme was the problem of living space, and he discussed various possible solutions, only to set them aside. He then said that the seizure of living space on the continent of Europe was therefore necessary, expressing himself in these words:

"It is not a case of conquering people, but of conquering agriculturally useful space. It would also be more to the purpose to seek raw material producing territory in Europe directly adjoining the Reich and not overseas, and this solution would have to be brought into effect for one or two generations. . . . The history of all times—Roman Empire, British Empire—has proved that every space expansion can only be effected by breaking resistance and taking risks. Even setbacks are unavoidable: neither formerly nor to-day has space been found without an owner; the attacker always comes up against the proprietor."

He concluded with this observation:

"The question for Germany is where the greatest possible conquest could be made at the lowest cost."

Nothing could indicate more plainly the aggressive intentions of Hitler, and the events which soon followed showed the reality of his purpose. It is impossible to accept the contention that Hitler did not actually mean war; for after pointing out that Germany might expect the opposition of England and France, and analysing the strength and the weakness of those powers in particular situations, he continued:

"The German question can be solved only by way of force, and this is never without risk. . . . If we place the decision to apply force with risk at the head of the following expositions, then we are left to reply to the questions 'when' and 'how'. In this regard we have to decide upon three different cases."

The first of these three cases set forth a hypothetical international situation, in which he would take action not later than 1943 to 1945, saying:

"If the Fuehrer is still living then it will be his irrevocable decision to solve the German space problem not later than 1943 to 1945. The necessity for action before 1943 to 1945 will come under consideration in Cases 2 and 3."

The second and third cases to which Hitler referred show the plain intention to seize Austria and Czechoslovakia, and in this connection Hitler said:

"For the improvement of our military-political position, it must be our first aim in every case of entanglement by war to conquer Czechoslovakia and Austria simultaneously in order to remove any threat from the flanks in case of a possible advance westwards."

He further added:

"The annexation of the two states to Germany militarily and politically would constitute a considerable relief, owing to shorter and better frontiers, the freeing of fighting personnel for other purposes, and the possibility of reconstituting new armies up to a strength of about twelve divisions."

This decision to seize Austria and Czechoslovakia was discussed in some detail; the action was to be taken as soon as a favourable opportunity presented itself.

The military strength which Germany had been building up since 1933 was now to be directed at the two specific countries, Austria and Czechoslovakia.

The defendant Goering testified that he did not believe at that time that Hitler actually meant to attack Austria and Czechoslovakia, and that the purpose of the conference was only to put pressure on von Fritsch to speed up the re-armament of the Army.

The defendant Raeder testified that neither he, nor von Fritsch, nor von Blomberg, believed that Hitler actually meant war, a conviction which the defendant Raeder claims that he held up to the 22nd August, 1939. The basis of this conviction was his hope that Hitler would obtain a "political solution" of Germany's problems. But all that this means, when examined, is the belief that Germany's position would be so good, and Germany's armed might so overwhelming, that the territory desired could be obtained without fighting for it. It must be remembered too that Hitler's declared intention with regard to Austria was actually carried out within a little over four months from the date of the meeting, and within less than a year the first portion of Czechoslovakia was absorbed, and Bohemia and Moravia a few months later. If any doubts had existed in the minds of any of his hearers in November, 1937, after March of 1939 there could no longer be any question that Hitler was in deadly earnest in his decision to resort to war. The Tribunal is satisfied that Lt.-Col. Hoszbach's account of the meeting is substantially correct, and that those present knew that Austria and Czechoslovakia would be annexed by Germany at the first possible opportunity.

THE PRESIDENT: The Tribunal will now adjourn for ten minutes.

(A recess was taken.)

THE PRESIDENT: I will now ask M. Donnedieu de Vabres to continue the reading of the judgment.

M. DONNEDIEU DE VABRES:

The invasion of Austria was a pre-mediated aggressive step in furthering the plan to wage aggressive wars against other countries. As a result Germany's flank was protected, that of Czechoslovakia being greatly weakened. The first step had been taken in the seizure of "Lebensraum"; many new divisions of trained fighting men had been acquired; and with the seizure of foreign exchange reserves, the re-armament programme had been greatly strengthened.

On the 21st May, 1935, Hitler announced in the Reichstag that Germany did not intend either to attack Austria or to interfere in her internal affairs. On the 1st May, 1936, he publicly coupled Czechoslovakia with Austria in his avowal of peaceful intentions; and so late as the 11th July, 1936, he recognised by treaty the full sovereignty of Austria.

Austria was in fact seized by Germany in the month of March, 1938. For a number of years before that date, the National Socialists in Germany had been cooperating with the National Socialists of Austria with the ultimate object of incorporating Austria into the German Reich. The Putsch of July 25th, 1934, which resulted in the assassination of Chancellor Dollfuss, had the seizure of Austria as its object; but the Putsch failed, with the consequence that the National Socialist Party was outlawed in Austria. On the 11th July, 1936, an agreement was entered into between the two countries, Article 1 of which stated:

"The German Government recognises the full sovereignty of the Federated State of Austria in the spirit of the pronouncements of the German Fuehrer and Chancellor of the 21st May, 1935."

Article 2 declared:

"Each of the two Governments regards the inner political order (including the question of Austrian National Socialism) obtaining in the other country as an internal affair of the other country, upon which it will exercise neither direct nor indirect influence."

The National Socialist movement in Austria however

continued its illegal activities under cover of secrecy; and the National Socialists of Germany gave the Party active support. The resulting "incidents" were seized upon by the German National Socialists as an excuse for interfering in Austrian affairs. After the conference of the 5th November, 1937, these "incidents" rapidly multiplied. The relationship between the two countries steadily worsened, and finally the Austrian Chancellor Schuschnigg was persuaded by the defendant von Papen and others to seek a conference with Hitler, which took place at Berchtesgaden on the 12th February, 1938. The defendant Keitel was present at the conference, and Dr. Schuschnigg was threatened by Hitler with an immediate invasion of Austria. Schuschnigg finally agreed to grant a political amnesty to various Nazis convicted of crime, and to appoint the Nazi Seyss-Inquart as Minister of the Interior and Security with control of the Police. On the 9th March, 1938, in an attempt to preserve the independence of his country, Dr. Schuschnigg decided to hold a plebiscite on the question of Austrian independence, which was fixed for the 13th March, 1938. Hitler, two days later, sent an ultimatum to Schuschnigg that the plebiscite must be withdrawn. In the afternoon and evening of the 11th March, 1938. the defendant Goering made a series of demands upon the Austrian Government, each backed up by the threat of invasion. After Schuschnigg had agreed to the cancellation of the plebiscite, another demand was put forward that Schuschnigg must resign, and that the defendant Seyss-Inquart should be appointed Chancellor. In consequence, Schuschnigg resigned, and President Miklas, after at first refusing to appoint Seyss-Inquart as Chancellor, gave way and appointed him.

Meanwhile Hitler had given the final order for the German troops to cross the border at dawn on the 12th of March and instructed Seyss-Inquart to use formations of

Austrian National Socialists to depose Miklas and to seize control of the Austrian Government. After the order to march had been given to the German troops, Goering telephoned the German Embassy in Vienna and dictated a telegram in which he wished Seyss-Inquart to send to Hitler to justify the military action which had already been ordered.

It was:

"The provisional Austrian Government, which, after the dismissal of the Schuschnigg Government, considers its task to establish peace and order in Austria, sends to the German Government the urgent request to support it in its task and to help it to prevent bloodshed. For this purpose it asks the German Government to send German troops as soon as possible."

Keppler, an official of the German Embassy, replied:

"Well, SA and SS are marching through the streets, but everything is quiet."

After some further discussion, Goering stated:

"Please show him (Seyss-Inquart) the text of the telegram, and do tell him that we are asking him—well, he doesn't even have to send the telegram. All he needs to do is to say 'Agreed'."

Seyss-Inquart never sent the telegram; he never even telegraphed "Agreed."

It appears that as soon as he was appointed Chancellor, some time after 10 p.m., he called Keppler and told him to call up Hitler and transmit his protests against the occupation. This action outraged the defendant Goering, because "it would disturb the rest of the Fuehrer, who wanted to go to Austria the next day." At 11.15 p.m. an official in the Ministry of Propaganda in Berlin telephoned the German Embassy in Vienna and was told by Keppler: "Tell the General Field Marshal that Seyss-Inquart agrees."

At daybreak on the 12th March, 1938, German troops marched into Austria, and met with no resistance. It was announced in the German press that Seyss-Inquart had been appointed the successor to Schuschnigg, and the telegram which Goering had suggested, but which was never sent, was quoted to show that Seyss-Inquart had requested the presence of German troops to prevent disorder. On the 13th March, 1938, a law was passed for the reunion of Austria in the German Reich. Seyss-Inquart demanded that President Miklas should sign this law, but he refused to do so, and resigned his office. He was succeeded by Seyss-Inquart, who signed the law in the name of Austria. This law was then adopted as a law of the Reich by a Reich Cabinet decree issued the same day, and signed by Hitler and the defendants Goering, Frick, von Ribbentrop and Hess.

It was contended before the Tribunal that the annexation of Austria was justified by the strong desire expressed in many quarters for the union of Austria and Germany; that there were many matters in common between the two peoples that made this union desirable; and that in the result the object was achieved without bloodshed.

These matters, even if true, are really immaterial, for the facts plainly prove that the methods employed to achieve the object were those of an aggressor. The ultimate factor was the armed might of Germany ready to be used if any resistance was encountered. Moreover, none of these considerations appear from the Hoszbach account of the meetings of the 5th November, 1937, to have been the motives which actuated Hitler; on the contrary, all the emphasis is there laid on the advantage to be gained by Germany in her military strength by the annexation of Austria.

The conference of the 5th November, 1937, made it quite plain that the seizure of Czechoslovakia by Germany had been definitely decided upon. The only question remaining was the selection of the suitable moment to do it. On the 4th March, 1938, the defendant Ribbentrop wrote to the defendant Keitel with regard to a suggestion made to Ribbentrop by the Hungarian Ambassador in Berlin, that possible war aims against Czechoslovakia should be discussed between the German and Hungarian armies. In the course of this letter Ribbentrop said:

"I have many doubts about such negotiations. In case we should discuss with Hungary possible war aims against Czechoslovakia, the danger exists that other parties as well would be informed about this."

On the 11th March, 1938, Goering made two separate statements to M. Mastny, the Czechoslovak Minister in Berlin, assuring him that the developments then taking place in Austria would in no way have any detrimental influence on the relations between the German Reich and Czechoslovakia, and emphasised the continued earnest endeavour on the part of the Germans to improve those mutual relations. On the 12th March, Goering asked M. Mastny to call on him, and repeated these assurances.

This design to keep Czechoslovakia quiet whilst Austria was absorbed was a typical manoeuvre on the part of the defendant Goering, which he was to repeat later in the case of Poland, when he made the most strenuous efforts to isolate Poland in the impending struggle. On the same day, the 12th March, the defendant von Neurath spoke with M. Mastny, and assured him on behalf of Hitler that Germany still considered herself bound by the

German–Czechoslovak Arbitration Convention concluded at Locarno in October, 1935.

The evidence shows that after the occupation of Austria by the German Army on the 12th March, and the annexation of Austria on the 13th March, Conrad Henlein, who was the leader of the Sudeten German party in Czechoslovakia, saw Hitler in Berlin on the 28th March. On the following day, at a conference in Berlin, when Ribbentrop was present with Henlein, the general situation was discussed, and later the defendant Jodl recorded in his diary:

"After the annexation of Austria the Fuehrer mentions that there is no hurry to solve the Czech question, because Austria has to be digested first. Nevertheless, preparations for Case Gruen (that is, the plan against Czechoslovakia) will have to be carried out energetically; they will have to be newly prepared on the basis of the changed strategic position because of the annexation of Austria."

On the 21st April, 1938, a discussion took place between Hitler and the defendant Keitel with regard to "Case Gruen", showing quite clearly that the preparations for the attack on Czechoslovakia were being fully considered. On the 28th May, 1938, Hitler ordered that preparations should be made for military action against Czechoslovakia by the 2nd October, and from then onwards the plan to invade Czechoslovakia was constantly under review. On the 30th May, 1938, a directive signed by Hitler declared his "unalterable decision to smash Czechoslovakia by military action in the near future."

In June, 1938, as appears from a captured document taken from the files of the SD in Berlin, an elaborate plan for the employment of the SD in Czechoslovakia had been proposed. This plan provided that "the SD follow, if possible, immediately after the leading troops, and take upon themselves the duties similar to their tasks in Germany . . .".

Gestapo officials were assigned to co-operate with the SD in certain operations. Special agents were to be trained beforehand to prevent sabotage, and these agents were to be notified "before the attack in due time . . . . in order to give them the possibility to hide themselves, avoid arrest and deportation . . .".

"At the beginning, guerrilla or partisan warfare is to be expected, therefore weapons are necessary . . .".

Files of information were to be compiled with notations as follows: "To arrest" . . . "To liquidate" . . . "To confiscate" . . . "To deprive of passport" etc.

The plan provided for the temporary division of the country into larger and smaller territorial units, and considered various "suggestions", as they were termed, for the incorporation into the German Reich of the inhabitants and districts of Czechoslovakia. The final "suggestion" included the whole country, together with Slovakia and Carpathian Russia, with a population of nearly 15 millions.

The plan was modified in some respects in September after the Munich Conference, but the fact that the plan existed in such exact detail and was couched in such war-like language indicated a calculated design to resort to force.

On the 31st August, 1938, Hitler approved a memorandum by Jodl dated 24th August, 1938, concerning the timing of the order for the invasion of Czechoslovakia and the question of defence measures. This memorandum contained the following:

"Operation Gruen will be set in motion by means of an 'incident' in Czechoslovakia, which will give Germany provocation for military intervention. The fixing of the *exact time* for this incident is of the utmost importance."

These facts demonstrate that the occupation of Czechoslovakia had been planned in detail long before the Munich conference.

In the month of September, 1938, the conferences and talks with military leaders continued. In view of the extra-ordinarily critical situation which had arisen, the British Prime Minister, Mr. Chamberlain, flew to Munich and then went to Berchtesgaden to see Hitler. On the 22nd September Mr. Chamberlain met Hitler for further dis-cussions at Bad Godesberg. On the 26th September, 1938, Hitler said in a speech in Berlin, with reference to his con-versation:

"I assured him, moreover, and I repeat it here, that when this problem is solved there will be no more territorial problems for Germany in Europe; and I further assured him that from the moment when Czechoslovakia solves its other problems, that is to say, when the Czechs have come to an arrangement with their other minorities, peacefully and without oppression, I will be no longer interested in the Czech State, and that as far as I am concerned I will guarantee it. We don't want any Czechs."

On the 29th September, 1938, after a conference between Hitler and Mussolini and the British and French Prime Ministers in Munich, the Munich Pact was signed, by which Czechoslovakia was required to acquiesce in the cession of the Sudetenland to Germany. The "piece of paper" which the British Prime Minister brought back to London, signed by himself and Hitler, expressed the hope that for the future Britain and Germany might live with-out war. That Hitler never intended to adhere to the Munich Agreement is shown by the fact that a little later he asked the defendant Keitel for information with regard to the military force which in his opinion would be required to break all Czech resistance in Bohemia and Moravia. Keitel gave his reply on the 11th October 1938. On the 21st October, 1938, a directive was issued by Hitler, and countersigned by the defendant Keitel, to the armed forces on their future tasks, which stated:

"Liquidation of the remainder of Czechoslovakia. It must be possible to smash at any time the remainder of Czechoslovakia if her policy should become hostile towards Germany."

On the 14th March, 1939, the Czech President Hacha and his Foreign Minister Chvalkovsky came to Berlin at the suggestion of Hitler, and attended a meeting at which the defendants Ribbentrop, Goering and Keitel were present, with others. The proposal was made to Hacha that if he would sign an agreement consenting to the incorporation of the Czech people in the German Reich at once, Bohemia and Moravia would be saved from destruction. He was informed that German troops had already received orders to march and that any resistance would be broken with physical force. The defendant Goering added the threat that he would destroy Prague completely from the air. Faced by this dreadful alternative, Hacha and his Foreign Minister put their signatures to the necessary agreement at 4.30 in the morning, and Hitler and Ribbentrop signed on behalf of Germany.

On the 15th March German troops occupied Bohemia and Moravia, and on the 16th March the German decree was issued incorporating Bohemia and Moravia in the Reich as a protectorate, and this decree was signed by the defendants Ribbentrop and Frick.

By March, 1939, the plan to annex Austria and Czechoslovakia, which had been discussed by Hitler at the meeting of the 5th November, 1937, had been accomplished. The time had now come for the German leaders to consider further acts of aggression, made more possible of attainment because of that accomplishment.

On the 23rd May, 1939, a meeting was held in Hitler's study in the new Reich Chancellery in Berlin. Hitler announced his decision to attack Poland and gave his reasons, and discussed the effect the decision might have on other countries. In point of time, this was the second of the important meetings to which reference has already been made, and in order to appreciate the full significance of what was said and done, it is necessary to state shortly some of the main events in the history of German-Polish relations.

As long ago as the year 1925 an Arbitration Treaty between Germany and Poland had been made at Locarno, providing for the settlement of all disputes between the two countries. On the 26th January, 1934, a German-Polish declaration of non-aggression was made, signed on behalf of the German Government by the defendant von Neurath. On the 30th January, 1934, and again on the 30th January, 1937, Hitler made speeches in the Reichstag in which he expressed his view that Poland and Germany could work together in harmony and peace. On the 20th February, 1938, Hitler made a third speech in the Reichstag in the course of which he said with regard to Poland:

"And so the way to a friendly understanding has been successfully paved, an understanding which, beginning with Danzig, has today, in spite of the attempts of certain mischief makers, succeeded in finally taking the poison out of the relations between Germany and Poland and transforming them into a sincere, friendly cooperation. Relying on her friendships, Germany will not leave a stone unturned to save that ideal which provides the foundation for the task which is ahead of us—peace."

On the 26th September, 1938, in the middle of the crisis over the Sudetenland, Hitler made the speech in Berlin which has already been quoted, and announced that he had informed the British Prime Minister that when the Czechoslovakian problem has been solved there would be no more territorial problems for Germany in Europe. Nevertheless, on the 24th November of the same year, an OKW directive was issued to the German armed forces to make preparations for an attack upon Danzig; it stated:

"The Feuhrer has ordered:

(1) Preparations are also to be made to enable the Free State of Danzig to be occupied by German troops by surprise."

In spite of having ordered military preparations for the occupation of Danzig, Hitler, on the 30th January, 1939, said in a speech in the Reichstag:

"During the troubled months of the past year, the friendship between Germany and Poland has been one of the most reassuring factors in the political life of Europe."

Five days previously, on the 25th January, 1939, Ribbentrop said in the course of a speech in Warsaw:

"Thus Poland and Germany can look forward to the future with full confidence in the solid basis of their mutual relations."

Following the occupation of Bohemia and Moravia by Germany on the 15th March, 1939, which was a flagrant breach of the Munich Agreement, Great Britain gave an assurance to Poland on the 31st March, 1939, that in the event of any action which clearly threatened Polish independence, and which the Polish Government accordingly considered it vital to resist with their national forces, Great Britain would feel itself bound at once to lend Poland all the support in its power. The French Government took the same stand. It is interesting to note in this connection, that one of the arguments frequently presented by the defence in the present case is that the defendants were influenced to think that their conduct was not in breach of international law by the acquiescence of other Powers. The declarations of Great Britain and France showed, at least, that this view could be held no longer.

On the 3rd April, 1939, a revised OKW directive was issued to the armed forces, which after referring to the question of Danzig made reference to Fall Weiss (the military code name for the German invasion of Poland) and stated:

"The Fuehrer had added the following directions to Fall Weiss:

(1) Preparations must be made in such a way that the operation can be carried out at any time from the 1st September, 1939, onwards.

(2) The High Command of the Armed Forces has been directed to draw up a precise timetable for Fall Weiss and to arrange by conferences the synchronised timings between the three branches of the Armed Forces."

On the 11th April, 1939, a further directive was signed by Hitler and issued to the armed forces, and in one of the annexes to that document the words occur:

"Quarrels with Poland should be avoided. Should Poland however adopt a threatening attitude towards Germany, "a final settlement" will be necessary, notwithstanding the pact with Poland. The aim is then to destroy Polish military strength, and to create in the East a situation which satisfies the requirements of defence. The Free State of Danzig will be incorporated into Germany at the outbreak of the conflict at the latest. Policy aims at limiting the war to Poland, and this is considered possible in view of the internal crisis in France, and British restraint as a result of this."

In spite of the contents of these two directives, Hitler made a speech in the Reichstag on the 28th April, 1939, in which, after describing the Polish Government's alleged rejection of an offer he had made with regard to Danzig and the Polish Corridor, he stated:

"I have regretted greatly this incomprehensible attitude of the Polish Government, but that alone is not the decisive fact; the worst is that now Poland like Czechoslovakia a year ago believes, under the pressure of a lying international campaign, that it must call up its troops, although Germany on her part has not called up a single man, and had not thought of proceeding in any way against Poland. ...The intention to attack on the part of Germany which was merely invented by the international Press ..."

It was four weeks after making this speech that Hitler, on the 23rd May, 1939, held the important military conference to which reference has already been made. Among the persons present were the defendants Goering, Raeder and Keitel. The adjutant on duty that day was Lieutenant-Colonel Schmundt, and he made a record of what happened, certifying it with his signature as a correct record.

The purpose of the meeting was to enable Hitler to

inform the heads of the armed forces and their staffs of his views on the political situation and his future aims. After analysing the political situation and reviewing the course of events since 1933, Hitler announced his decision to attack Poland. He admitted that the quarrel with Poland over Danzig was not the reason for this attack, but the necessity for Germany to enlarge her living space and secure her food supplies. He said:

"The solution of the problem demands courage. The principle by which one evades solving the problem by adapting oneself to circumstances is inadmissible. Circumstances must rather be adapted to. This is impossible without invasion of foreign states or attacks upon foreign property."

Later in his address he added:

"There is therefore no question of sparing Poland, and we are left with the decision to attack Poland at the first suitable opportunity. We cannot expect a repetition of the Czech affair. There will be war. Our task is to isolate Poland. The success of the isolation will be decisive . . . The isolation of Poland is a matter of skilful politics."

Lt.-Col. Schmundt's record of the meeting reveals that Hitler fully realised the possibility of Great Britain and France coming to Poland's assistance. If, therefore, the isolation of Poland could not be achieved, Hitler was of opinion that Germany should attack Great Britain and France first, or at any rate should concentrate primarily on the war in the West, in order to defeat Great Britain and France quickly, or at least to destroy their effectiveness. Nevertheless, Hitler stressed that war with England and France would be a life and death struggle, which might last a long time, and that preparations must be made accordingly.

During the weeks which followed this conference, other meetings were held and directives were issued in preparation for the war. The defendant Ribbentrop was sent to Moscow to negotiate a non-aggression pact with the Soviet Union.

On the 22nd August, 1939, there took place the important meeting of that day, to which reference has already been made. The Prosecution have put in *evidence two unsigned captured documents which appear to be records made of this meeting by persons who were present. The first document is headed: "The Fuehrer's speech to the Commanders-in-Chief on the 22nd August, 1939 . . ." The purpose of the speech was to announce the decision to make war on Poland at once, and Hitler began by saying:

"It was clear to me that a conflict with Poland had to come sooner or later. I had already made this decision in the Spring, but I thought that I would first turn against the West in a few years, and only afterwards against the East . . . I wanted to establish an acceptable relationship with Poland in order to fight first against the West. But this plan, which was agreeable to me, could not be executed since essential points have changed. It became clear to me that Poland would attack us in case of a conflict with the West."

Hitler then went to to explain why he had decided that the most favourable moment had arrived for starting the war. "Now," said Hitler, "Poland is in the position in which I wanted her . . . I am only afraid that at the last moment some Schweinehund will make a proposal for mediation . . . A beginning has been made for the destruction of England's hegemony."

This document closely resembles one of the documents put in evidence on behalf of the defendant Raeder. This latter document consists of a summary of the same speech, compiled on the day it was made, by one Admiral Boehm, from notes he had taken during the meeting. In substance it says that the moment had arrived to settle the dispute with Poland by military invasion, that although a conflict between Germany and the West was unavoidable in the long run, the likelihood of Great Britain and France coming to Poland's assistance was not great, and that even if a war in the West should come about, the first aim should be the crushing of the Polish military strength. It also contains a statement by Hitler that an appropriate propaganda reason for invading Poland would be given, the truth or falsehood of which was unimportant, since "the Right lies in Victory."

The second unsigned document put in evidence by the Prosecution is headed: "Second Speech by the Fuehrer on the 22nd August, 1939," and it is in the form of notes of the main points made by Hitler. Some of these are as follows:

"Everybody shall have to make a point of it that we were determined from the beginning to fight the Western Powers. Struggle for life or death . . . destruction of Poland in the foreground. The aim is elimination of living forces, not the arrival at a certain line. Even if war should break out in the West, the destruction of Poland shall be the primary objective. I shall give a propagandist cause for starting the war—never mind whether it be plausible or not. The victor shall not be asked later on whether we told the truth or not. In starting and making a war, not the Right is what matters, but Victory . . . The start will be ordered probably by Saturday morning." (That is to say, the 26th August.)

In spite of it being described as a second speech, there are sufficient points of similarity with the two previously mentioned documents to make it appear very probable that this is an account of the same speech, not as detailed as the other two, but in substance the same.

These three documents establish that the final decision as to the date of Poland's destruction, which had been agreed upon and planned earlier in the year, was reached by Hitler shortly before the 22nd August, 1939. They also show that although he hoped to be able to avoid having to fight Great Britain and France as well, he fully realised there was a risk of this happening, but it was a risk which he was determined to take.

The events of the last days of August confirm this determination. On the 22nd August, 1939, the same day as the speech just referred to, the British Prime Minister wrote a letter to Hitler, in which he said:

"Having thus made our position perfectly clear, I wish to repeat to you my conviction that war between our two peoples would be the greatest calamity that could occur." On the 23rd August Hitler replied:

"The question of the treatment of European problems on a peaceful basis is not a decision which rests with Germany, but primarily on those who since the crime committed by the Versailles Diktat have stubbornly and consistently opposed any peaceful revision. Only after a change of spirit on the part of the responsible Powers can there be any real change in the relationship between England and Germany."

There followed a number of appeals to Hitler to refrain from forcing the Polish issue to the point of war. These were from President Roosevelt on the 24th and 25th August; from His Holiness the Pope on the 24th and 31st August; and from M. Daladier, the Prime Minister of France, on the 26th August. All these appeals fell on deaf ears.

On the 25th August, Great Britain signed a pact of mutual assistance with Poland, which reinforced the understanding she had given to Poland earlier in the year. This coupled with the news of Mussolini's unwillingness to enter the war on Germany's side, made Hitler hesitate for a moment. The invasion of Poland, which was timed to start on the 26th August, was postponed until a further attempt had been made to persuade Great Britain not to intervene. Hitler offered to enter into a comprehensive agreement with Great Britain, once the Polish question had been settled. In reply to this, Great Britain made a counter-suggestion for the settlement of the Polish dispute by negotiation. On the 29th August Hitler informed the British Ambassador that the German Government, though sceptical as to the result, would be prepared to enter into direct negotiations with a Polish emissary, provided he arrived in Berlin with plenipotentiary powers by midnight for the following day, August 30th. The Polish Government were informed of this, but with the example of Schuschnigg and Hacha before them, they decided not to send such an emissary. At midnight on the 30th August the defendant Ribbentrop read to the British Ambassador at top speed a document containing the first precise formulation of the German demands against Poland. He refused, however, to give the Ambassador a copy of this, and stated that in any case it was too late now, since no Polish plenipotentiary had arrived.

In the opinion of the Tribunal, the manner in which these negotiations were conducted by Hitler and Ribbentrop showed that they were not entered into in good faith or with any desire to maintain peace, but solely in the attempt to prevent Great Britain and France from honouring their obligations to Poland.

Parallel with these negotiations were the unsuccessful attempts made by Goering to effect the isolation of Poland by persuading Great Britain not to stand by her pledged word, through the services of one Birger Dahlerus, a Swede. Dahlerus, who was called as a witness by Goering, had a considerable knowledge of England and of things English, and in July, 1939, was anxious to bring about a better understanding between England and Germany, in the hope of preventing a war between the two countries. He got into contact with Goering as well as with official circles in London, and during the latter part of August, Goering used him as an unofficial intermediary to try and deter the British Government from their opposition to Germany's intentions towards Poland. Dahlerus, of course, had no knowledge at the time of the decision which Hitler had secretly announced on the 22nd August, nor of the German military directives for the attack on Poland which were already in existence. As he admitted in his evidence, it was not until the 26th September, after the conquest of Poland was virtually complete, that he first realised that Goering's aim all along had been to get Great Britain's consent to Germany's seizure of Poland.

After all attempts to persuade Germany to agree to a settlement of her dispute with Poland on a reasonable basis had failed, Hitler, on the 31st August, issued his final directive, in which he announced that the attack on Poland would start in the early morning hours of the 1st September, and gave instructions as to what action would be taken if Great Britain and France should enter the war in defence of Poland.

In the opinion of the Tribunal, the events of the days immediately preceding the 1st September, 1939, demonstrate the determination of Hitler and his associates to carry out the declared intention of invading Poland at all costs, despite appeals from every quarter. With the ever increasing evidence before him that this intention would lead to war with Great Britain and France as well, Hitler was resolved not to depart from the course he had set for himself. The Tribunal is fully satisfied by the evidence that the war initiated by Germany against Poland on the 1st September, 1939, was most plainly an aggressive war, which was to develop in due course into a war which embraced almost the whole world, and resulted in the commission of countless crimes, both against the laws and customs of war, and against humanity.

The PRESIDENT: Now I shall ask M. Falco to continue the reading of the judgment.

M. FALCO:

The aggressive war against Poland was but the beginning. The aggression of Nazi Germany quickly spread from country to country. In point of time the first two countries to suffer were Denmark and Norway.

On the 31st May, 1939, a Treaty of Non-Aggression was made between Germany and Denmark, and signed by the defendant Ribbentrop. It was there solemnly stated that the parties to the Treaty were "firmly resolved to maintain peace between Denmark and Germany under all circumstances." Nevertheless, Germany invaded Denmark on the 9th April, 1940.

On the 2nd September, 1939, after the outbreak of war with Poland, Germany sent a solemn assurance to Norway in these terms:

"The German Reich Government is determined in view of the friendly relations which exist between Norway and Germany, under no circumstance to prejudice the inviolability and integrity of Norway, and to respect the territory of the Norwegian State. In making this declaration the Reich Government naturally expects, on its side, that Norway will observe an unimpeachable neutrality towards the Reich and will not tolerate any breaches of Norwegian neutrality by any third party which might occur. Should the attitude of the Royal Norwegian Government differ from this so that any such breach of neutrality by a third party occurs, the Reich Government would then obviously be compelled to safeguard the interests of the Reich in such a way as the resulting situation might dictate."

On the 9th April, 1940, in pursuance of her plan of campaign, Norway was invaded by Germany.

The idea of attacking Norway originated, it appears, with the defendants Raeder and Rosenberg. On the 3rd October, 1939, Raeder prepared a memorandum on the subject of "gaining bases in Norway," and amongst the questions discussed was the question: "Can bases be gained by military force against Norway's will, if it is impossible to carry this out without fighting?" Despite this fact, three days later, further assurances were given to Norway by Germany, which stated:

"Germany has never had any conflicts of interest or even points of controversy with the Northern States, and neither has she any to-day."

Three days later again, the defendant Doenitz prepared a memorandum on the same subject, namely, bases in Norway, and suggested the establishment of a base in Trondheim with an alternative of supplying fuel in Narvik. At the same time the defendant Raeder was in correspondence with Admiral Karls, who pointed out to him the importance of an occupation of the Norwegian coast by Germany. On the 10th October, Raeder reported to Hitler the disadvantages to Germany which an occupation by the British would have. In the months of October and November Raeder continued to work on the possible occupation of Norway, in conjunction with the "Rosenberg Organisation." The "Rosenberg

Organisation" was the Foreign Affairs Bureau of the NSDAP, and Rosenberg as Reichsleiter was in charge of it. Early in December, Quisling, the notorious Norwegian traitor, visited Berlin and was seen by the defendants Rosenberg and Raeder. He put forward a plan for a *coup d'etat* in Norway. On the 12th December, the defendant Raeder and the naval staff, together with the defendants Keitel and Jodl, had a conference with Hitler, when Raeder reported on his interview with Quisling, and set out Quisling's views. On the 16th December, Hitler himself interviewed Quisling on all these matters. In the report of the activities of the Foreign Affairs Bureau of the NSDAP for the years 1933–1943, under the heading of "Political preparations for the military occupation of Norway," it is stated that at the interview with Quisling Hitler said that he would prefer a neutral attitude on the part of Norway as well as the whole of Scandinavia, as he did not desire to extend the theater of war, or to draw other nations into the conflict. If the enemy attempted to extend the war he would be compelled to guard himself against that undertaking; however he promised Quisling financial support, and assigned to a special military staff the examination of the military questions involved.

On the 27th January, 1940, a memorandum was prepared by the defendant Keitel regarding the plans for the invasion of Norway. On the 28th February, 1940, the defendant Jodl entered in his diary:

"I proposed first to the Chief of OKW and then to the Fuehrer that "Case Yellow" (that is the operation against the Netherlands) and Weser Exercise (that is the operation against Norway and Denmark) must be prepared in such a way that they will be independent of one another as regard both time and forces employed."

On the 1st March Hitler issued a directive regarding the Weser Exercise which contained the words:

"The development of the situation in Scandinavia requires the making of all preparations for the occupation of Denmark and Norway by a part of the German Armed Forces. This operation should prevent British encroachment on Scandinavia and the Baltic; further, it should guarantee our ore base in Sweden and give our Navy and Air Force a wider start line against Britain . . . The crossing of the Danish border and the landings in Norway must take place simultaneously . . . It is most important that the Scandinavian States as well as the Western opponents should be taken by surprise by our measures."

On the 24th March, the naval operation orders for the Weser Exercise were issued, and on the 30th March the defendant Doenitz as Commander-in-Chief of U-boats issued his operational order for the occupation of Denmark and Norway. On the 9th April, 1940, the German forces invaded Norway and Denmark.

From this narrative it is clear that as early as October, 1939, the question of invading Norway was under consideration. The defence that has been made here is that Germany was compelled to attack Norway to forestall an Allied invasion, and her action was therefore preventive.

It must be remembered that preventive action in foreign territory is justified only in case of "an instant and overwhelming necessity for self-defence, leaving no choice of means, and no moment of deliberation." (The Caroline Case, 1808.6.C.Rob.461). How widely the view was held in influential German circles that the Allies intended to occupy Norway cannot be determined with exactitude. Quisling asserted that the Allies would intervene in Norway with the tacit consent of the Norwegian Government. The German Legation at Oslo disagreed with this view, although the Naval Attaché at that Legation shared it.

The War Diary of the German Naval Operations Staff for 13th January, 1940, stated that the Chief of the Naval Operations Staff thought that the most favourable solution would be the maintenance of the neutrality of Norway, but he harboured the firm conviction that England intended to occupy Norway in the near future relying on the tacit agreement of the Norwegian Government.

The directive of Hitler issued on 1st March, 1940, for the attack on Denmark and Norway stated that the operation "should prevent British encroachment on Scandinavia and the Baltic."

It is, however, to be remembered that the defendant Raeder's memorandum of the 3rd October, 1939, makes no reference to forestalling the Allies, but it is based upon "the aim of improving our strategical and operational position."

The memorandum itself is headed "Gaining of Bases in Norway." The same observation applies *mutatis mutandis* to the memorandum of the defendant Doenitz of 9th October, 1939.

Furthermore, on the 13th March, the defendant Jodl recorded in his diary:

"Fuehrer does not give order yet for 'W' (Weser Exercise). He is still looking for an excuse." (Justification?)

On the 14th March, 1940, he again wrote:

"Fuehrer has not yet decided what reason to give for 'Weser Exercise'."

On the 21st March, 1940, he recorded the misgivings of Task Force XXI about the long interval between taking up readiness positions and the close of the diplomatic negotiations, and added:

"Fuehrer rejects any earlier negotiations, as otherwise calls for help go out to England and America. If resistance is put up it must be ruthlessly broken."

On 2nd April he records that all the preparations are completed; on 4th April the Naval Operation Order was issued; and on the 9th April, the invasion was begun.

From all this it is clear that when the plans for an attack on Norway were being made, they were not made for the purpose of forestalling an imminent Allied landing, but, at the most, that they might prevent an Allied occupation at some future date.

When the final orders for the German invasion of Norway were given, the diary of the Naval Operations Staff for 23rd March, 1940, records:

"A mass encroachment by the English into Norwegian territorial waters . . . is not to be expected at the present time."

And Admiral Assmann's entry for 26th March says:

"British landing in Norway not considered serious."

Documents which were subsequently captured by the Germans are relied on to show that the Allied plan to occupy harbours and airports in Western Norway was a definite plan, although in all points considerably behind the German plans under which the invasion was actually carried out. These documents indicate that an altered plan had been finally agreed upon on 20th March, 1940, that a convoy should leave England on 5th April, and that mining in Norwegian waters would begin the same day; and that on 5th April the sailing time had been postponed until 8th April. But these plans were not the cause of the German invasion of Norway. Norway was occupied by Germany to afford her bases from which a more effective attack on England and France might be made, pursuant to plans prepared long in advance of the Allied plans which are now relied on to support the argument of self-defence.

It was further argued that Germany alone could decide, in accordance with the reservations made by many of the Signatory Powers at the time of the conclusion of the Briand-Kellogg Pact, whether preventive action was a necessity, and that in making her decision her judgment was conclusive. But whether action taken under the claim of self-defence was in fact aggressive or defensive must ultimately be subject to investigation and adjudication if international law is ever to be enforced.

No suggestion is made by the defendants that there was any plan by any belligerent, other than Germany, to occupy Denmark. No excuse for that aggression has ever been offered.

As the German armies entered Norway and Denmark, German memoranda were handed to the Norwegian and Danish Governments which gave the assurance that the German troops did not come as enemies, that they did not intend to make use of the points occupied by German troops as bases for operations against England, as long as they were not forced to do so by measures taken by England and France, and that they had come to protect the North against the proposed occupation of Norwegian strong points by English-French forces.

The memoranda added that Germany had no intention of infringing the territorial integrity and political independence of the Kingdom of Norway then or in the future. Nevertheless, on the 3rd June, 1940, a German Naval memorandum discussed the use to be made of

Norway and Denmark, and put forward one solution for consideration, that the territories of Denmark and Norway acquired during the course of the war should continue to be occupied and organised so that they could in the future be considered as German possessions.

In the light of all the available evidence it is impossible to accept the contention that the invasions of Denmark and Norway were defensive, and in the opinion of the Tribunal they were acts of aggressive war.

The plan to seize Belgium and the Netherlands was considered in August, 1938, when the attack on Czechoslovakia was being formulated, and the possibility of war with France and England was contemplated. The advantage to Germany of being able to use these countries for their own purposes, particularly as air bases in the war against England and France, was emphasised. In May of 1939, when Hitler made his irrevocable decision to attack Poland, and foresaw the possibility at least of a war with England and France in consequence, he told his military commanders:

"Dutch and Belgian air bases must be occupied. . . . Declarations of neutrality must be ignored."

On August 22nd in the same year, he told his military commanders that England and France, in his opinion, would not "violate the neutrality of these countries." At the same time he assured Belgium and Holland and Luxemburg that he would respect their neutrality; and on the 6th October, 1939, after the Polish campaign, he repeated this assurance. On the 7th October General von Brauchitsch directed Army Group B to prepare "for the immediate invasion of Dutch and Belgian territory, if the political situation so demands." In a series of orders, which were signed by the defendants Keitel and Jodl, the attack was fixed for the 10th November, 1939, but it was post-poned from time to time until May of 1940 on account of weather conditions and transport problems.

At the conference on the 23rd November, 1939, Hitler said:

"We have an Achilles heel: The Ruhr. The progress of the war depends on the possession of the Ruhr. If England and France push through Belgium and Holland into the Ruhr, we shall be in the greatest danger. . . . Certainly England and France will assume the offensive against Germany when they are armed. England and France have means of pressure to bring Belgium and Holland to request English and French help. In Belgium and Holland the sympathies are all for France and England. . . . If the French Army marches into Belgium in order to attack us, it will be too late for us. We must anticipate them. . . . We shall sow the English coast with mines which cannot be cleared. This mine war-fare with the Luftwaffe demands a different starting point. England cannot live without its imports. We can feed ourselves. The permanent sowing of mines on the English coasts will bring England to her knees. However, this can only occur if we have occupied Belgium and Holland . . . My decision is unchangeable; I shall attack France and England at the most favourable and quickest moment. Breach of the neutrality of Belgium and Holland is meaningless. No one will question that when we have won. We shall not bring about the breach of neutrality as idiotically as it was in 1914. If we do not break the neu-trality, then England and France will. Without attack, the war is not to be ended victoriously."

On the 10th May, 1940, the German forces invaded the Netherlands, Belgium and Luxemburg. On the same day the German Ambassadors handed to the Netherlands and Belgian Governments a memorandum alleging that the British and French armies, with the consent of Belgium and Holland, were planning to march through those countries to attack the Ruhr, and justifying the invasion on these grounds. Germany, however, assured the Netherlands and Belgium that their integrity and their possessions would be respected. A similar memorandum was delivered to Luxemburg on the same date.

There is no evidence before the Tribunal to justify the contention that the Netherlands, Belgium and Luxemburg were invaded by Germany because their occupation had been planned by England and France. British and French staffs had been cooperating in making certain plans for military operations in the Low Countries, but the purpose of this planning was to defend these countries in the event of a German attack.

The invasion of Belgium, Holland and Luxemburg was entirely without justification.

It was carried out in pursuance of policies long considered and prepared, and was plainly an act of aggressive war. The resolve to invade was made without any other consideration than the advancement of the aggressive policies of Germany.

On the 12th August, 1939, Hitler had a conversation with Ciano and the defendant Ribbentrop at Obersalzberg. He said then:

"Generally speaking, the best thing to happen would be for the neutrals to be liquidated one after the other. The process could be carried out more easily if on every occasion one partner of the Axis covered the other while it was dealing with the uncertain neutral. Italy might well regard Yugoslavia as a neutral of this kind."

This observation was made only two months after Hitler had given assurances to Yugoslavia that he would

regard her frontier as final and inviolable. On the occasion
of the visit to Germany of the Prince Regent of Yugoslavia
on 1st June, 1939, Hitler had said in a public speech:

"The firmly established reliable relationship of Germany
to Yugoslavia now that owing to historical events we have
become neighbours with common boundaries fixed for all
time, will not only guarantee lasting peace between our
two peoples and countries, but can also represent an element of calm to our nerveracked continent. This peace is
the goal of all who are disposed to perform really con-
structive work."

On the 6th October, 1939, Germany repeated these
assurances to Yugoslavia, after Hitler and Ribbentrop had
unsuccessfully tried to persuade Italy to enter the war on
the side of Germany by attacking Yugoslavia. On the 28th
October, 1940, Italy invaded Greece, but the military
operations met with no success. In November Hitler
wrote to Mussolini with regard to the invasion of Greece,
and the extension of the war in the Balkans, and pointed
out that no military operations could take place in the
Balkans before the following March, and therefore
Yugoslavia must if at all possible be won over by other
means, and in other ways. But on the 12th November,
1940, Hitler issued a directive for the prosecution of the
war, and it included the words:

"The Balkans: The Commander-in-Chief of the Army
will make preparations for occupying the Greek mainland
north of the Aegean Sea, in case of need entering through
Bulgaria."

On the 13th December he issued a directive concerning the operation "Marita," the code name for the
invasion of Greece, in which he stated:

"1. The result of the battles in Albania is not yet decisive. Because of a dangerous situation in Albania, it is doubly necessary that the British endeavour be foiled to create air bases under the protection of a Balkan front, which would be dangerous above all to Italy as to the Roumanian oil-fields.

2. My plan therefore is (a) to form a slowly increasing task force in Southern Roumania within the next month, (b) after the setting in of favourable weather, probably in March, to send a task force for the occupation of the Aegean north coast by way of Bulgaria and if necessary to occupy the entire Greek mainland."

On the 20th January, 1941, at a meeting between Hitler and Mussolini, at which the defendants Ribbentrop, Keitel, Jodl and others were present, Hitler stated:

"The massing of troops in Roumania serves a threefold purpose.

(a) An operation against Greece;
(b) Protection of Bulgaria against Russia and Turkey;
(c) Safeguarding the guarantee to Roumania . . .

It is desirable that this deployment be completed without interference from the enemy. Therefore, disclose the game as late as possible. The tendency will be to cross the Danube at the last possible moment, and to line up for attack at the earliest possible moment."

On the 19th February, 1941, an OKW directive re the operation "Marita" stated:

"On the 18th February the Fuehrer made the following decision regarding the carrying out of Operation Marita: the following dates are envisaged: Commencement of building bridge, 28th February: Crossing of the Danube, 2nd March."

On the 3rd March, 1941, British troops landed in Greece to assist the Greeks to resist the Italians: and on the 18th March, at a meeting between Hitler and the defendant Raeder, at which the defendants Keitel and Jodl were also present, the defendant Raeder asked for confirmation that the "whole of Greece will have to be occupied, even in the event of a peaceful settlement," to which Hitler replied, "The complete occupation is a prerequisite of any settlement."

On the 25th March, on the occasion of the adherence of Yugoslavia to the Tripartite Pact at a meeting in Vienna, the defendant Ribbentrop, on behalf of the German Government, confirmed the determination of Germany to respect the sovereignty and territorial integrity of Yugoslavia at all times. On the 26th March the Yugoslav Ministers, who had adhered to the Tripartite Pact, were removed from office by a *coup d'etat* in Belgrade on their return from Vienna, and the new Government repudiated the Pact. Thereupon on 27th March, at a conference in Berlin with the High Command at which the defendants Goering, Keitel and Jodl were present, and the defendant Ribbentrop part of the time, Hitler stated that Yugoslavia was an uncertain factor in regard to the contemplated attack on Greece, and even more so with regard to the attack upon Russia which was to be conducted later on. Hitler announced that he was determined, without waiting for possible loyalty declarations of the new Government, to make all preparations in order to destroy Yugoslavia militarily and as a national unit. He stated that he would act with "unmerciful harshness."

On the 6th April German forces invaded Greece and Yugoslavia without warning, and Belgrade was bombed by the Luftwaffe. So swift was this particular invasion that there had not been time to establish any "incidents" as a usual preliminary, or to find and publish any adequate "political" explanations. As the attack was starting on the 6th April, Hitler proclaimed to the German people that this attack was necessary because the British forces in Greece (who were helping the Greeks to defend themselves against the Italians) represented a British attempt to extend the war to the Balkans.

It is clear from this narrative that aggressive war against Greece and Yugoslavia had long been in contemplation, certainly as early as August of 1939. The fact that Great Britain had come to the assistance of the Greeks, and might thereafter be in a position to inflict great damage upon German interests was made the occasion for the occupation of both countries.

On the 23rd August, 1939, Germany signed the non-aggression pact with the Union of Soviet Socialist Republics.

The evidence has shown unmistakably that the Soviet Union on their part conformed to the terms of this pact; indeed the German Government itself had been assured of this by the highest German sources. Thus, the German Ambassador in Moscow informed his Government that the Soviet Union would go to war only if attacked by Germany, and this statement is recorded in the German War Diary under the date of June 6th, 1941.

Nevertheless, as early as the late summer of 1940, Germany began to make preparations for an attack on the U.S.S.R., in spite of the non-aggression pact. This operation was secretly planned under the code name "Case Barbarossa", and the former Field Marshal Paulus testified that on the 3rd September, 1940, when he joined the German General Staff, he continued developing "Case Barbarossa", which was finally completed at the beginning of November, 1940; and that even then, the German General Staff had no information that the Soviet Union was preparing for war.

On the 18th of December, 1940, Hitler issued directive No. 21, initialled by Keitel and Jodl, which called for the completion of all preparations connected with the realisation of "Case Barbarossa" by the 15th May, 1941. This directive stated:

"The German armed forces must be prepared to crush Soviet Russia in a quick campaign before the end of the war against England . . . Great caution has to be exercised that the intention of an attack will not be recognised."

Before the directive of the 18th December had been made, the defendant Goering had informed General Thomas, chief of the Office of War Economy of the OKW, of the plan, and General Thomas made surveys of the economic possibilities of the USSR including its raw materials, its power and transport system, and its capacity to produce arms.

In accordance with these surveys, an economic staff for the Eastern territories with many military-economic units (inspectorates, Commandos, groups) was created under the supervision of the defendant Goering. In conjunction with the military command, these units were to achieve the most complete and efficient economic exploitation of the occupied territories in the interest of Germany.

The framework of the future political and economic organisation of the occupied territories was designed by the defendant Rosenberg over a period of three months, after conferences with and assistance by the defendants Keitel, Jodl, Raeder, Funk, Goering, Ribbentrop, and Frick or their representatives. It was made the subject of a most detailed report immediately after the invasion.

These plans outlined the destruction of the Soviet Union as an independent State, and its partition, the creation of so-called Reich Commissariats, and the conversion of Esthonia, Latvia, Byelorussia and other territories into German colonies.

At the same time Germany drew Hungary, Roumania and Finland into the war against the U.S.S.R. In December 1940 Hungary agreed to participate on the promise of Germany that she should have certain territories at the expense of Yugoslavia.

In May 1941 a final agreement was concluded with Antonescu, the Prime Minister of Roumania, regarding the attack on the U.S.S.R., in which Germany promised to Roumania, Bessarabia, Northern Bukovina and the right to occupy Soviet territory up to the Dnieper.

On the 22nd June, 1941, without any declaration of war, Germany invaded Soviet territory in accordance with the plans so long made.

The evidence which has been given before this Tribunal proves that Germany had the design carefully thought out, to crush the U.S.S.R. as a political and military power, so that Germany might expand to the east according to her own desire. In "Mein Kampf", Hitler had written:

"If new territory were to be acquired in Europe, it must have been mainly at Russia's cost, and once again the new German Empire should have set out on its march along the same road as was formerly trodden by the Teutonic Knights, this time to acquire soil for the German plough by means of the German sword and thus provide the nation with its daily bread."

But there was a more immediate purpose, and in one of the memoranda of the OKW, that immediate purpose was stated to be to feed the German armies from Soviet territory in the third year of the war, even if "as a result many millions of people, as the defendant Rosenberg said, will be starved to death if we take out of the country the things necessary for us."

The final aims of the attack on the Soviet Union were formulated at a conference with Hitler on July 16, 1941, in which the defendants Goering, Keitel, Rosenberg and Bormann participated:

"There can be no talk of the creation of a military power west of the Urals, even if we should have to fight 100 years to achieve this . . . All the Baltic regions must become part of the Reich. The Crimea and adjoining regions (North of the Crimea) must likewise be incorporated into the Reich. The region of the Volga as well as the Baku district must likewise be incorporated into the Reich. The Finns want Eastern Karelia. However, in view of the large deposits of nickel, the Kola peninsula must be ceded to Germany."

It was contended for the defendants that the attack upon the U.S.S.R., was justified because the Soviet Union was contemplating an attack upon Germany, and making preparations to that end. It is impossible to believe that this view was ever honestly entertained.

The plans for the economic exploitation of the U.S.S.R., for the removal of masses of the population, for the murder of Commissars and political leaders, were all part of the carefully prepared scheme launched on the

22nd June without warning of any kind, and without the shadow of legal excuse. It was plain aggression.

Four days after the attack launched by the Japanese on the United States fleet in Pearl Harbour on December 7, 1941, Germany declared war on the United States.

The Tripartite Pact between Germany, Italy, and Japan, had been signed on the 27th September, 1940, and from that date until the attack upon the U.S.S.R., the defendant Ribbentrop, with other defendants, was endeavouring to induce Japan to attack British possessions in the Far East. This, it was thought, would hasten England's defeat, and also keep the United States out of the war.

The possibility of a direct attack on the United States was considered and discussed as a matter for the future. Major von Falkenstein, the Luftwaffe Liaison officer with the Operations Staff of the OKW, summarising military problems which needed discussion in Berlin in October of 1940, spoke of the possibility "of the prosecution of the war against America at a later date." It is clear, too, that the German policy of keeping America out of the war, if possible, did not prevent Germany promising support to Japan even against the United States. On the 4th April, 1941, Hitler told Matsuoka, the Japanese Foreign Minister, in the presence of the defendant Ribbentrop, that Germany would "strike without delay" if a Japanese attack on Singapore should lead to war between Japan and the United States. The next day Ribbentrop himself urged Matsuoka to bring Japan into the war.

On the 28th November, 1941, ten days before the attack on Pearl Harbour, Ribbentrop encouraged Japan, through her Ambassador in Berlin, to attack Great Britain and the United States, and stated that should Japan become engaged in a war with the United States, Germany would join the war immediately. A few days later, Japanese representatives told Germany and Italy that Japan was preparing to attack the United States, and asked for their support. Germany and Italy agreed to do this, although in the Tripartite Pact, Italy and Germany had undertaken to assist Japan only if she were attacked. When the assault on Pearl Harbour did take place, the defendant Ribbentrop is reported to have been "overjoyed," and later, at a ceremony in Berlin, when a German medal was awarded to Oshima, the Japanese Ambassador, Hitler indicated his approval of the tactics which the Japanese had adopted of negotiating with the United States as long as possible, and then striking hard without any declaration of war.

Although it is true that Hitler and his colleagues originally did not consider that a war with the United States would be beneficial to their interest, it is apparent that in the course of 1941 that view was revised, and Japan was given every encouragement to adopt a policy which would almost certainly bring the United States into the war. And when Japan attacked the United States fleet in Pearl Harbour and thus made aggressive war against the United States, the Nazi Government caused Germany to enter that war at once on the side of Japan by declaring war themselves on the United States.

The PRESIDENT: The Tribunal will adjourn until a quarter past two.

(A recess was taken until 2.15 p.m.)

The PRESIDENT: I now ask Mr. Biddle to continue the reading of the judgment.

Mr. BIDDLE:

The Charter defines as a crime the planning or waging of war that is a war of aggression or a war in violation of international treaties. The Tribunal has decided that certain of the defendants planned and waged aggressive wars against twelve nations, and were therefore guilty of this series of crimes. This makes it unnecessary to discuss the subject in further detail, or even to consider at any length the extent to which these aggressive wars were also "wars in violation of international treaties, agreements or assurances." These treaties are set out in the Indictment. Those of principal importance are the following.

HAGUE CONVENTIONS

In the 1899 Convention the signatory powers agreed: "before an appeal to arms ... to have recourse, as far as circumstances allow, to the good offices or mediation of one or more friendly powers." A similar clause was inserted in the Convention for Pacific Settlement of International Disputes of 1907. In the accompanying Convention Relative to Opening of Hostilities, Article I contains this far more specific language:

"The Contracting Powers recognise that hostilities between them must not commence without a previous and explicit warning, in the form of either a declaration of war, giving reasons, or an ultimatum with a conditional declaration of war."
Germany was a party to these conventions.

VERSAILLES TREATY

Breaches of certain provisions of the Versailles Treaty are also relied on by the Prosecution—not to fortify the left bank of the Rhine (Art. 42–44); to "respect strictly the independence of Austria" (Art. 80); renunciation of any rights in Memel (Art. 99), and the Free City of Danzig (Art. 100); the recognition of the independence of the

Czecho-Slovak State; and the Military, Naval and Air Clauses against German rearmament found in Part V. There is no doubt that action was taken by the German Government contrary to all these provisions, the details of which are set out in Appendix C. With regard to the Treaty of Versailles, the matters relied on are:

1.   The violation of Articles 42 to 44 in respect of the demilitarised zone of the Rhineland.
2.   The annexation of Austria on the 13th March, 1938, in violation of Article 80;
3.   The incorporation of the district of Memel on the 22nd March, 1939, in violation of Article 99;
4.   The incorporation of the Free City of Danzig on the 1st September, 1939, in violation of Article 100;
5.   The incorporation of the provinces of Bohemia and Moravia on the 16th March, 1939, in violation of Article 81;
6.   The repudiation of the military naval and air clauses of the Treaty, in or about March of 1935.

On the 21st May, 1935, Germany announced that, whilst renouncing the disarmament clauses of the Treaty, she would still respect the territorial limitations, and would comply with the Locarno Pact. [With regard to the first five breaches alleged, therefore, the Tribunal finds the allegation proved.]

It is unnecessary to discuss in any detail the various treaties entered into by Germany with other powers. Treaties of Mutual Guarantee were signed by Germany at Locarno in 1925, with Belgium, France, Great Britain and Italy, assuring the maintenance of the territorial *status quo*. Arbitration treaties were also executed by Germany at Locarno with Czechoslovakia, Belgium and Poland.

Article I of the latter treaty is typical, providing:

"All disputes of every kind between Germany and Poland ... which it may not be possible to settle amicably by the normal methods of diplomacy, shall be submitted for decision to an arbitral tribunal ..."

Conventions of Arbitration and Conciliation were entered into between Germany, the Netherlands and Denmark in 1926; and between Germany and Luxemberg in 1929. Non-aggression treaties were executed by Germany with Denmark and Russia in 1939.

KELLOGG-BRIAND PACT

The Pact of Paris was signed on the 27th August, 1928, by Germany, the United States, Belgium, France, Great Britain, Italy, Japan, Poland and other countries; and subsequently by other powers. The Tribunal has made full reference to the nature of this Pact and its legal effect in another part of this judgment. It is therefore not necessary to discuss the matter further here, save to state that in the opinion of the Tribunal this Pact was violated by Germany in all the cases of aggressive war charged in the Indictment. It is to be noted that on the 26th January, 1930, Germany signed a Declaration for the Maintenance of Permanent Peace with Poland, which was explicitly based on the Pact of Paris, and in which the use of force was outlawed for a period of ten years.

The Tribunal does not find it necessary to consider any of the other treaties referred to in the Appendix, or the repeated agreements and assurances of her peaceful intentions entered into by Germany.

The jurisdiction of the Tribunal is defined in the Agreement and Charter, and the crimes coming within the jurisdiction of the Tribunal, for which there shall be individual responsibility, are set out in Article 6. The law of the Charter is decisive, and binding upon the Tribunal.

The making of the Charter was the exercise of the sovereign legislative power by the countries to which the German Reich unconditionally surrendered; and the undoubted right of these countries to legislate for the occupied territories has been recognised by the civilised world. The Charter is not an arbitrary exercise of power on the part of the victorious nations, but in the view of the Tribunal, as will be shown, it is the expression of international law existing at the time of its creation; and to that extent is itself a contribution to international law.

The Signatory Powers created this Tribunal, defined the law it was to administer, and made regulations for the proper conduct of the Trial. In doing so, they have done together what any one of them might have done singly; for it is not to be doubted that any nation has the right thus to set up special courts to administer law. With regard to the constitution of the court, all that the defendants are entitled to ask is to receive a fair trial on the facts and law.

The Charter makes the planning or waging of a war of aggression or a war in violation of international treaties a crime; and it is therefore not strictly necessary to consider whether and to what extent aggressive war was a crime before the execution of the London Agreement. But in view of the great importance of the questions of law involved, the Tribunal has heard full argument from the Prosecution and the Defence, and will express its view on the matter.

It was urged on behalf of the defendants that a fundamental principle of all law—international and domestic— is that there can be no punishment of crime without a pre-existing law. "*Nullum crimen sine lege, nulla poena sine lege.*" It was submitted that *ex post facto* punishment is abhorent to the law of all civilised nations, that no sovereign power had made aggressive war a crime at the time the alleged criminal acts were committed, that no statute had defined aggressive war, that no penalty had been fixed for its commission, and no court had been created to try and punish offenders.

In the first place, it is to be observed that the maxim *nullum crimen sine lege* is not a limitation of sovereignty, but is in general a principle of justice. To assert that it is unjust to punish those who in defiance of treaties and assurances have attacked neighbouring states without warning is obviously untrue, for in such circumstances the attacker must know that he is doing wrong, and so far from it being unjust to punish him, it would be unjust if his wrong were allowed to go unpunished. Occupying the positions they did in the government of Germany, the defendants, or at least some of them must have known of the treaties signed by Germany, outlawing recourse to war for the settlement of international disputes; they must have known that they were acting in defiance of all international law when in complete deliberation they carried out their designs of invasion and aggression. On this view of the case alone, it would appear that the maxim has no application to the present facts.

This view is strongly reinforced by a consideration of the state of international law in 1939, so far as aggressive war is concerned. The General Treaty for the Renunciation of War of 27th August, 1928, more generally known as the Pact of Paris or the Kellogg-Briand Pact, was binding on sixty-three nations, including Germany, Italy and Japan at the outbreak of war in 1939. In the preamble, the signatories declared that they were:-

"Deeply sensible of their solemn duty to promote the welfare of mankind; persuaded that the time has come when a frank renunciation of war as an instrument of national policy should be made to the end that the peaceful and friendly relations now existing between their peoples should be perpetuated . . . . all changes in their relations with one another should be sought only by pacific means . . . . thus uniting civilised nations of the world in a common renunciation of war as an instrument of their national policy . . . ."

The first two Articles are as follows:-

"Article I: The High Contracting Parties solemnly declare in the names of their respective peoples that they condemn recourse to war for the solution of international controversies and renounce it as an instrument of national policy in their relations to one another."

"Article II: The High Contracting Parties agree that the settlement or solution of all disputes or conflicts of whatever nature or of whatever origin they may be, which may arise among them, shall never be sought except by pacific means."

The question is, what was the legal effect of this Pact? The nations who signed the Pact or adhered to it unconditionally condemned recourse to war for the future as an instrument of policy, and expressly renounced it. After the signing of the Pact, any nation resorting to war as an instrument of national policy breaks the Pact. In the opinion of the Tribunal, the solemn renunciation of war as an instrument of national policy necessarily involves the proposition that such a war is illegal in international law; and that those who plan and wage such a war, with its inevitable and terrible consequences, are committing a crime in so doing. War for the solution of international controversies undertaken as an instrument of national policy certainly includes a war of aggression, and such a war is therefore outlawed by the Pact. As Mr. Henry L. Stimson, then Secretary of State of the United States, said in 1932:—

"War between nations was renounced by the signatories of the Kellogg-Briand Treaty. This means that it has become throughout practically the entireworld . . . . an illegal thing. Hereafter, when nations engage in armed conflict, either one or both of them must be termed violators of this general treaty law. . . . We denounce them as law breakers."

But it is argued that the Pact does not expressly enact that such wars are crimes, or set up courts to try those who make such wars. To that extent the same is true with regard to the laws of war contained in the Hague Convention. The Hague Convention of 1907 prohibited resort to certain methods of waging war. These included the inhumane treatment of prisoners, the employment of poisoned weapons, the improper use of flags of truce, and similar matters. Many of these prohibitions had been enforced long before the date of the Convention; but since 1907 they have certainly been crimes, punishable as offences against the laws of war; yet the Hague Convention nowhere designates such practices as criminal, nor is any sentence prescribed, nor any mention made of a court to try and punish offenders. For many years past, however, military tribunals have tried and punished individuals guilty of violating the rules of land warfare laid down by this Convention. In the opinion of the Tribunal, those who wage aggressive war are doing that which is equally illegal, and of much greater moment than a breach of one of the rules of the Hague Convention. In interpreting the words of the Pact, it must be remembered that international law is not the product of an international legislature, and that such international agreements as the Pact of Paris have to deal with general principles of law, and not with administrative matters of procedure. The law of war is to be found not only in treaties, but in the customs and practices of states which gradually obtained universal recognition, and from the general principles of justice applied by jurists and practised by military courts. This law is not static, but by continual adaptation follows the needs of a changing world. Indeed, in many cases treaties do no more than express and define for more accurate reference the principles of law already existing.

The view which the Tribunal takes of the true interpretation of the Pact is supported by the international history which preceded it. In the year 1923 the draft of a Treaty of Mutual Assistance was sponsored by the League of Nations. In Article I the Treaty declared "that aggressive war is an international crime," and that the parties would "undertake that no one of them will be guilty of its commission." The draft treaty was submitted to twenty-nine States, about half of whom were in favour of accepting the text. The principal objection appeared to be in the difficulty of defining the acts which would constitute "aggression," rather than any doubt as to the criminality of aggressive war. The preamble to the League of Nations 1924 Protocol for the Pacific Settlement of International Disputes ("Geneva Protocol"), after "recognising the solidarity of the members of the international community," declared that "a war of aggression constitutes a violation of this solidarity and is an international crime." It went on to declare that the contracting parties were "desirous of facilitating the complete application of the system provided in the Covenant of the League of Nations for the pacific settlement of disputes between the states and of ensuring the repression of international crimes." The Protocol was recommended to the members of the League of Nations by a unanimous resolution in the Assembly of the forty-eight members of the League. These members included Italy and Japan, but Germany was not then a member of the League.

Although the Protocol was never ratified, it was signed by the leading statesmen of the world, representing the vast majority of the civilised states and peoples, and may be regarded as strong evidence of the intention to brand aggressive war as an international crime.

At the meeting of the Assembly of the League of Nations on the 24th September, 1927, all the delegations then present (including the German, the Italian and the Japanese), unanimously adopted a declaration concerning wars of aggression. The preamble to the declaration stated:

"The Assembly:

Recognising the solidarity which unites the community of nations;

Being inspired by a firm desire for the maintenance of general peace;

Being convinced that a war of aggression can never serve as a means of settling international disputes, and is in consequence an international crime . . . ."

The unanimous resolution of the 18th February, 1928, of twenty-one American Republics of the Sixth (Havana) Pan-American Conference, declared that "war of aggression constitutes an international crime against the human species."

All these expressions of opinion, and others that could be cited, so solemnly made, reinforce the construction which the Tribunal placed upon the Pact of Paris, that resort to a war of aggression is not merely illegal, but is criminal. The prohibition of aggressive war demanded by the conscience of the world, finds its expression in the series of pacts and treaties to which the Tribunal has just referred.

It is also important to remember that Article 227 of the Treaty of Versailles provided for the constitution of a special Tribunal, composed of representatives of five of the Allied and Associated Powers which had been belligerents in the first World War opposed to Germany, to try the former German Emperor "for a supreme offence against international morality and the sanctity of treaties." The purpose of this trial was expressed to be "to vindicate the solemn obligations of international undertakings, and the validity of international morality." In Article 228 of the Treaty, the German Government expressly recognised the right of the Allied Powers "to bring before military tribunals persons accused of having committed acts in violation of the laws and customs of war."

It was submitted that international law is concerned with the action of sovereign States, and provides no punishment for individuals; and further, that where the act in question is an act of state, those who carry it out are not personally responsible, but are protected by the doctrine of the sovereignty of the State. In the opinion of the Tribunal, both these submissions must be rejected. That international law imposes duties and liabilities upon individuals as well as upon States has long been recognised. In the recent case of Ex Parte Quirin (1942 317 US 1), before the Supreme Court of the United States, persons were charged during the war with landing in the United States for purposes of spying and sabotage. The late Chief Justice Stone, speaking for the Court, said:

"From the very beginning of its history this Court has applied the law of war as including that part of the law of nations which prescribes for the conduct of war, the status, rights and duties of enemy nations as well as enemy individuals."

He went on to give a list of cases tried by the Courts, where individual offenders were charged with offences against the laws of nations, and particularly the laws of war. Many other authorities could be cited, but enough has been said to show that individuals can be punished for violations of international law. Crimes against international law are committed by men, not by abstract entities, and only by punishing individuals who commit such crimes can the provisions of international law be enforced.

The provisions of Article 228 of the Treaty of Versailles already referred to illustrate and enforce this view of individual responsibility.

The principle of international law, which under certain circumstances, protects the representatives of a state, cannot be applied to acts which are condemned as criminal by international law. The authors of these acts cannot shelter themselves behind their official position in order to be freed from punishment in appropriate proceedings. Article 7 of the Charter expressly declares:

"The official position of defendants, whether as Heads of State, or responsible officials in government departments, shall not be considered as freeing them from responsibility, or mitigating punishment."

On the other hand the very essence of the Charter is that individuals have international duties which transcend the national obligations of obedience imposed by the individual State. He who violates the laws of war cannot obtain immunity while acting in pursuance of the authority of the State if the State in authorising action moves outside its competence under international law.

It was also submitted on behalf of most of these defendants that in doing what they did they were acting under the orders of Hitler, and therefore cannot be held responsible for the acts committed by them in carrying out these orders. The Charter specifically provides in Article 8:

"The fact that the defendant acted pursuant to order of his Government or of a superior shall not free him from responsibility, but may be considered in mitigation of punishment."

The provisions of this Article are in conformity with the law of all nations. That a soldier was ordered to kill or torture in violation of the international law of war has never been recognised as a defence to such acts of brutality, though, as the Charter here provides, the order may be urged in mitigation of the punishment. The true test, which is found in varying degrees in the criminal law of most nations, is not the existence of the order, but whether moral choice was in fact possible.

In the previous recital of the facts relating to aggressive war, it is clear that planning and preparation had been carried out in the most systematic way at every stage of the history.

Planning and preparation are essential to the making of war. In the opinion of the Tribunal aggressive war is a crime under international law. The Charter defines this offence as planning, preparation, initiation or waging of a war of aggression "*or* participation in a common plan or conspiracy for the accomplishment . . . of the foregoing." The Indictment follows this distinction. Count One charges the common plan or conspiracy. Count Two charges the planning and waging of war. The same evidence has been introduced to support both counts. We shall therefore discuss both counts together, as they are in substance the same. The defendants have been charged under both counts, and their guilt under each count must be determined.

The "common plan or conspiracy" charged in the Indictment covers twenty-five years, from the formation of the Nazi party in 1919 to the end of the war in 1945. The party is spoken of as "the instrument of cohesion among the defendants" for carrying out the purposes of the conspiracy—the the overthrowing of the Treaty of Versailles, acquiring territory lost by Germany in the last war and "lebensraum" in Europe, by the use, if necessary, of armed force, of aggressive war. The "seizure of power" by the Nazis, the use of terror, the destruction of trade unions, the attack on Christian teaching and on churches, the persecution of the Jews, the regimentation of youth— all these are said to be steps deliberately taken to carry out the common plan. It found expression, so it is alleged, in secret rearmament, the withdrawal by Germany from the Disarmament Conference and the League of Nations, universal military service, and seizure of the Rhineland. Finally, according to the Indictment, aggressive action was planned and carried out against Austria and Czechoslovakia in 1936–1938, followed by the planning and waging of war against Poland; and, successively, against ten other countries.

The Prosecution says, in effect, that any significant participation in the affairs of the Nazi Party or Government is evidence of a participation in a conspiracy that is in itself criminal. Conspiracy is not defined in the Charter. But in the opinion of the Tribunal the conspiracy must be clearly outlined in its criminal purpose. It must not be too far removed from the time of decision and of action. The planning, to be criminal, must not rest merely on the declarations of a party programme, such as are found in the twenty-five points of the Nazi Party, announced in 1920, or the political affirmations expressed in "Mein Kampf" in later years. The Tribunal must examine whether a concrete plan to wage war existed, and determine the participants in that concrete plan.

It is not necessary to decide whether a single master conspiracy between the defendants has been established by the evidence. The seizure of power by the Nazi Party, and the subsequent domination by the Nazi State of all spheres of economic and social life must of course be remembered when the later plans for waging war are examined. That plans were made to wage wars, as early as 5th November, 1937, and probably before that, is apparent. And thereafter, such preparations continued in many directions, and against the peace of many countries. Indeed the threat of war—and war itself if necessary—was an integral part of the Nazi policy. But the evidence establishes with certainty the existence of many separate plans rather than a single conspiracy embracing them all. That Germany was rapidly moving to complete dictatorship from the moment that the Nazis seized power, and progressively in the direction of war, has been overwhelmingly shown in the ordered sequence of aggressive acts and wars already set out in this Judgment.

In the opinion of the Tribunal, the evidence establishes the common planning to prepare and wage war by certain of the defendants. It is immaterial to consider whether a single conspiracy to the extent and over the time set out in the Indictment has been conclusively proved. Continued planning, with aggressive war as the objective, has been established beyond doubt. The truth of the situation was well stated by Paul Schmidt, official interpreter of the German Foreign Office, as follows:

"The general objectives of the Nazi leadership were apparent from the start, namely the domination of the European Continent, to be achieved first by the incorporation of all German speaking groups in the Reich, and secondly, by territorial expansion under the slogan 'Lebensraum.' The execution of these basic objectives, however, seemed to be characterised by improvisation. Each succeeding step was apparently carried out as each new situation arose, but all consistent with the ultimate objectives mentioned above."

The argument that such common planning cannot exist where there is complete dictatorship is unsound. A plan in the execution of which a number of persons participate is still a plan, even though conceived by only one of them; and those who execute the plan do not avoid responsibility by showing that they acted under the direction of the man who conceived it. Hitler could not make aggressive war by himself. He had to have the co-operation of statesmen, military leaders, diplomats, and business men. When they, with knowledge of his aims, gave him their co-operation, they made themselves parties to the plan he had initiated. They are not to be deemed innocent because Hitler made use of them, if they knew what they were doing. That they were assigned to their tasks by a dictator does not absolve them from responsibility for their acts. The relation of leader and follower does not preclude responsibility here any more than it does in the comparable tyranny of organised domestic crime.

The PRESIDENT: I now ask Judge Parker to continue the reading of the Judgment.

Judge PARKER:

The evidence relating to war crimes has been overwhelming, in its volume and its detail. It is impossible for this Judgment adequately to review it, or to record the mass of documentary and oral evidence that has been presented. The truth remains that war crimes were committed on a vast scale, never before seen in the history of war.

They were perpetrated in all the countries occupied by Germany, and on the High Seas, and were attended by every conceivable circumstance of cruelty and horror. There can be no doubt that the majority of them arose from the Nazi conception of "total war", with which the aggressive wars were waged. For in this conception of "total war", the moral ideas underlying the conventions which seek to make war more humane are no longer regarded as having force or validity. Everything is made subordinate to the overmastering dictates of war. Rules, regulations, assurances and treaties all alike are of no moment; and so, freed from the restraining influence of international law, the aggressive war is conducted by the Nazi leaders in the most barbaric way. Accordingly, war crimes were committed when and wherever the Fuehrer and his close associates thought them to be advantageous. They were for the most part the result of cold and criminal calculation.

On some occasions, war crimes were deliberately planned long in advance. In the case of the Soviet Union, the plunder of the territories to be occupied, and the ill-treatment of the civilian population, were settled in minute detail before the attack was begun. As early as the Autumn of 1940, the invasion of the territories of the Soviet Union was being considered. From that date onwards, the methods to be employed in destroying all possible opposition were continuously under discussion.

Similarly, when planning to exploit the inhabitants of the occupied countries for slave labour on the very greatest scale, the German Government conceived it as an integral part of the war economy, and planned and organised this particular war crime down to the last elaborate detail.

Other war crimes, such as the murder of prisoners of war who had escaped and been recaptured, or the murder of Commandos or captured airmen, or the destruction of the Soviet Commissars, were the result of direct orders circulated through the highest official channels.

The Tribunal proposes, therefore, to deal quite generally with the question of war crimes, and to refer to them later when examining the responsibility of the individual defendants in relation to them. Prisoners of war were illtreated and tortured and murdered, not only in defiance of the well-established rules of international law, but in complete disregard of the elementary dictates of humanity. Civilian populations in occupied territories suffered the same fate. Whole populations were deported to Germany for the purposes of slave labour upon defence works, armament production and similar tasks connected with the war effort. Hostages were taken in very large numbers from the civilian populations in all the occupied countries, and were shot as suited the German purposes. Public and private property was systematically plundered and pillaged in order to enlarge the resources of Germany at the expense of the rest of Europe. Cities and towns and villages were wantonly destroyed without military justification or necessity.

Article 6 (*b*) of the Charter defines war crimes in these words:

"War crimes: namely, violations of the laws or customs of war. Such violations shall include, but not be limited to, murder, ill-treatment or deportation to slave labour or for any other purpose of civilian population of or in occupied territory, murder or ill-treatment of prisoners of war or persons on the seas, killing of hostages, plunder of public or private property, wanton destruction of cities, towns, or villages, or devastation not justified by military necessity."

In the course of the war, many Allied soldiers who had

surrendered to the Germans were shot immediately, often as a matter of deliberate, calculated policy. On the 18th October, 1942, the defendant Keitel circulated a directive authorised by Hitler, which ordered that all members of Allied "Commando" units, often when in uniform and whether armed or not, were to be "slaughtered to the last man", even if they attempted to surrender. It was further provided that if such Allied troops came into the hands of the military authorities after being first captured by the local police, or in any other way, they should be handed over immediately to the SD. This order was supplemented from time to time, and was effective throughout the remainder of the war, although after the Allied landings in Normandy in 1944 it was made clear that the order did not apply to "Commandos" captured within the immediate battle area. Under the provisions of this order, Allied "Commando" troops, and other military units operating independently, lost their lives in Norway, France, Czechoslovakia and Italy. Many of them were killed on the spot, and in no case were those who were executed later in concentration camps ever given a trial of any kind. For example, an American military mission which landed behind the German front in the Balkans in January, 1945, numbering about twelve to fifteen men and wearing uniform, were taken to Mauthausen under the authority of this order, and according to the affidavit of Adolf Zutte, the adjutant of the Mauthausen Concentration Camp, all of them were shot.

In March, 1944, the OKH issued the "Kugel" or "Bullet" decree, which directed that every escaped officer and NCO prisoner of war who had not been put to work, with the exception of British and American prisoners of war, should on recapture be handed over to the SIPO and SD. This order was distributed by the SIPO and SD to their regional offices. These escaped officers and NCOs were to be sent to the concentration camp at Mauthausen, to be executed upon arrival, by means of a bullet shot in the neck.

In March, 1944, fifty officers of the British Royal Air Force, who escaped from the camp at Sagan where they were confined as prisoners, were shot on recapture, on the direct orders of Hitler. Their bodies were immediately cremated, and the urns containing their ashes were returned to the camp. It was not contended by the defendants that this was other than plain murder, in complete violation of international law.

When Allied airmen were forced to land in Germany, they were sometimes killed at once by the civilian population. The police were instructed not to interfere with these killings, and the Ministry of Justice was informed that no one should be prosecuted for taking part in them.

The treatment of Soviet prisoners of war was characterised by particular inhumanity. The death of so many of them was not due merely to the action of individual guards, or to the exigencies of life in the camps. It was the result of systematic plans to murder. More than a month before the German invasion of the Soviet Union, the OKW were making special plans for dealing with political representatives serving with the Soviet armed forces who might be captured. One proposal was that "political Commissars *of the Army* are not recognised as *Prisoners of War*, and are to be *liquidated* at the latest in the transient prisoner of war camps." The defendant Keitel gave evidence that instructions incorporating this proposal were issued to the German army.

On the 8th September, 1941, regulations for the treatment of Soviet prisoners of war in all prisoner of war camps were issued, signed by General Reinecke, the head of the prisoner of war department of the High Command. These orders stated:

"The Bolshevist soldier has therefore lost all claim to treatment as an honourable opponent, in accordance with the Geneva Convention. . . . The order for ruthless and energetic action must be given at the slightest indication of insubordination, especially in the case of Bolshevist fanatics. Insubordination, active or passive resistance, must be broken immediately by force of arms (bayonets, butts and firearms) . . . Anyone carrying out the order who does not use his weapons, or does so with insufficient energy, is punishable . . . Prisoners of war attempting escape are to be fired on without previous challenge. No warning shot must ever be fired. . . . The use of arms against prisoners of war is as a rule legal."

The Soviet prisoners of war were left without suitable clothing. The wounded without medical care; they were starved, and in many cases left to die.

On the 17th July, 1941, the Gestapo issued an order providing for the killing of all Soviet prisoners of war who were or might be dangerous to National Socialism. The order recited:

"The mission of the Commanders of the SIPO and SD stationed in Stalags is the political investigation of all camp inmates, the elimination and further 'treatment' (*a*) of all political, criminal or in some other way unbearable elements among them, (*b*) of those persons who could be used for the reconstruction of the occupied territories . . . Further, the commanders must make efforts from the beginning to seek out among the prisoners elements which appear reliable, regardless if there are Communists concerned or not, in order to use them for Intelligence purposes inside of the camp, and if advisable, later in the occupied territories also. By use of such informers, and by use of all other existing possibilities, the discovery of all elements to be eliminated among the prisoners must proceed step by step at once . . .

"Above all, the following must be discovered: all important functionaries of State and Party, especially professional revolutionaries . . . all People's Commissars in the Red Army, leading personalities of the State . . . leading personalities of the business world, members of the Soviet Russian Intelligence, all Jews, all persons who are found to be agitators or fanatical Communists. Executions are not to be held in the camp or in the immediate vicinity of the camp . . . The prisoners are to be taken for special treatment if possible into the former Soviet Russian territory."

The affidavit of Warlimont, deputy Chief of Staff of the Wehrmacht, and the testimony of Ohlendorf, former Chief of Amt III of the RSHA, and of Lahousen, the head of one of the sections of the Abwehr, the Wehrmacht's Intelligence Service, all indicate the thoroughness with which this order was carried out.

The affidavit of Kurt Lindown, a former Gestapo official, states:

". . . There existed in the prisoner of war camps on the Eastern Front small screening teams (Einsatz commandos) headed by lower ranking members of the Secret Police (Gestapo). These teams were assigned to the camp commanders and had the job to segregate the prisoners of war who were candidates for execution according to the orders that had been given, and to report them to the office of the Secret Police."

On the 23rd October, 1941, the camp commander of the Gross Rosen concentration camp reported to Mueller, chief of the Gestapo, a list of the Soviet prisoners of war who had been executed there on the previous day.

An account of the general conditions and treatment of

Soviet prisoners of war during the first eight months after the German attack upon Russia was given in a letter which the defendant Rosenberg sent to the defendant Keitel on the 28th February, 1942:

"The fate of the Soviet prisoners of war in Germany is on the contrary a tragedy of the greatest extent . . . A large part of them has starved, or died because of the hazards of the weather. Thousands also died from spotted fever.

"The camp commanders have forbidden the civilian population to put food at the disposal of the prisoners, and they have rather let them starve to death.

"In many cases, when prisoners of war could no longer keep up on the march because of hunger and exhaustion, they were shot before the eyes of the horrified population, and the corpses were left.

"In numerous camps, no shelter for the prisoners of war was provided at all. They lay under the open sky during rain or snow. Even tools were not made available to dig holes or caves."

In some cases Soviet prisoners of war were branded with a special permanent mark. There was put in evidence the OKW order dated the 20th July, 1942, which laid down that:

"The brand is to take the shape of an acute angle of about 45 degrees, with the long side to be 1 cm. in length, pointing upwards and burnt on the left buttock . . . This brand is made with the aid of a lancet available in any military unit. The colouring used is Chinese ink."

The carrying out of this order was the responsibility of the military authorities, though it was widely circulated by the

Chief of the SIPO and the SD to German police officials for information.

Soviet prisoners of war were also made the subject of medical experiments of the most cruel and inhuman kind. In July, 1943, experimental work was begun in preparation for a campaign of bacteriological warfare; Soviet prisoners of war were used in these medical experiments, which more often than not proved fatal. In connection with this campaign for bacteriological warfare, preparations were also made for the spreading of bacterial emulsions from planes, with the object of producing widespread failures of crops and consequent starvation. These measures were never applied, possibly because of the rapid deterioration of Germany's military position.

The argument in defence of the charge with regard to the murder and ill-treatment of Soviet prisoners of war, that the U.S.S.R. was not a party to the Geneva Convention, is quite without foundation. On the 15th September 1941 Admiral Canaris protested against the regulations for the treatment of Soviet prisoners of war, signed by General Reinecke on the 8th September 1941. He then stated:

"The Geneva Convention for the treatment of prisoners of war is not binding in the relationship between Germany and the U.S.S.R. Therefore only the principles of general international law on the treatment of prisoners of war apply. Since the 18th century these have gradually been established along the lines that war captivity, is neither revenge nor punishment, but solely protective custody, the only purpose of which is to prevent the prisoners of war from further participation in the war. This principle was developed in accordance with the view held by all armies that it is contrary to military tradition to kill or injure helpless people . . . The decrees for the treatment of Soviet prisoners of war enclosed are based on a fundamentally different view-point."

This protest, which correctly stated the legal position, was ignored. The defendant Keitel made a note on this memorandum:

"The objections arise from the military concept of chivalrous warfare. This is the destruction of an ideology. Therefore I approve and back the measures."

Article 6(*b*) of the Charter provides that "ill-treatment . . . of civilian population of or in occupied territory . . . killing of hostages . . . wanton destruction of cities, towns or villages" shall be a war crime. In the main, these provisions are merely declaratory of the existing laws of war as expressed by the Hague Convention, Article 46, which stated:

"Family honour and rights, the lives of persons and private property, as well as religious convictions and practices must be respected."

The territories occupied by Germany were administered in violation of the laws of war. The evidence is quite
overwhelming of a systematic rule of violence, brutality
and terror. On the 7th December, 1941, Hitler issued the
directive since known as the "Nacht und Nebel Erlass"
(Night and Fog Decree), under which persons who committed offences against the Reich or the German forces in
occupied territories, except where the death sentence was
certain, were to be taken secretly to Germany and handed
over to the SIPO and SD for trial or punishment in
Germany. This decree was signed by the defendant Keitel.
After these civilians arrived in Germany, no word of them
was permitted to reach the country from which they
came, or their relatives; even in cases when they died
awaiting trial the families were not informed, the purpose
being to create anxiety in the minds of the family of the
arrested person. Hitler's purpose in issuing this decree was
stated by the defendant Keitel in a covering letter, dated
12th December, 1941, to be as follows:

"Efficient and enduring intimidation can only be achieved
either by capital punishment or by measures by which the
relatives of the criminal and the population do not know
the fate of the criminal. This aim is achieved when the
criminal is transferred to Germany."

Even persons who were only suspected of opposing
any of the policies of the German occupation authorities
were arrested, and on arrest were interrogated by the
Gestapo and the SD in the most shameful manner. On the
12th June 1942 the Chief of the SIPO and SD published,
through Mueller, the Gestapo Chief, an order authorising
the use of "third degree" methods of interrogation, where
preliminary investigation had indicated that the person
could give information on important matters, such as subversive activities, though not for the purpose of extorting

confessions of the prisoner's own crimes. This order provided:

". . . Third degree may, under this supposition, only be employed against Communists, Marxists, Jehovah's Witnesses, saboteurs, terrorists, members of resistance movements, parachute agents, anti-social elements, Polish or Soviet Russian loafers or tramps; in all other cases my permission must first be obtained . . . Third degree can, according to circumstances, consist amongst other methods of very simple diet (bread and water), hard bunk, dark cell, deprivation of sleep, exhaustive drilling, also in flogging (for more than twenty strokes a doctor must be consulted)."

The brutal suppression of all opposition to the German occupation was not confined to severe measures against suspected members of resistance movements themselves, but was also extended to their families. On the 19th July, 1944, the Commander of the SIPO and SD in the district of Radom, in Poland, published an order, transmitted through the Higher SS and Police leaders, to the effect that in all cases of assassination or attempted assassination of Germans, or where saboteurs had destroyed vital installations not only the guilty person, but also all his or her male relatives should be shot, and female relatives over sixteen years of age put into a concentration camp.

In the summer of 1944, the Einsatz Commando of the SIPO and SD at Lusemburg caused persons to be confined at Sachsenhausen concentration camp because they were relatives of deserters, and were therefore "expected to endanger the interest of the German Reich if allowed to go free."

The practice of keeping hostages to prevent and to punish any form of civil disorder was resorted to by the

Germans; an order issued by the defendant Keitel on the 16th September, 1941, spoke in terms of fifty or a hundred lives from the occupied areas of the Soviet Union for one German life taken. The order stated that "it should be remembered that a human life in unsettled countries frequently counts for nothing, and a deterrent effect can be obtained only by unusual severity." The exact number of persons killed as a result of this policy is not known, but large number were killed in France and the other occupied territories in the West, while in the East the slaughter was on an even more extensive scale. In additions to the killing of hostages, entire towns were destroyed in some cases; st massacres as those of Oradour-sur-Glane in France and Lidice in Czecl slovakia, both of which were described to the Tribunal in detail, examples of the organised use of terror by the occupying forces to be down and destroy all opposition to their rule.

One of the most notorious means of terrorising the people in occupation territories was the use of concentration camps. They were first establish in Germany at the moment of the seizure of power by the Nazi Government. Their original purpose was to imprison without trial all those persons who were opposed to the Government, or who were in any way obnoxi to German authority. With the aid of a secret police force, this practice was widely extended and in course of time concentration camps because places of organised and systematic murder, where millions of people was destroyed.

In the administration of the occupied territories the concentration can were used to destroy all opposition groups. The persons arrested by Gestapo were as a rule sent to concentration camps. They were conveyed the camps in many cases without any care whatever being taken for the and great numbers died on the way. Those who arrived at the camp was subject to systematic cruelty. They were given hard physical labour, inadequate food, clothes and shelter, and were subject at all times to the rigo of a soulless régime, and the private whims of individual guards. In report of the War Crimes Branch of the Judge Advocate's Section of 3rd U.S. Army, under date 21st June, 1945, the conditions at the Flossenburg concentration camp were investigated, and one passage may be quoted:

"Flossenburg concentration camp can be described as a factory dealing in death. Although this camp had in view the primary object of putting to work the mass slave labour, another of its primary objects was the elimination of human lives by the methods employed in handling the prisoners. Hunger and starvation rations, sadism, inadequate clothing, medical neglect, disease, beatings, hangings, freezing, forced suicides, shooting, etc., all played a major rôle in obtaining their object. Prisoners were murdered at random; spite killings against Jews were common, injections of poison and shooting in the neck were everyday occurrences; epidemics of typhus and spotted fever were permitted to run rampant as a means of eliminating prisoners; life in this camp meant nothing. Killing became a common thing, so common that a quick death was welcomed by the unfortunate ones."

A certain number of the concentration camps were equipped with gas chambers for the wholesale destruction of the inmates, and with furnaces for the burning of the bodies. Some of them were in fact used for the extermination of Jews as part of the "final solution" of the Jewish problem. Most of the non-Jewish inmates were used for labour, although the conditions under which they worked made labour and death almost synonymous tern Those inmates who became ill and were unable to work were either destroyed in the gas chambers or sent to special infirmaries, where they were given entirely inadequate medical treatment, worse food if possible than the working inmates, and left to die.

The murder and ill-treatment of civilian populations reached its height in the treatment of the citizens of the Soviet Union and Poland. Some four weeks before the invasion of Russia began, special task forces of the SIPO and SD, called Einsatz Groups, were formed on the orders of Himmler for the purpose of following the German armies into Russia, combating partisans and members of Resistance Groups, and exterminating the Jews and communist leaders and other sections of the population. In the beginning, four such Einsatz Groups were formed, one operating in the Baltic States, one towards Moscow, one towards Kiev, and one operating in the south of Russia. Ohlendorf, former chief of Amt III of the RSHA, who led the fourth group, stated in his affidavit:

"When the German army invaded Russia, I was leader of Einsatzgruppe D, in the southern sector, and in the course of the year during which I was leader of the Einsatzgruppe D it liquidated approximately 90,000 men, women and children. The majority of those liquidated were Jews, but there were also among them some communist functionaries."

In an order issued by the defendant Keitel on the 23rd July, 1941, and drafted by the defendant Jodl, it was stated that

"in view of the vast size of the occupied areas in the East, the forces available for establishing security in these areas will be sufficient only if all resistance is punished, not by legal prosecution of the guilty, but by the spreading of such terror by the armed forces as is alone appropriate to eradicate every inclination to resist among the population . . .

Commanders must find the means of keeping order by applying suitable draconian measures."

The evidence has shown that this order was ruthlessly carried out in the territory of the Soviet Union and in Poland. A significant illustration of the measures actually applied occurs in the document which was sent in 1943 to the defendant Rosenberg by the Reich Commissar for Eastern Territories, who wrote:

"It should be possible to avoid atrocities and to bury those who have been liquidated. To lock men, women and children into barns and set fire to them does not appear to be a suitable method of combating bands, even if it is desired to exterminate the population. This method is not worthy of the German cause, and hurts our reputation severely."

The Tribunal has before it an affidavit of one Hermann Graebe, dated 10th November, 1945, describing the immense mass murders which he witnessed. He was the manager and engineer in charge of the branch of the Solingen firm of Josef Jung in Spolbunow, Ukraine, from September, 1941, to January, 1944. He first of all described the attack upon the Jewish ghetto at Rowno:

". . . Then the electric floodlights which had been erected all round the ghetto were switched on. SS and militia details of four to six members entered or at least tried to enter the houses. Where the doors and windows were closed, and the inhabitants did not open upon the knocking, the SS men and militia broke the windows, forced the doors with beams and crowbars, and entered the dwelling. The owners were driven on to the street just as they were, regardless of whether they were dressed or whether they had been in bed. . . . Car after car was filled. Over it hung the screaming of women and children, the cracking of whips and rifle shots."

Graebe then described how a mass execution at Dubno, which he witnessed on the 5th October, 1942, was carried out:

". . . Now we heard shots in quick succession from behind one of the earth mounds. The people who had got off the trucks, men, women and children of all ages, had to undress upon the orders of an SS man, who carried a riding or dog whip. . . . Without screaming or crying, these people undressed, stood around by families, kissed each other, said farewells, and waited for the command of another SS man, who stood near the excavation, also with a whip in his hand. . . . At that moment the SS man at the excavation called something to his comrade. The latter counted off about 20 persons, and instructed them to walk behind the earth mound. . . . I walked around the mound and stood in front of a tremendous grave; closely pressed together, the people were lying on top of each other so that only their heads were visible. The excavation was already two-thirds full; I estimated that it contained about a thousand people. . . . Now already the next group approached, descended into the excavation, lined themselves up against the previous victims and were shot."

The foregoing crimes against the civilian population are sufficiently appalling, and yet the evidence shows that at any rate in the East, the mass murders and cruelties were not committed solely for the purpose of stamping out opposition or resistance to the German occupying forces. In Poland and the Soviet Union these crimes were part of a plan to get rid of whole native populations by expulsion and annihilation, in order that their territory could be used for colonisation by Germans. Hitler had written in "Mein Kampf" on these lines, and the plan was clearly stated by Himmler in July, 1942, when he wrote:

"It is not our task to Germanise the East in the old sense, that is to teach the people there the German language and the German law, but to see to it that only people of purely Germanic blood live in the East."

In August, 1942, the policy for the Eastern Territories as laid down by Bormann was summarised by a subordinate of Rosenberg as follows:

"The Slavs are to work for us. In so far as we do not need them, they may die. Therefore, compulsory vaccination and Germanic health services are superfluous. The fertility of the Slavs is undesirable."

It was Himmler again who stated in October, 1943:

"What happens to a Russian, a Czech, does not interest me in the slightest. What the nations can offer in the way of good blood of our type, we will take. If necessary, by kidnapping their children and raising them here with us. Whether nations live in prosperity or starve to death interests me only in so far as we need them as slaves for our Kultur, otherwise it is of no interest to me."

In Poland the intelligentsia had been marked down for extermination as early as September, 1939, and in May, 1940, the defendant Frank wrote in his diary of "taking advantage of the focusing of world interest on the Western Front, by wholesale liquidation of thousands of Poles, first leading representatives of the Polish intelligentsia." Earlier, Frank had been directed to reduce the "entire Polish economy to absolute minimum necessary for bare existence. The Poles shall be the slaves of the Greater German World Empire." In January, 1940, he recorded in his diary that "cheap labour must be removed from the General Government by hundreds of thousands. This will hamper the native biological propagation." So successfully did the Germans carry out this policy in Poland that by the end of the war one third of the population had been killed, and the whole of the country devastated.

It was the same story in the occupied area of the Soviet Union. At the time of the launching of the German attack in June, 1941, Rosenberg told his collaborators:

"The object of feeding the German people stands this year without a doubt at the top of the list of Germany's claims on the East, and there the southern territories and the northern Caucasus will have to serve as a balance for the feeding of the German people. . . . A very extensive evacuation will be necessary, without any doubt, and it is sure that the future will hold very hard years in store for the Russians."

Three or four weeks later Hitler discussed with Rosenberg, Goering, Keitel and others his plan for the exploitation of the Soviet population and territory which included among other things the evacuation of the inhabitants of the Crimea and its settlement by Germans.

A somewhat similar fate was planned for Czechoslovakia by the defendant von Neurath, in August, 1940; the intelligentsia were to be "expelled," but the rest of the population was to be Germanised rather than expelled or exterminated, since there was a shortage of Germans to replace them.

In the West the population of Alsace were the victims of a German "expulsion action." Between July and December, 1940, 105,000 Alsatians were either deported from their homes or prevented from returning to them. A captured German report dated 7th August, 1942, with regard to Alsace states that:

"The problem of race will be given first consideration, and this in such a manner that persons of racial value will be deported to Germany proper, and racially inferior persons to France."

THE PRESIDENT: The Tribunal will adjourn for ten minutes.

(A recess was taken.)

THE PRESIDENT: I now ask General Nikitchenko to continue the reading of the judgment.

General NIKITCHENKO: Article 49 of the Hague Convention provides that an occupying power may levy a contribution of money from the occupied territory to pay for the needs of the army of occupation, and for the administration of the territory in question. Article 52 of the Hague Convention provides that an occupying power may make requisitions in kind only for the needs of the army of occupation, and that these requisitions shall be in proportion to the resources of the country. These Articles, together with Article 48, dealing with the expenditure of money collected in taxes, and Articles 53, 55 and 56, dealing with public property, make it clear that under the rules of war, the economy of an occupied country can only be required to bear the expenses of the occupation, and these should not be greater than the economy of the country can reasonably be expected to bear. Article 56 reads as follows:

"The property of municipalities, of religious, charitable, educational, artistic and scientific institutions, although belonging to the State, is to be accorded the same standing as private property. All pre-meditated seizure, destruction or damage of such institutions, historical monuments, works of art and science, is prohibited and should be prosecuted."

The evidence in this case has established, however, that the territories occupied by Germany were exploited for the German war effort in the most ruthless way, without consideration of the local economy, and in consequence of a deliberate design and policy. There was in truth a systematic "plunder of public or private property", which was criminal under Article 6 (*b*) of the Charter. The German occupation policy was clearly stated in a speech made by the defendant Goering on the 6th August, 1942, to the various German authorities in charge of occupied territories:

"God knows, you are not sent out there to work for the welfare of the people in your charge, but to get the utmost out of them, so that the German people can live. That is what I expect of your exertions. This everlasting concern about foreign people must cease now, once and for all. I have here before me reports on what you are expected to deliver. It is nothing at all, when I consider your territories. It makes no difference to me in this connection if you say that your people will starve."

The methods employed to exploit the resources of the occupied territories to the full varied from country to country. In some of the occupied countries in the East and the West, this exploitation was carried out within the framework of the existing economic structure. The local industries were put under German supervision, and the distribution of war materials was rigidly controlled. The industries thought to be of value to the German war effort were compelled to continue, and most of the rest were closed down altogether. Raw materials and the finished products alike were confiscated for the needs of the Germany industry. As early as the 19th October, 1939, the defendant Goering had issued a directive giving detailed instructions for the administration of the occupied territories; it provided:

"The task for the economic treatment of the various administrative regions is different, depending on whether the country is involved which will be incorporated politically into the German Reich, or whether we will deal with the Government-General, which in all probability will not be made a part of Germany. In the first mentioned territories, the . . . safeguarding of all their productive facilities and supplies must be aimed at, as well as a complete incorporation into the Greater German economic system, at the earliest possible time. On the other hand, there must be removed from the territories of the Government-General all raw materials, scrap materials, machines, etc., which are of use for the German war economy. Enterprises which are not absolutely necessary for the meagre maintenance of the naked existence of the population must be transferred to Germany, unless such transfer would require an unreasonably long period of time, and would make it more practicable to exploit those enterprises by giving them German orders, to be executed at their present location."

As a consequence of this order, agricultural products, raw materials needed by German factories, machine tools, transportation equipment, other finished products and even foreign securities and holdings of foreign exchange were all requisitioned and sent to Germany. These resources were requisitioned in a manner out of all proportion to the economic resources of those countries, and resulted in famine, inflation and an active black market. At first the German occupation authorities attempted to suppress the black market, because it was a channel of distribution keeping local products out of German hands. When attempts at suppression failed, a German purchasing agency was organised to make purchases for Germany on the black market, thus carrying out the assurance made by the defendant Goering that it was "necessary that all should know that if there is to be famine anywhere, it shall in no case be in Germany."

In many of the occupied countries of the East and the West, the authorities maintained the pretence of paying for all the property which they seized. This elaborate pretence of payment merely disguised the fact that the goods sent to Germany from these occupied countries were paid for by the occupied countries themselves, either by the device of excessive occupation costs or by forced loans in return for a credit balance on a "clearing account" which was an account merely in name.

In most of the occupied countries of the East even this pretence of legality was not maintained; economic exploitation became deliberate plunder. This policy was first put into effect in the administration of the Government-General in Poland. The main exploitation of the raw materials in the East was centered on agricultural products and very large amounts of food were shipped from the Government-General to Germany.

The evidence of the widespread starvation among the Polish people in the Government-General indicates the ruthlessness and the severity with which the policy of exploitation was carried out.

The occupation of the territories of the U.S.S.R., was characterised by premeditated and systematic looting. Before the attack on the U.S.S.R., an economic staff— Oldenburg—was organised to ensure the most efficient exploitation of Soviet territories. The German armies were to be fed out of Soviet territory, even if "many millions of people will be starved to death." An OKW directive issued before the attack said:

"To obtain the greatest possible quantity of food and crude oil for Germany—that is the main economic purpose of the campaign."

Similarly, a declaration by the defendant Rosenberg of the 20th June, 1941, had advocated the use of the produce from Southern Russia and of the Northern Caucasus to feed the German people, saying:

"We see absolutely no reason for any obligation on our part to feed also the Russian people with the products of that surplus territory. We know that this is a harsh necessity, bare of any feelings."

When the Soviet territory was occupied, this policy was put into effect; there was a large scale confiscation of agricultural supplies, with complete disregard of the needs of the inhabitants of the occupied territory.

In addition to the seizure of raw materials and manufactured articles, a wholesale seizure was made of art treasures, furniture, textiles and similar articles in all the invaded countries.

The defendant Rosenberg was designated by Hitler on the 29th January, 1940, Head of the Centre for National Socialist Ideological and Educational Research, and thereafter the organisation known as the "Einsatzstab Rosenberg" conducted its operations on a very great scale. Originally designed for the establishment of a research library, it developed into a project for the seizure of cultural treasures. On the 1st March, 1942, Hitler issued a further decree, authorising Rosenberg to search libraries, lodges and cultural establishments, to seize material from these establishments, as well as culture treasures owned by Jews. Similar directions were given where the ownership could not be clearly established. The decree directed the co-operation of the Wehrmacht High Command, and indicated that Rosenberg's activities in the West were to be conducted in his capacity as Reichsleiter, and in the East in his capacity as Reichsminister. Thereafter, Rosenberg's activities were extended to the occupied countries. The report of Robert Scholz, Chief of the special staff for Pictorial Art, stated:

"During the period from March, 1941, to July, 1944, the special staff for Pictorial Art brought into the Reich 29 large shipments, including 137 freight cars with 4,174 cases of art works."

The report of Scholz refers to 25 portfolios of pictures of the most valuable works of the art collection seized in the West, which portfolios were presented to the Fuehrer. Thirty-nine volumes, prepared by the Einsatzstab, contained photographs of paintings, textiles, furniture, candelabra and numerous other objects of art, and illustrated the value and magnitude of the collection which had been made. In many of the occupied countries private collections were robbed, libraries were plundered and private houses were pillaged.

Museums, palaces and libraries in the occupied territories of the U.S.S.R. were systematically looted. Rosenberg's Einsatzstab, Ribbentrop's special "Battalion", the Reichscommissars and representatives of the Military Command seized objects of cultural and historical value belonging to the people of the Soviet Union, which were sent to Germany. Thus, the Reichscommissar of the Ukraine removed paintings and objects of any from Kiev and Kharkov and sent them to East Prussia. Rare volume and objects of art from the palaces of Peterhof, Tsarskoye Selo, and Pavlovsk were shipped to Germany. In his letter to Rosenberg of the 3rd October, 1941, Reichscommissar Kube stated that the value of the objects of art taken from Byelorussia ran into millions of roubles. The scale of this plundering can also be seen in the letter sent from Rosenberg's department to von Milde-Schreden in which it is stated that during the month of October, 1943, alone, about 40 box-cars loaded with objects of cultural value were transported to the Reich.

With regard to the suggestion that the purpose of the seizure of any treasures was protective and meant for their preservation, it is necessary to say a few words. On the 1st December, 1939, Himmler, as the Reich Commissioner for the "strengthening of Germanism", issued a decree to the regional officers of the secret police in the annexed eastern territories and to the commanders of the security service in Radom, Warsaw and Lublin. This decree contained administrative directions for carrying out the art seizure programme, and in Clause 1 it is stated:

"To strengthen Germanism in the defence of the Reich, all articles mentioned in Section 2 of this decree are hereby confiscated. . . . They are confiscated for the benefit of the German Reich, and are at the disposal of the Reich Commissioner for the strengthening of Germanism."

The intention to enrich Germany by the seizures, rather than to protect the seized objects, is indicated in an undated report by Dr. Hans Posse, director of the Dresden State Picture Gallery:

"I was able to gain some knowledge on the public and private collections, as well as clerical property, in Cracow and Warsaw. It is true that we cannot hope too much to enrich ourselves from the acquisition of great art works of paintings and sculptures, with the exception of the Veit-Stoss altar, and the plates of Hans von Kulnback in the Church of Maria in Cracow . . . and several other works from the national museum in Warsaw."

Article 6 (*b*) of the Charter provides that the "ill-treatment or deportation to slave labour or for any other purpose, of civilian population of or in occupied territory" shall be a war crime. The laws relating to forced labour by the inhabitants of occupied territories are found in Article 52 of The Hague Convention, which provides:—

"Requisition in kind and services shall not be demanded from municipalities or inhabitants except for the needs of the army of occupation. They shall be in proportion to the resources of the country, and of such a nature as not to involve the inhabitants in the obligation of taking part in military operations against their own country."

The policy of the German occupation authorities was in flagrant violation of the terms of this Convention. Some idea of this policy may be gathered from the statement made by Hitler in a speech on 9th November, 1941:—

"The territory which now works for us contains more than 250,000,000 men, but the territory which works indirectly for us includes now more than 350,000,000. In the measure in which it concerns German territory, the domain which we have taken under our administration, it is not doubtful that we shall succeed in harnessing the very last man to this work."

The actual results achieved were not so complete as this, but the German occupation authorities did succeed in forcing many of the inhabitants of the occupied territories to work for the German war effort, and in deporting at least 5,000,000 persons to Germany to serve German industry and agriculture.

In the early stages of the war, manpower in the occupied territories was under the control of various occupation authorities, and the procedure varied from country to country. In all the occupied territories compulsory labour service was promptly instituted. Inhabitants of the occupied countries were conscripted and compelled to work in local occupations, to assist the German war economy. In many cases they were forced to work on German fortifications and military installations. As local supplies of raw materials and local industrial capacity became inadequate to meet the German requirements, the system of deporting labourers to Germany was put into force. By the middle of April, 1940, compulsory deportation of labourers to Germany had been ordered in the Government General; and a similar procedure was followed in other eastern territories as they were occupied. A description of this compulsory deportation from Poland was given by Himmler. In an address to SS officers he recalled how in weather 40 degrees below zero they had to "haul away thousands, tens of thousands, hundreds of thousands." On a later occasion Himmler stated:—

"Whether ten thousand Russian females fall down from exhaustion while digging an anti-tank ditch interests me only in so far as the anti-tank ditch for Germany is finished. . . . We must realise that we have 6–7 million foreigners in Germany. . . . They are none of them dangerous so long as we take severe measures at the merest trifles."

During the first two years of the German occupation of France, Belgium, Holland and Norway, however, an attempt was made to obtain the necessary workers on a voluntary basis. How unsuccessful this was may be seen from the report of the meeting of the Central Planning Board on the 1st March, 1944. The representative of the defendant Speer, one Koehrl, speaking of the situation in France, said:—

"During all this time a great number of Frenchmen were recruited, and voluntarily went to Germany."
He was interrupted by the defendant Sauckel:

"Not only voluntary, some were recruited forcibly."
To which Koehrl replied:

"The calling up started after the recruitment no longer yielded enough results."
To which the defendant Sauckel replied:

"Out of the five million workers who arrived in Germany, not even 200,000 came voluntarily,"

and Koehrl rejoined:—

"Let us forget for the moment whether or not some slight pressure was used. Formally, at least, they were volunteers."

Committees were set up to encourage recruiting, and a vigorous propaganda campaign was begun to induce workers to volunteer for service in Germany. This propaganda campaign included, for example, the promise that a prisoner of war would be returned for every labourer who volunteered to go to Germany. In some cases it was supplemented by withdrawing the ration cards of labourers who refused to go to Germany, or by discharging them from their jobs and denying them unemployment benefit or an opportunity to work elsewhere. In some cases workers and their families were threatened with reprisals by the police if they refused to go to Germany. It was on the 21st March, 1942, that the defendant Sauckel was appointed Plenipotentiary-General for the Utilisation of Labour, with authority over "all available manpower, including that of workers recruited abroad, and of prisoners of war."

The defendant Sauckel was directly under the defendant Goering as Commissioner of the Four Year Plan, and a Goering decree of the 27th March, 1942, transferred all his authority over manpower to Sauckel. Sauckel's instructions, too, were that foreign labour should be recruited on a voluntary basis, but also provided that "where, however, in the occupied territories the appeal for volunteers does not suffice, obligatory service and drafting must under all circumstances be resorted to." Rules requiring labour service in Germany were published in all the occupied territories. The number of labourers to be supplied was fixed by Sauckel, and the local authorities were instructed to meet these requirements by conscription if necessary. That conscription was the rule rather than the exception is shown by the statement of Sauckel already quoted, on the 1st March, 1944.

The defendant Sauckel frequently asserted that the workers belonging to foreign nations were treated humanely, and that the conditions in which they lived were good. But whatever the intention of Sauckel may have been, and however much he may have desired that foreign labourers should be treated humanely, the evidence before the Tribunal establishes the fact that the conscription of labour was accomplished in many cases by drastic and violent methods. The "mistakes and blunders" were on a very great scale. Man-hunts took place in the streets, at motion picture houses, even at churches and at night in private houses. Houses were sometimes burnt down, and the families taken as hostages, practices which were described by the defendant Rosenberg as having their origin "in the blackest periods of the slave trade." The methods used in obtaining forced labour from the Ukraine appear from an order issued to SD officers which stated:

"It will not be possible always to refrain from using force. . . . When searching villages, especially when it has been necessary to burn down a village, the whole population will be put at the disposal of the Commissioner by force. . . . As a rule no more children will be shot. . . . If we limit harsh measures through the above orders for the time being, it is only done for the following reason. . . . The most important thing is the recruitment of workers."

The resources and needs of the occupied countries were completely disregarded in carrying out this policy. The treatment of the labourers was governed by Sauckel's instructions of the 20th April, 1942, to the effect that:

"All the men must be fed, sheltered and treated in such a way as to exploit them to the highest possible extent, at the lowest conceivable degree of expenditure."

The evidence showed that workers destined for the Reich

were sent under guard to Germany, often packed in trains without adequate heat, food, clothing or sanitary facilities. The evidence further showed that the treatment of the labourers in Germany in many cases was brutal and degrading. The evidence relating to the Krupp Works at Essen showed that punishments of the most cruel kind were inflicted on the workers. Theoretically at least the workers were paid, housed and fed by the DAF, and even permitted to transfer their savings and to send mail and parcels back to their native country; but restrictive regulations took a proportion of the pay; the camps in which they were housed were insanitary; and the food was very often less than the minimum necessary to give the workers strength to do their jobs. In the case of Poles employed on farms in Germany, the employers were given authority to inflict corporal punishment and were ordered, if possible, to house them in stables, not in their own homes. They were subject to constant supervision by the Gestapo and the SS, and if they attempted to leave their jobs they were sent to correction camps or concentration camps. The concentration camps were also used to increase the supply of labour. Concentration camp commanders were ordered to work their prisoners to the limits of their physical power. During the latter stages of the war the concentration camps were so productive in certain types of work that the Gestapo was actually instructed to arrest certain classes of labourers so that they could be used in this way. Allied prisoners of war were also regarded as a possible source of labour. Pressure was exercised on non-commissioned officers to force them to consent to work, by transferring to disciplinary camps those who did not consent. Many of the prisoners of war were assigned to work directly related to military operations, in violation of Article 31 of the Geneva Convention. They were put to work in munition factories and even made to load bombers, to carry ammunition and to dig trenches, often under the most hazardous conditions. This condition applied particularly to the Soviet prisoners of war. On the 16th February, 1943, at a meeting of the Central Planning Board, at which the defendants Sauckel and Speer were present, Milch said:

"We have made a request for an order that a certain percentage of men in the Ack-Ack artillery must be Russians; 50,000 will be taken altogether, 30,000 are already employed as gunners. This is an amusing thing, that Russians must work the guns."

And on the 4th October, 1943, at Posen, Himmler, speaking of the Russian prisoners, captured in the early days of the war, said:

"At that time we did not value the mass of humanity as we value it to-day, as raw material, as labour. What, after all, thinking in terms of generations, is not to be regretted, but is now deplorable by reason of the loss of labour, is that the prisoners died in tens and hundreds of thousands of exhaustion and hunger."

The general policy underlying the mobilisation of slave labour was stated by Sauckel on the 20th April, 1942. He said:

"The aim of this new gigantic labour mobilisation is to use all the rich and tremendous sources conquered and secured for us by our fighting armed forces under the leadership of Adolf Hitler, for the armament of the armed forces, and also for the nutrition of the Homeland. The raw materials, as well as the fertility of the conquered territories and their human labour power, are to be used completely and conscientiously to the profit of Germany and her Allies. . . . All prisoners of war from the territories of the West, as well as the East, actually in Germany, must be completely incorporated into the German armament and nutrition industries. . . . Consequently it is an immediate necessity to use the human reserves of the conquered Soviet territory to the fullest extent. Should we not succeed in obtaining the necessary amount of labour on a voluntary basis, we must immediately institute conscription or forced labour. . . . The complete employment of all prisoners of war, as well as the use of a gigantic number of new foreign civilian workers, men and women, has become an indisputable necessity for the solution of the mobilisation of the labour programme in this war."

Reference should also be made to the policy which was in existence in Germany by the summer of 1940, under which all aged, insane, and incurable people, "useless eaters," were transferred to special institution where they were killed, and their relatives informed that they had died from natural causes. The victims were not confined to German citizens but included foreign labourers, who were no longer able to work, and were therefore useless to the German war machine. It has been estimated that at least some 275,000 people were killed in this manner in nursing homes, hospitals and asylums, which were under the jurisdiction of the defendant Frick, in his capacity as Minister of the Interior. How many foreign workers were included in this total it has been quite impossible to determine.

∞◦◊◦∞

The persecution of the Jews at the hands of the Nazi Government has been proved in the greatest detail before the Tribunal. It is a record of consistent and systematic inhumanity on the greatest scale. Ohlendorf. chief of Amt III in the RSHA from 1939 to 1943, and who was in command of one of the Einsatz groups in the campaign against the Soviet Union testified as to the methods employed in the extermination of the Jews. He said that he employed firing squads to shoot the victims in order to lessen the sense of individual guilt on the part of his men; and the 90,000 men, women and children who were murdered in one year by his particular group were mostly Jews.

When the witness Bach Zelewski was asked how Ohlendorf could admit the murder of 90,000 people, he replied:

"I am of the opinion that when, for years, for decades, the doctrine is preached that the Slav race is an inferior race, and Jews not even human, then such an outcome is inevitable."

But the defendant Frank spoke the final words of this chapter of Nazi history when he testified in this court:

"We have fought against Jewry; we have fought against it for years: and we have allowed ourselves to make utterances and my own diary has become a witness against me in this connection—utterances which are terrible. . . . A thousand years will pass and this guilt of Germany will not be erased."

The anti-Jewish policy was formulated in Point 4 of the Party Programme which declared "Only a member of the race can be a citizen. A member of the race can only be one who is of German blood, without consideration of creed. Consequently, no Jew can be a member of the race." Other points of the programme declared that Jews should be treated as foreigners, that they should not be permitted to hold public office, that they should be expelled from the Reich if it were impossible to nourish the entire population of the State, that they should be denied any further immigration into Germany, and that they should be prohibited from publishing German newspapers. The Nazi Party preached these doctrines throughout its history. "Der Stuermer" and other publications were allowed to disseminate hatred of the Jews, and in the speeches and public declarations of the Nazi leaders, the Jews were held up to public ridicule and contempt.

With the seizure of power, the persecution of the Jews was intensified. A series of discriminatory laws were passed, which limited the offices and professions permitted to Jews; and restrictions were placed on their family life and their rights of citizenship. By the autumn of 1938, the Nazi policy towards the Jews had reached the stage where it was directed towards the complete exclusion of Jews from German life. Pogroms were organised, which included the burning and demolishing of synagogues, the looting of Jewish businesses, and the arrest of prominent Jewish business men. A collective fine of one billion marks was imposed on the Jews, the seizure of Jewish assets was authorised, and the movement of Jews was restricted by regulations to certain specified districts and hours. The creation of ghettoes was carried out on an extensive scale, and by an order of the Security Police Jews were compelled to wear a yellow star to be worn on the breast and back.

It was contended for the Prosecution that certain aspects of this anti-Semitic policy were connected with the plans for aggressive war. The violent measures taken against the Jews in November, 1938, were nominally in retaliation for the killing of an official of the German Embassy in Paris. But the decision to seize Austria and Czechoslovakia had been made a year before. The imposition of a fine of one billion marks was made, and the confiscation of the financial holdings of the Jews was decreed, at a time when German armament expenditure had put the German treasury in difficulties, and when the reduction of expenditure on armaments was being considered. These steps were taken, moreover, with the approval of the defendant Goering, who had been given responsibility for economic matters of this kind, and who was the strongest advocate of an extensive rearmament programme notwithstanding the financial difficulties.

It was further said that the connection of the anti-Semitic policy with aggressive war was not limited to economic matters. The German Foreign Office circular, in an article of 25th January, 1939, entitled "Jewish question as a factor in German Foreign Policy in the year 1938", described the new phase in the Nazi anti-Semitic policy in these words:

"It is certainly no coincidence that the fateful year 1938 has brought nearer the solution of the Jewish question simultaneously with the realisation of the idea of Greater Germany, since the Jewish policy was both the basis and consequence of the events of the year 1938. The advance made by Jewish influence and the destructive Jewish spirit in politics, economy, and culture, paralysed the power and the will of the German people to rise again, more perhaps even than the power policy opposition of the former enemy Allied powers of the first World War. The healing of this sickness among the people was therefore certainly one of the most important requirements for exerting the force which, in the year 1938, resulted in the joining together of Greater Germany in defiance of the world."

The Nazi persecution of Jews in Germany before the war, severe and repressive as it was, cannot compare, however, with the policy pursued during the war in the occupied territories. Originally the policy was similar to that which had been in force inside Germany. Jews were required to register, were forced to live in ghettoes, to wear the yellow star, and were used as slave labourers. In the summer of 1941, however, plans were made for the "final solution" of the Jewish question in all of Europe. This "final solution" meant the extermination of the Jews, which early in 1939 Hitler had threatened would be one of the consequences of an outbreak of war, and a special section in the Gestapo under Adolf Eichmann, as head of Section B4 of the Gestapo, was formed to carry out the policy.

The plan for exterminating the Jews was developed shortly after the attack on the Soviet Union. Einsatzgruppen of the Security Police and SD, formed for the purpose of breaking the resistance of the population of the areas lying behind the German armies in the East, were given the duty of exterminating the Jews in those areas. The effectiveness of the work of the Einsatzgruppen is shown by the fact that in February, 1942, Heydrich was able to report that Estonia had already been cleared of Jews and that in Riga the number of Jews had been reduced from 29,500 to 2,500. Altogether the Einsatzgruppen operating in the occupied Baltic States killed over 135,000 Jews in three months.

Nor did these special units operate completely independently of the German Armed Forces. There is clear evidence that leaders of the Einsatzgruppen obtained the co-operation of Army Commanders. In one case the relations between an Einsatzgruppe and the military authorities was described at the time as being "very close, almost cordial"; in another case the smoothness of an Einsatz-commando's operation was attributed to the "understanding for this procedure" shown by the army authorities.

Units of the Security Police and SD in the occupied territories of the East, which were under civil administration, were given a similar task. The planned and systematic character of the Jewish persecutions is best illustrated by the original report of the SS Brigadier-General Stroop, who was in charge of the destruction of the ghetto in Warsaw, which took place in 1943. The Tribunal received in evidence that report, illustrated with photographs, bearing on its title page: "The Jewish Ghetto in Warsaw no longer exists." The volume records a series of reports sent by Stroop to the Higher SS and Police Fuehrer East. In April and May, 1943, in one report, Stroop wrote:

"The resistance put up by the Jews and bandits could only be suppressed by energetic actions of our troops day and night. The Reichsfuehrer SS ordered therefore on the 23rd April, 1943 the cleaning out of the ghetto with utter ruthlessness and merciless tenacity. I therefore decided to destroy and burn down the entire ghetto, without regard to the armament factories. These factories were systematically dismantled and then burnt. Jews usually left their hideouts, but frequently remained in the burning buildings, and jumped out of the windows only when the heat became unbearable. They then tried to crawl with broken bones across the street into buildings which were not afire. . . . Life in the sewers was not pleasant after the first week. Many times we could hear loud voices in the sewers. . . . Tear gas bombs were thrown into the manholes, and the Jews driven out of the sewers and captured. Countless numbers of Jews were liquidated in sewers and bunkers through blasting. The longer the resistance continued, the tougher became the members of the Waffen SS, Police and Wehrmacht, who always discharged their duties in an exemplary manner."

Stroop recorded that his action at Warsaw eliminated "a proved total of 56,065 people. To that we have to add the number of those killed through blasting, fire, etc., which cannot be counted." Grim evidence of mass murders of Jews was also presented to the Tribunal in cinematograph films depicting the communal graves of hundreds of victims which were subsequently discovered by the Allies.

These atrocities were all part and parcel of the policy

inaugurated in 1941, and it is not surprising that there should be evidence that one or two German officials entered vain protests against the brutal manner in which the killings were carried out. But the methods employed never conformed to a single pattern. The massacres of Rowno and Dubno, of which the German engineer Graebe spoke, were examples of one method, the systematic extermination of Jews in concentration camps, was another. Part of the "final solution" was the gathering of Jews from all German occupied Europe in concentration camps. Their physical condition was the test of life or death. All who were fit to work were used as slave labourers in the concentration camps; all who were not fit to work were destroyed in gas chambers and their bodies burnt. Certain concentration camps such as Treblinka and Auschwitz were set aside for this main purpose. With regard to Auschwitz, the Tribunal heard the evidence of Hoess, the Commandant of the camp from 1st May, 1940, to 1st December, 1943. He estimated that in the camp of Auschwitz alone in that time 2,500,000 persons were exterminated, and that a further 500,000 died from disease and starvation. Hoess described the screening for extermination by stating in evidence:

"We had two SS doctors on duty at Auschwitz to examine the incoming transports of prisoners. The prisoners would be marched by one of the doctors who would make spot decisions as they walked by. Those who were fit for work were sent into the camp. Others were sent immediately to the extermination plants. Children of tender years were invariably exterminated since by reason of their youth they were unable to work. Still another improvement we made over Treblinka was that at Treblinka the victims almost always knew that they were to be exterminated and at Auschwitz we endeavoured to fool the victims into thinking that they were to go through a delousing process. Of course, frequently they realised our true intensions and we sometimes had riots and difficulties due to that fact. Very frequently women would hide their children under their clothes, but of course when we found them we would send the children in to be exterminated."

He described the actual killing by stating:

"It took from three to fifteen minutes to kill the people in the death chamber, depending upon climatic conditions. We knew when the people were dead because their screaming stopped. We usually waited about one half-hour before we opened the doors and removed the bodies. After the bodies were removed our special commandos took off the rings and extracted the gold from the teeth of the corpses."

Beating, starvation, torture, and killing were general. The inmates were subjected to cruel experiments at Dachau in August, 1942, victims were immersed in cold water until their body temperature was reduced to 28° Centigrade, when they died immediately. Other experiments included high altitude experiments in pressure chambers, experiments to determine how long human beings could survive in freezing water, experiments with poison bullets, experiments with contagious diseases, and experiments dealing with sterilisation of men and women by X-rays and other methods.

Evidence was given of the treatment of the inmates before and after their extermination. There was testimony that the hair of women victims was cut off before they were killed, and shipped to Germany, there to be used in the manufacture of mattresses. The clothes, money and valuables of the inmates were also salvaged and sent to the appropriate agencies for disposition. After the extermination the gold teeth and fillings were taken from the heads of the corpses and sent to the Reichsbank.

After cremation the ashes were used for fertilizer, and in some instances attempts were made to utilise the fat from the bodies of the victims in the commercial manufacture of soap. Special groups travelled through Europe to find Jews and subject them to the "final solution." German missions were sent to such satellite countries as Hungary and Bulgaria, to arrange for the shipment of Jews to extermination camps and it is known that by the end of 1944, 400,000 Jews from Hungary had been murdered at Auschwitz. Evidence has also been given of the evacuation of 110,000 Jews from part of Roumania for "liquidation." Adolf Eichmann, who had been put in charge of this programme by Hitler, has estimated that the policy pursued resulted in the killing of 6,000,000 Jews, of which 4,000,000 were killed in the extermination institutions.

∘⊸⊱⊰⊶∘

Article 6 of the Charter provides:

"(b) War Crimes: namely, violations of the laws or customs of war. Such violations shall include, but not be limited to, murder, ill-treatment or deportation to slave labour or for any other purpose of civilian population of or in occupied territory, murder or ill-treatment of prisoners of war or persons on the seas, killing of hostages, plunder of public or private property, wanton destruction of cities, towns or villages, or devastation not justified by military necessity;

"(c) Crimes against Humanity: namely, murder, extermination, enslavement, deportation, and other inhuman acts committed against any civilian population, before or during the war; or persecutions on political, racial or religious grounds in execution of or in connection with any crime within the jurisdiction of the Tribunal, whether or not in violation of the domestic law of the country where perpetrated."

As heretofore stated, the Charter does not define as a separate crime any conspiracy except the one set out in Article 6 (*a*), dealing with crimes against peace.

The Tribunal is of course bound by the Charter, in the definition which it gives both of war crimes and crimes against humanity. With respect to war crimes, however, as has already been pointed out, the crimes defined by Article 6, section (*b*), of the Charter were already recognised as war crimes under international law. They were covered by Articles 46, 50, 52, and 56 of the Hague Convention of 1907, and Articles 2, 3, 4, 46, and 51 of the Geneva Convention of 1929. That violations of these provisions constituted crimes for which the guilty individuals were punishable is too well settled to admit of argument.

But it is argued that the Hague Convention does not apply in this case, because of the "general participation" clause in Article 2 of the Hague Convention of 1907. That clause provided:

"The provisions contained in the regulations (Rules of Land Warfare) referred to in Article I as well as in the present Convention do not apply except between contracting powers, and then only if all the belligerents are parties to the Convention."

Several of the belligerents in the recent war were not parties to this Convention.

In the opinion of the Tribunal it is not necessary to decide this question. The rules of land warfare expressed in the Convention undoubtedly represented an advance over existing international law at the time of their adoption. But the Convention expressly stated that it was an attempt "to revise the general laws and customs of war," which it thus recognised to be then existing, but by 1939 these rules laid down in the Convention were recognised by all civilised nations, and were regarded as being declaratory of the laws and customs of war which are referred to in Article 6 (*b*) of the Charter.

A further submission was made that Germany was no longer bound by the rules of land warfare in many of the territories occupied during the war, because Germany had completely subjugated those countries and incorporated them into the German Reich, a fact which gave Germany authority to deal with the occupied countries as though they were part of Germany. In the view of the Tribunal it is unnecessary in this case to decide whether this doctrine of subjugation, dependent as it is upon military conquest, has any application where the subjugation is the result of the crime of aggressive war. The doctrine was never considered to be applicable so long as there was an army in the field attempting to restore the occupied countries to their true owners, and in this case, therefore, the doctrine could not apply to any territories occupied after the 1st September, 1939. As to the war crimes committed in Bohemia and Moravia, it is a sufficient answer that these territories were never added to the Reich, but a mere protectorate was established over them.

With regard to crimes against humanity, there is no doubt whatever that political opponents were murdered in Germany before the war, and that many of them were kept in concentration camps in circumstances of great horror and cruelty. The policy of terror was certainly carried out

on a vast scale, and in many cases was organised and systematic. The policy of persecution, repression and murder
of civilians in Germany before the war of 1939, who were
likely to be hostile to the Government, was most ruthlessly
carried out. The persecution of Jews during the same
period is established beyond all doubt. To constitute crimes
against humanity, the acts relied on before the outbreak of
war must have been in execution of, or in connection
with, any crime within the jurisdiction of the Tribunal.
The Tribunal is of the opinion that revolting and horrible
as many of these crimes were, it has not been satisfactorily
proved that they were done in execution of, or in connection with, any such crime. The Tribunal therefore
cannot make a general declaration that the acts before
1939 were crimes against humanity within the meaning of
the Charter, but from the beginning of the war in 1939
war crimes were committed on a vast scale, which were
also crimes against humanity; and insofar as the inhumane
acts charged in the Indictment, and committed after the
beginning of the war, did not constitute war crimes, they
were all committed in execution of, or in connection
with, the aggressive war, and therefore constituted crimes
against humanity.

The PRESIDENT: I now ask Colonel Volchkov to continue
the reading of the Judgment.

Colonel VOLCHKOV:

Article 9 of the Charter provides:

"At the trial of any individual member of any group or
organisation the Tribunal may declare (in connection with
any act of which the individual may be convicted) that the
group or organisation of which the individual was a member was a criminal organisation.

"After receipt of the Indictment the Tribunal shall give such notice as it thinks fit that the prosecution intends to ask the Tribunal to make such declaration and any member of the organisation will be entitled to apply to the Tribunal for leave to be heard by the Tribunal upon the question of the criminal character of the organisation. The Tribunal shall have power to allow or reject the application. If the application is allowed, the Tribunal may direct in what manner the applicants shall be represented and heard."

Article 10 of the Charter makes clear that the declaration of criminality against an accused organisation is final, and cannot be challenged in any subsequent criminal proceeding against a member of that organisation. Article 10 is as follows:

"In cases where a group or organisation is declared criminal by the Tribunal, the competent national authority of any Signatory shall have the right to bring individuals to trial for membership therein before national, military or occupation courts. In any such case the criminal nature of the group or organisation is considered proved and shall not be questioned."

The effect of the declaration of criminality by the Tribunal is well illustrated by Law Number 10 of the Control Council of Germany passed on the 20th day of December, 1945, which provides:

"Each of the following acts is recognised as a crime:

. . .

"(*d*) Membership in categories of a criminal group or organisation declared criminal by the International Military Tribunal.

. . .

"(3) Any person found guilty of any of the crimes above mentioned may upon conviction be punished as shall be determined by the Tribunal to be just. Such punishment may consist of one or more of the following:

(*a*) Death.

(*b*) Imprisonment for life or a term of years, with or without hard labour.

(*c*) Fine, and imprisonment with or without hard labour, in lieu thereof."

In effect, therefore, a member of an organisation which the Tribunal has declared to be criminal may be subsequently convicted of the crime of membership and be punished for that crime by death. This is not to assume that international or military courts which will try these individuals will not exercise appropriate standards of justice. This is a far-reaching and novel procedure. Its application, unless properly safeguarded, may produce great injustice.

Article 9, it should be noted, uses the words "The Tribunal may declare" so that the Tribunal is vested with discretion as to whether it will declare any organisation criminal. This discretion is a judicial one and does not permit arbitrary action, but should be exercised in accordance with well settled legal principles one of the most important of which is that criminal guilt is personal, and that mass punishments should be avoided. If satisfied of the criminal guilt of any organisation or group, this Tribunal should not hesitate to declare it to be criminal because the theory of "group criminality" is new, or because it might be unjustly applied by some subsequent tribunals. On the other hand, the Tribunal should make such declaration of criminality so far as possible in a manner to insure that innocent persons will not be punished.

A criminal organisation is analogous to a criminal conspiracy in that the essence of both is cooperation for criminal purposes. There must be a group bound together and organised for a common purpose. The group must be formed or used in connection with the commission of crimes denounced by the Charter. Since the declaration with respect to the organisations and groups will, as has been pointed out, fix the criminality of its members, that definition should exclude persons who had no knowledge of the criminal purposes or acts of the organisation and those who were drafted by the State for membership, unless they were personally implicated in the commission of acts declared criminal by Article 6 of the Charter as members of the organisation. Membership alone is not enough to come within the scope of these declarations.

Since declarations of criminality which the Tribunal makes will be used by other courts in the trial of persons on account of their membership in the organisations found to be criminal, the Tribunal feels it appropriate to make the following recommendations:

1. That so far as possible throughout the four zones of occupation in Germany the classifications, sanctions and penalties be standardised. Uniformity of treatment so far as practical should be a basic principle. This does not, of course, mean that discretion in sentencing should not be vested in the court; but the discretion should be within fixed limits appropriate to the nature of the crime.

2. Law No. 10, to which reference has already been made, leaves punishment entirely in the discretion of the trial court even to the extent of inflicting the death penalty.

The De-Nazification Law of 5th March, 1946, however, passed for Bavaria, Greater-Hesse and Wuerttemberg-Baden, provides definite sentences for punishment in each type of offence. The Tribunal recommends that in no case should punishment imposed under Law No. 10 upon any members of an organisation or group declared by the Tribunal to be criminal exceed the punishment fixed by the De-Nazification Law. No person should be punished under both laws.

3. The Tribunal recommends to the Control Council that Law No. 10 be amended to prescribe limitations on the punishment which may be imposed for membership in a criminal group or organisation so that such punishment shall not exceed the punishment prescribed by the De-Nazification Law.

The Indictment asks that the Tribunal declare to be criminal the following organisations: The Leadership Corps of the Nazi Party; The Gestapo; The S.D.; The S.S.; The S.A.; The Reich Cabinet, and The General Staff and High Command of the German Armed Forces.

∞∞⟨⟩∞∞

The Indictment has named the Leadership Corps of the Nazi Party as a group or organisation which should be declared criminal. The Leadership Corps of the Nazi Party consisted, in effect, of the official organisation of the Nazi Party, with Hitler as Fuehrer at its head. The actual work of running the Leadership Corps was carried out by the Chief of the Party Chancellery (Hess, succeeded by Bormann) assisted by the Party Reich Directorate, or Reichsleitung, which was composed of the Reichleiters, the heads of the functional organisations of the Party, as well as of the heads of the various main departments and offices which were attached to the Party Reich

Directorate. Under the Chief of the Party Chancellery were the Gauleiters, with territorial jurisdiction over the main administrative regions of the Party, the Gaus. The Gauleiters were assisted by a Party Gau Directorate or Gauleitung, similar in composition and in function to the Party Reich Directorate. Under the Gauleiters in the Party hierarchy were the Kreisleiters with territorial jurisdiction over a Kreis, usually consisting of a single county, and assisted by a Party of Kreis Directorate, or Kreisleitung. The Kreisleiters were the lowest members of the Party hierarchy who were full time paid employees. Directly under the Kreisleiters were the Ortsgruppenleiters, then the Zellenleiters and then the Blockleiters. Directives and instructions were received from the Party Reich Directorate. The Gauleiters had the function of interpreting such orders and issuing them to lower formations. The Kreisleiters had a certain discretion in interpreting orders, but the Ortsgruppenleiters had not, but acted under definite instructions. Instructions were only issued in writing down as far as the Ortsgruppenleiters. The Block and Zellenleiters usually received instructions orally. Membership in the Leadership Corps at all levels was voluntary.

On 28th February, 1946, the Prosecution excluded from the declaration all members of the staffs of the Ortsgruppenleiters and all assistants of the Zellenleiters and Blockleiters. The declaration sought against the Leadership Corps of the Nazi Party thus includes the Fuehrer, the Reichsleitung, the Gauleiters and their staff officers, the Kreisleiters and their staff officers, the Ortsgruppenleiters, the Zellenleiters and the Blockleiters, a group estimated to contain at least 600,000 people.

The primary purposes of the Leadership Corps from its beginning was to assist the Nazis in obtaining and, after

30th January, 1933, in retaining, control of the German State. The machinery of the Leadership Corps was used for the widespread dissemination of Nazi propaganda and to keep a detailed check on the political attitudes of the German people. In this activity the lower Political Leaders played a particularly important rôle. The Blockleiters were instructed by the Party Manual to report to the Ortsgruppenleiters, all persons circulating damaging rumours or criticism of the régime. The Ortsgruppenleiters, on the basis of information supplied them by the Blockleiters and Zellenleiters, kept a card index of the people within their Ortsgruppe which recorded the factors which would be used in forming a judgment as to their political reliability. The Leadership Corps was particularly active during plebiscites. All members of the Leadership Corps were active in getting out the vote and insuring the highest possible proportion of "yes" votes. Ortsgruppenleiters and Political Leaders of higher ranks often collaborated with the Gestapo and SD in taking steps to determine those who refused to vote or who voted "no", and in taking steps against them which went as far as arrest and detention in a concentration camp.

These steps, which relate merely to the consolidation of control of the Nazi Party, are not criminal under the view of the conspiracy to wage aggressive war which has previously been set forth. But the Leadership Corps was also used for similar steps in Austria and those parts of Czechoslovakia, Lithuania, Poland, France, Belgium, Luxembourg and Yugoslavia which were incorporated into the Reich and within the Gaus of the Nazi Party In those territories the machinery of the Leadership Corps was used for their Germanisation through the elimination of local customs and the detection and arrest of persons who opposed German occupation. This was criminal under Article 6 (*b*) of the Charter in those areas governed by the Hague Rules of Land Warfare and criminal under Article 6 (*c*) of the Charter as to the remainder.

The Leadership Corps played its part in the persecution of the Jews. It was involved in the economic and political discrimination against the Jews, which was put into effect shortly after the Nazis came into power. The Gestapo and SD were instructed to co-ordinate with the Gauleiters and Kreisleiters the measures taken in the pogroms of the 9th and 10th November in the year 1938. The Leadership Corps was also used to prevent German public opinion from reacting against the measures taken against the Jews in the East. On the 9th October, 1942, a confidential information bulletin was sent to all Gauleiters and Kreisleiters entitled "Preparatory Measures for the Final Solution of the Jewish Question in Europe. Rumours concerning the Conditions of the Jews in the East." This bulletin stated that rumours were being started by returning soldiers concerning the conditions of Jews in the East which some Germans might not understand, and outlined in detail the official explanation to be given. This bulletin contained no explicit statement that the Jews were being exterminated, but it did indicate they were going to labour camps, and spoke of their complete segregation and elimination and the necessity of ruthless severity. Thus, even at its face value, it indicated the utilisation of the machinery of the Leadership Corps to keep German public opinion from rebelling at a programme which was stated to involve condemning the Jews of Europe to a lifetime of slavery. This information continued to be available to the Leadership Corps. The August, 1944, edition of "Die Lage", a publication which was circulated among the

Political Leaders, described the deportation of 430,000 Jews from Hungary.

The Leadership Corps played an important part in the administration of the Slave Labour Programme. A Sauckel decree dated 6th April 1942, appointed the Gauleiters as Plenipotentiary for Labour Mobilisation for their Gaus with authority to co-ordinate all agencies dealing with labour questions in their Gaus, with specific authority over the employment of foreign workers, including their conditions of work, feeding and housing. Under this authority the Gauleiters assumed control over the allocation of labour in their Gaus, including the forced labourers from foreign countries. In carrying out this task the Gauleiters used many Party offices within their Gaus, including subordinate Political Leaders. For example, Sauckel's decree of the 8th September, 1942, relating to the allocation for household labour of 400,000 women labourers brought in from the East, established a procedure under which applications filed for such workers should be passed on by the Kreisleiters, whose judgment was final.

Under Sauckel's directive the Leadership Corps was directly concerned with the treatment given foreign workers, and the Gauleiters were specifically instructed to prevent "politically inept factory heads" from giving too much consideration to the care of Eastern workers. The type of question which was considered in their treatment included reports by the Kreisleiters on pregnancies among the female slave labourers, which would result in an abortion if the child's parentage would not meet the racial standards laid down by the SS and usually detention in a concentration camp for the female slave labourer. The evidence has established that under the supervision of the Leadership Corps, the industrial workers were housed in camps under atrocious sanitary conditions, worked long hours and were inadequately fed. Under similar supervision, the agricultural workers, who were somewhat better treated were prohibited transportation, entertainment and religious worship, and were worked without any time limit on their working hours and under regulations which gave the employer the right to inflict corporal punishment. The Political Leaders, at least down to the Ortsgruppenleiters, were responsible for this supervision. On the 5th May, 1943, a memorandum of Bormann instructing that mistreatment of slave labourers cease was distributed down to the Ortsgruppenleiters. Similarly on the 10th November, 1944, a Speer circular transmitted a Himmler directive which provided that all members of the Nazi Party, in accordance with instructions from the Kreisleiter, would be warned by the Ortsgruppenleiters of their duty to keep foreign workers under careful observation.

The Leadership Corps was directly concerned with the treatment of prisoners of war. On 5th November, 1941, Bormann transmitted a directive down to the level of Kreisleiter instructing them to insure compliance by the Army with the recent directives of the Department of the Interior ordering that dead Russian prisoners of war should be buried wrapped in tar paper in a remote place without any ceremony or any decorations of their graves. On 25th November, 1943, Bormann sent a circular instructing the Gauleiters to report any lenient treatment of prisoners of war. On 13th September, 1944, Bormann sent a directive down to the level of Kreisleiter ordering that liaison be established between the Kreisleiters and the guards of the prisoners of war in order "to better assimilate the commitment of the prisoners of war to the political and economic demands". On 17th October, 1944, an OKW directive instructed the officer in charge of the prisoners of war to confer with the Kreisleiters on questions of the productivity of labour. The use of prisoners of war, particularly those from the East, was accompanied by a widespread violation of the rules of land warfare. This evidence establishes that the Leadership Corps down to the level of Kreisleiter was a participant in this illegal treatment.

The machinery of the Leadership Corps was also utilised in attempts made to deprive Allied airmen of the protection to which they were entitled under the Geneva Convention. On 13th March, 1940, a directive of Hess transmitted instructions through the Leadership Corps down to the Blockleiter for the guidance of the civilian population in case of the landing of enemy planes or parachutists, which stated that enemy parachutists were to be immediately arrested or "made harmless". On 30th May, 1944, Bormann sent a circular letter to all Gau and Kreisleiters reporting instances of lynchings of Allied low level fliers in which no police action was taken. It was requested that Ortsgruppenleiters be informed orally of the contents of this letter. This letter accompanied a propaganda drive which had been instituted by Goebbels to induce such lynchings, and clearly amounted to instructions to induce such lynchings or at least to violate the Geneva Convention by withdrawing any police protection. Some lynchings were carried out pursuant to this programme, but it does not appear that they were carried out throughout all of Germany. Nevertheless, the existence of this circular letter shows that the heads of the Leadership Corps were utilising it for a purpose which was patently illegal and which involved the use of the machinery of the Leadership Corps at least through the Ortsgruppenleiter.

The Leadership Corps was used for purposes which were criminal under the Charter and involved the Germanisation of incorporated territory, the persecution of the Jews, the administration of the slave labour programme, and the mistreatment of prisoners of war. The defendants Bormann and Sauckel, who were members of this organisation, were among those who used it for these purposes. The Gauleiters, the Kreisleiters, and the Ortsgruppenleiters participated, to one degree or another, in these criminal programmes. The Reichsleitung as the staff organisation of the Party is also responsible for these criminal programmes as well as the heads of the various staff organisations of the Gauleiters and Kreisleiters. The decision of the Tribunal on these staff organisations includes only the Amtsleiters who were heads of offices on the staffs of the Reichsleitung, Gauleitung and Kreisleitung. With respect to other staff officers and party organisations attached to the Leadership Corps other than the Amtsleiters referred to above, the Tribunal will follow the suggestion of the Prosecution in excluding them from the declaration.

The Tribunal declares to be criminal within the meaning of the Charter the group composed of those members of the Leadership Corps holding the positions enumerated in the preceding paragraph who became or remained members of the organisation with knowledge that it was being used for the commission of acts declared criminal by Article 6 of the Charter, or who were personally implicated as members of the organisation in the commission of such crimes. The basis of this finding is the participation of the organisation in war crimes and crimes against humanity connected with the war; the group declared criminal cannot include, therefore, persons who had ceased to hold the positions enumerated in the preceding paragraph prior to 1st September, 1939.

The Prosecution has named Die Geheime Staatspolizei (Gestapo) and Die Sicherheitsdienst des Reichsfuehrer SS (SD) as groups or organisations which should be declared criminal. The Prosecution presented the cases against the Gestapo and SD together, stating that this was necessary because of the close working relationship between them. The Tribunal permitted the SD to present its defence separately because of a claim of conflicting interests, but after examining the evidence has decided to consider the case of the Gestapo and SD together.

The Gestapo and the SD were first linked together on

26th June, 1936, by the appointment of Heydrich, who was the Chief of the SD, to the position of Chief of the Security Police, which was defined to include both the Gestapo and the Criminal Police. Prior to that time the SD had been the intelligence agency, first of the SS, and, after 4th June, 1934, of the entire Nazi Party. the Gestapo had been composed of the various political police forces of the several German Federal states which had been unified under the personal leadership of Himmler, with the assistance of Goering. Himmler had been appointed Chief of the German Police in the Ministry of the Interior on 17th June, 1936, and in his capacity as Reichsfuehrer SS and Chief of the German Police issued his decree of 26th June, 1936, which placed both the Criminal Police, or Kripo, and the Gestapo in the Security Police, and placed both the Security Police and the SD under the command of Heydrich.

This consolidation under the leadership of Heydrich of the Security Police, a State organisation, and the SD, a Party organisation, was formalised by the decree of 27th September, 1939, which united the various state and Party offices which were under Heydrich as Chief of the Security Police and SD into one administrative unit, the Reichs Security Head Office (RSHA) which was at the same time both one of the principal offices (Hauptamter) of the SS under Himmler as Reichsfuehrer SS and an office in the Ministry of the Interior under Himmler as Chief of the German Police. The internal structure of the RSHA shows the manner in which it consolidated the offices of the Security Police with those of the SD. The RSHA was divided into seven offices (Amter), two of which (Amt I and Amt II) dealt with administrative matters. The Security Police were represented by Amt IV, the head office of the Gestapo, and by Amt V, the head office of the Criminal Police. The SD were represented by Amt

III, the head office for SD activities inside Germany, by Amt VI, the head office for SD activities outside of Germany, and by Amt VII, the office for ideological research. Shortly after the creation of the RSHA, in November, 1939, the Security Police was "coordinated" with the SS by taking all officials of the Gestapo and Criminal Police into the SS at ranks equivalent to their positions.

The creation of the RSHA represented the formalisation, at the top level, of the relationship under which the SD served as the intelligence agency for the Security Police. A similar coordination existed in the local offices. Within Germany and areas which were incorporated within the Reich for the purpose of civil administration, local offices of the Gestapo, Criminal Police and SD were formally separate. They were subject to coordination by Inspectors of the Security Police and SD on the staffs of the local Higher SS and Police Leaders, however, and one of the principal functions of the local SD units was to serve as the intelligence agency for the local Gestapo units. In the occupied territories the formal relationship between local units of the Gestapo, Criminal Police and SD was slightly closer. They were organised into local units of the Security Police and SD and were under the control of both the RSHA and of the Higher SS and Police Leader who was appointed by Himmler to serve on the staff of the occupying authority. The offices of the Security Police and SD in occupied territory were composed of departments corresponding to the various Amts of the RSHA. In occupied territories which were still considered to be operational military areas or where German control had not been formally established, the organisation of the Security Police and SD was only slightly changed. Members of the Gestapo, Kripo and SD were joined together into military type organisations known as Einsatz

Kommandos and Einsatzgruppen in which the key positions were held by members of the Gestapo, Kripo, and SD and in which members of the Order Police, the Waffen SS and even the Wehrmacht were used as auxiliaries. These organisations were under the over-all control of the RSHA, but in front line areas were under the operational control of the appropriate Army Commander.

It can thus be seen that from a functional point of view both the Gestapo and the SD were important and closely related groups within the organisation of the Security Police and the SD. The Security Police and SD was under a single command, that of Heydrich and later Kaltenbrunner, as Chief of the Security Police and SD; it had a single headquarters, the RSHA; it had its own command channels and worked as one organisation both in Germany, in occupied territories and in the areas immediately behind the front lines. During the period with which the Tribunal is primarily concerned, applicants for positions in the Security Police and SD received training in all its components, the Gestapo, Criminal Police and SD. Some confusion has been caused by the fact that part of the organisation was technically a formation of the Nazi Party while another part of the organisation was an office in the Government, but this is of no particular significance in view of the law of 1st December, 1933, declaring the unity of the Nazi Party and the German State.

The Security Police and SD was a voluntary organisation. It is true that many civil servants and administrative officials were transferred into the Security Police. The claim that this transfer was compulsory amounts to nothing more than the claim that they had to accept the transfer or resign their positions, with a possibility of having incurred official disfavour. During the war a member of the Security Police and SD did not have a free choice of assignments within that organisation and the refusal to accept a particular position, especially when serving in occupied territory, might have led to serious punishment. The fact remains, however, that all members of the Security Police and SD joined the organisation voluntarily under no other sanction than the desire to retain their positions as officials.

The organisation of the Security Police and SD also included three special units which must be dealt with separately. The first of these was the Frontier Police or Grenzpolizei which came under the control of the Gestapo in 1937. Their duties consisted in the control of passage over the borders of Germany. They arrested persons who crossed the borders illegally. It is also clear from the evidence presented that they received directives from the Gestapo to transfer foreign workers whom they apprehended to concentration camps. They could also request the local office of the Gestapo for permission to commit persons arrested to concentration camps. The Tribunal is of the opinion that the Frontier Police must be included in the charge of criminality against the Gestapo.

The border and customs protection of Zollgrenzschutz became part of the Gestapo in the summer of 1944. The functions of this organisation were similar to the Frontier Police in enforcing border regulations with particular respect to the prevention of smuggling. It does not appear, however, that their transfer was complete but that about half of their personnel of 54,000 remained under the Reich Finance Administration or the Order Police. A few days before the end of the war the whole organisation was transferred back to the Reich Finance Administration. The transfer of the organisation to the Gestapo was so late and it participated so little in the overall activities of the organisation that the Tribunal does not feel that it should be dealt with in considering the criminality of the Gestapo.

The third organisation was the so-called Secret Field Police which was originally under the Army but which in 1942 was transferred by military order to the Security Police. The Secret Field Police was concerned with security matters within the Army in occupied territory, and also with the prevention of attacks by civilians on military installations or units, and committed war crimes and crimes against humanity on a wide scale. It has not been proved, however, that it was a part of the Gestapo and the Tribunal does not consider it as coming within the charge of criminality contained in the Indictment, except such members as may have been transferred to Amt IV of the RSHA or were members of organisations declared criminal by this Judgment.

Originally, one of the primary functions of the Gestapo was the prevention of any political opposition to the Nazi régime, a function which it performed with the assistance of the SD. The principal weapon used in performing this function was the concentration camp. The Gestapo did not have administrative control over the concentration camps, but, acting through the RSHA, was responsible for the detention of political prisoners in those camps. Gestapo officials were usually responsible for the interrogation of political prisoners at the camps.

The Gestapo and the SD also dealt with charges of treason and with questions relating to the Press, the Churches and the Jews. As the Nazi programme of anti-Semitic persecution increased in intensity the role played by these groups became increasingly important. In the early morning of 10th November, 1938, Heydrich sent a telegram to all offices of the Gestapo and SD giving instructions for the organisation of the pogroms of that date and instructing them to arrest as many Jews as the prisons could hold "especially rich ones," but to be careful that those arrested were healthy and not too old. By 11th November, 1938, 20,000 Jews had been arrested and many were sent to concentration camps. On 24th January, 1939, Heydrich, the Chief of the Security Police and SD, was charged with furthering the emigration and evacuation of Jews from Germany, and on 31st July, 1941, with bringing about a complete solution of the Jewish problem in German dominated Europe. A special section of the Gestapo office of the RSHA under Standartenfuehrer Eichmann was set up with responsibility for Jewish matters which employed its own agents to investigate the Jewish problem in occupied territory. Local offices of the Gestapo were used first to supervise the emigration of Jews and later to deport them to the East both from Germany and from the territories occupied during the war. Einsatzgruppen of the Security Police and SD operating behind the lines of the Eastern front engaged in the wholesale massacre of Jews. A special detachment from Gestapo headquarters in the RSHA was used to arrange for the deportation of Jews from Axis satellites to Germany for the "final solution."

Local offices of the Security Police and SD played an important role in the German administration of occupied territories. The nature of their participation is shown by measures taken in the summer of 1938 in preparation for the attack on Czechoslovakia which was then in contemplation. Einsatzgruppen of the Gestapo and SD were organised to follow the Army into Czechoslovakia to provide for the security of political life in the occupied territories. Plans were made for the infiltration of SD men into the area in advance, and for the building up of a system of files to indicate what inhabitants should be placed under surveillance, deprived of passports of liquidated. These plans were considerably altered due to the cancellation of the attack on Czechoslovakia, but in the military operations which actually occurred, particularly in the war against U.S.S.R., Einsatzgruppen of the Security Police and SD went into operation, and combined brutal measures for the pacification of the civilian population with the wholesale slaughter of Jews. Heydrich gave orders to fabricate incidents on the Polish-German frontier in 1939 which would give Hitler sufficient provocation to attack Poland. Both Gestapo and SD personnel were involved in these operations.

The local units of the Security Police and SD continued their work in the occupied territories after they had ceased to be an area of operations. The Security Police and SD engaged in widespread arrests of the civilian population of these occupied countries, imprisoned many of them under inhumane conditions, subjected them to brutal third degree methods, and sent many of them to concentration camps. Local units of the Security Police and SD were also involved in the shooting of hostages, the imprisonment of relatives, the execution of persons charged as terrorists and saboteurs without a trial, and the enforcement of the "Nacht und Nebel" decrees under which persons charged with a type of offence believed to endanger the security of the occupying forces were either executed within a week or secretly removed to Germany without being permitted to communicate with their family and friends.

Offices of the Security Police and SD were involved in the administration of the Slave Labour Programme. In some occupied territories they helped local labour authorities to meet the quotas imposed by Sauckel. Gestapo offices inside of Germany were given surveillance over slave labourers and responsibility for apprehending those who were absent from their place of work. The Gestapo also had charge of the so-called work training camps. Although both German and foreign workers could be committed to these camps, they played a significant rôle in forcing foreign labourers to work for the German war effort. In the latter stages of the war as the SS embarked on a slave labour programme of its own, the Gestapo was used to arrest workers for the purpose of insuring an adequate supply in the concentration camps.

The local offices of the Security Police and SD were also involved in the commission of war crimes involving the mistreatment and murder of prisoners of war. Soviet prisoners of war in prisoner of war camps in Germany were screened by Einsatz Kommandos acting under the directions of the local Gestapo offices. Commissars, Jews, members of the intelligentsia, "fanatical Communists" and even those who were considered incurably sick were classified as "intolerable," and exterminated. The local offices of the Security Police and SD were involved in the enforcement of the "Bullet" decree, put into effect on 4th March, 1944, under which certain categories of prisoners of war, who were recaptured, were not treated as prisoners of war but taken to Mauthausen in secret and shot. Members of the Security Police and the SD were charged with the enforcement of the decree for the shooting of parachutists and commandos.

The Gestapo and SD were used for purposes which were criminal under the Charter involving the persecution and extermination of the Jews, brutalities and killings in concentration camps, excesses in the administration of occupied territories, the administration of the slave labour programme and the mistreatment and murder of prisoners of war. The defendant Kaltenbrunner, who was a member of this organisation, was among those who used it for these purposes. In dealing with the Gestapo the Tribunal includes all executive and administrative officials of Amt IV of the RSHA or concerned with Gestapo administration in other departments of the RSHA and all local

Gestapo officials serving both inside and outside of
Germany, including the members of the Frontier Police,
but not including the members of the Border and
Customs Protection or the Secret Field Police, except such
members as have been specified above. At the suggestion
of the Prosecution the Tribunal does not include persons
employed by the Gestapo for purely clerical, stenographic,
janitorial or similar unofficial routine tasks. In dealing with
the SD the Tribunal includes Amts III, VI and VII of the
RSHA and all other members of the SD, including all
local representatives and agents, honorary or otherwise,
whether they were technically members of the SS or not.

The Tribunal declares to be criminal within the
meaning of the Charter the group composed of those
members of the Gestapo and SD holding the positions
enumerated in the preceding paragraph who became or
remained members of the organisation with knowledge
that it was being used for the commission of acts declared
criminal by Article 6 of the Charter, or who were personally implicated as members of the organisation in the
commission of such crimes. The basis for this finding is the
participation of the organisation in war crimes and crimes
against humanity connected with the war; this group
declared criminal cannot include, therefore, persons who
had ceased to hold the positions enumerated in the preceding paragraph prior to 1st September, 1939.

The PRESIDENT:

The Prosecution has named Die Schutzstaffeln Der
Nationalsocialistischen Deutschen Arbeiterpartei (commonly known as the SS) as an organisation which should
be declared criminal. The portion of the Indictment dealing with the SS also includes the Die Sicherheitsdienst des
Reichsfuehrer—SS (commonly known as the SD). This

latter organisation, which was originally an intelligence branch of the SS, later became an important part of the organisation of Security Police and SD and is dealt with in the Tribunal's Judgment on the Gestapo.

The SS was originally established by Hitler in 1925 as an elite section of the SA for political purposes under the pretext of protecting speakers at public meetings of the Nazi Party. After the Nazis had obtained power the SS was used to maintain order and control audiences at mass demonstrations and was given the additional duty of "internal security" by a decree of the Fuehrer. The SS played an important role at the time of the Roehm purge of 30th June, 1934, and, as a reward for its services, was made an independent unit of the Nazi Party shortly thereafter.

In 1929, when Himmler was first appointed as Reichs Fuehrer the SS consisted of 280 men who were regarded as especially trustworthy. In 1933, it was composed of 52,000 men drawn from all walks of life. The original formation of the SS was the Allgemeine SS, which by 1939 had grown to a corps of 240,000 men, organised on military lines into divisions and regiments. During the war its strength declined to well under 40,000.

The SS originally contained two other formations, the SS Verfuegungstruppe, a force consisting of SS members who volunteered for four years' armed service in lieu of compulsory service with the Army, and the SS Totenkopf Verbaende, special troops employed to guard concentration camps, which came under the control of the SS in 1934. The SS Verfuegungstruppe was organised as an armed unit to be employed with the Army in the event of mobilisation. In the summer of 1939, the Verfuegungstruppe was equipped as a motorised division to form the nucleus of the forces which came to be known in 1940 as the Waffen SS. In that year the Waffen SS comprised 100,000 men, 56,000 coming from the

Verfuegungstruppe and the rest from the Allgemeine SS
and the Totenkopf Verbaende. At the end of the war it is
estimated to have consisted of about 580,000 men and 40
divisions. The Waffen SS was under the tactical command
of the Army, but was equipped and supplied through the
administrative branches of the SS and under SS disciplinary control.

The SS Central Organisation had 12 main offices. The
most important of these were the RSHA, which has
already been discussed, the WVHA or Economic
Administration Main Office which administered concentration camps along with its other duties, a Race and
Settlement Office together with auxiliary offices for repa-
triation of racial Germans (Volksdeutschemit-telstelle).
The SS Central Organisation also had a legal office and
the SS possessed its own legal system; and its personnel
were under the jurisdiction of special courts. Also attached
to the SS main offices was a research foundation known as
the Experiments Ahnenerbe. The scientists attached to this
organisation are stated to have been mainly honorary
members of the SS. During the war an institute for military scientific research became attached to the Ahnenerbe
which conducted extensive experiments involving the use
of living human beings. An employee of this institute was
a certain Dr. Rascher, who conducted these experiments
with the full knowledge of the Ahnenerbe, which was sub-
sidised and under the patronage of the Reichsfuehrer SS
who was a trustee of the foundation.

Beginning in 1933 there was a gradual but thorough
amalgamation of the police and SS. In 1936 Himmler, the
Reichs Fuehrer SS, became Chief of the German Police
with authority over the regular uniformed police as well
as the Security Police. Himmler established a system under
which Higher SS and Police Leaders, appointed for each
Wehrkreis, served as his personal representatives in coordi-

nating the activities of the Order Police, Security Police and SD and Allgemeine SS within their jurisdictions. In 1939 the SS and police systems were coordinated by taking into the SS all officials of the Security and Order Police, at SS ranks equivalent to their rank in the police.

Until 1940 the SS was an entirely voluntary organisation. After the formation of the Waffen SS in 1940 there was a gradually increasing number of conscripts into the Waffen SS. It appears that about a third of the total number of people joining the Waffen SS were conscripts, that the proportion of conscripts was higher at the end of the war than at the beginning, but that there continued to be a high proportion of volunteers until the end of the war.

SS units were active participants in the steps leading up to aggressive war. The Verfuegungstruppe was used in the occupation of the Sudetenland, of Bohemia and Moravia and of Memel. The Henlein Free Corps was under the jurisdiction of the Reichs Fuehrer SS for operations in the Sudetenland in 1938 and the Volksdeutschemittelstelle financed fifth column activities there.

The SS was even a more general participant in the commission of war crimes and crimes against humanity. Through its control over the organisation of the Police, particularly the Security Police and SD, the SS was involved in all the crimes which have been outlined in the section of this Judgment dealing with the Gestapo and SD. Other branches of the SS were equally involved in these criminal programmes. There is evidence that the shooting of unarmed prisoners of war was the general practice in some Waffen SS divisions. On 1st October, 1944, the custody of prisoners of war and interned persons was transferred to Himmler, who in turn transferred prisoner of war affairs to SS Obergruppenfuehrer Berger and to SS Obergruppenfuehrer Pohl. The Race and Settlement

Office of the SS together with the Volksdeutsche-mittelstelle were active in carrying out schemes for Germanisation of occupied territories according to the racial principles of the Nazi Party and were involved in the deportation of Jews and other foreign nationals. Units of the Waffen SS and Einsatzgruppen operating directly under the SS main office were used to carry out these plans. These units were also involved in the widespread murder and ill-treatment of the civilian population of occupied territories. Under the guise of combatting partisan units, units of the SS exterminated Jews and people deemed politically undesirable by the SS, and their reports record the execution of enormous numbers of persons. Waffen SS divisions were responsible for many massacres and atrocities in occupied territories such as the massacres at Oradour and Lidice.

From 1934 onwards the SS was responsible for the guarding and administration of concentration camps. The evidence leaves no doubt that the consistently brutal treatment of the inmates of concentration camps was carried out as a result of the general policy of the SS, which was that the inmates were racial inferiors to be treated only with contempt. There is evidence that where manpower considerations permitted, Himmler wanted to rotate guard battalions so that all members of the SS would be instructed as to the proper attitude to take to inferior races. After 1942 when the concentration camps were placed under the control of the WVHA they were used as a source of slave labour. An agreement made with the Ministry of Justice on 18th September, 1942, provided that anti-social elements who had finished prison sentences were to be delivered to the SS to be worked to death. Steps were continually taken, involving the use of the Security Police and SD and even the Waffen SS, to insure that the SS had an adequate supply of concentration camp labour for its projects. In connection with the administration of the concentration camps, the SS embarked on a series of experiments on human beings which were performed on prisoners of war or concentration camp inmates. These experiments included freezing to death, and killing by poison bullets. The SS was able to obtain an allocation of Government funds for this kind of research on the grounds that they had access to human material not available to other agencies.

The SS played a particularly significant rôle in the persecution of the Jews. The SS was directly involved in the demonstrations of 10th November, 1938. The evacuation of the Jews from occupied territories was carried out under the directions of the SS with the assistance of SS Police units. The extermination of the Jews was carried out under the direction of the SS central organisation. It was actually put into effect by SS formations. The Einsatzgruppen engaged in wholesale massacres of the Jews. SS police units were also involved. For example, the massacre of Jews in the Warsaw Ghetto was carried out under the directions of the SS Brigadefuehrer and Major General of the Police Stroup. A special group from the SS central organisation arranged for the deportation of Jews from various Axis satellites and their extermination was carried out in the concentration camps run by the WVHA.

It is impossible to single out any one portion of the SS which was not involved in these criminal activities. The Allgemeine SS was an active participant in the persecution of the Jews and was used as a source of concentration camp guards. Units of the Waffen SS were directly involved in the killing of prisoners of war and the atrocities in occupied countries. It supplied personnel for the Einsatzgruppen, and had command over the concentration camp guards after its absorption of the Totenkopf SS, which originally controlled the system. Various SS Police units were also widely used in the atrocities in occupied countries and the extermination of the Jews there. The SS central organisation supervised the activities of these various formations and was responsible for such special projects as the human experiments and "final solution" of the Jewish question.

The Tribunal finds that knowledge of these criminal activities was sufficiently general to justify declaring that the SS was a criminal organisation to the extent hereinafter described. It does appear that an attempt was made to keep secret some phases of its activities, but its criminal programmes were so widespread, and involved slaughter on such a gigantic scale, that its criminal activities must have been widely known. It must be recognised, moreover, that the criminal activities of the SS followed quite logically from the principles on which it was organised. Every effort had been made to make the SS a highly disciplined organisation composed of the elite of National Socialism. Himmler had stated that there were people in Germany "who become sick when they see these black coats" and that he did not expect that "they should be loved by too many". Himmler also indicated his view that the SS was concerned with perpetuating the elite racial stock with the object of making Europe a Germanic Continent and the SS was instructed that it was designed to assist the Nazi Government in the ultimate domination of Europe and the elimination of all inferior races. This mystic and fanatical belief in the superiority of the Nordic German developed into the studied contempt and even hatred of other races which led to criminal activities of the type outlined above being considered as a matter of course if not a matter of pride. The actions of a soldier in the Waffen SS who in September, 1939, acting entirely on his own initiative, killed fifty Jewish labourers whom he had been guarding, were described by the statement that as an SS man, he was "particularly sensitive to the sight of Jews", and had acted "quite thoughtlessly in a youthful spirit of adventure" and a sentence of three years' imprisonment imposed on him was dropped under an amnesty. Hess wrote with truth that the Waffen SS were more suitable for the specific tasks to be solved in occupied territory owing to their extensive training in questions of race and nationality. Himmler, in a series of speeches made in 1943, indicated his pride in the ability of the SS to carry out these criminal acts. He encouraged his men to be "tough and ruthless" he spoke of shooting "thousands of leading Poles", and thanked them for their cooperation and lack of squeamishness at the sight of hundreds and thousands of corpses of their victims. He extolled ruthlessness in exterminating the Jewish race and later described this process as "delousing". These speeches show the general attitude prevailing; the SS was consistent with these criminal acts.

The SS was utilised for the purposes which were criminal under the Charter involving the persecution and extermination of the Jews, brutalities and killings in concentration camps, excesses in the administration of occupied territories, the administration of the slave labour programme and the mistreatment and murder of prisoners of war. The defendant Kaltenbrunner was a member of the SS implicated in these activities. In dealing with the SS the Tribunal includes all persons who had been officially accepted as members of the SS including the members of the Allgemeine SS, members of the Waffen SS, members of the SS Totenkopf Verbaende and the members of any of the different police forces who were members of the SS. The Tribunal does not include the so-called SS riding units. The Sicherheitsdienst des Reichsfuhrer SS (commonly known as the SD) is dealt with in the Tribunal's Judgment on the Gestapo and SD.

The Tribunal declares to be criminal within the meaning of the Charter the group composed of those persons who had been officially accepted as members of the SS as enumerated in the preceding paragraph who became or remained members of the organisation with knowledge that it was being used for the commission of acts declared criminal by Article 6 of the Charter, or who were personally implicated as members of the organisation in the commission of such crimes, excluding, however, those who were drafted into membership by the State in such a way as to give them no choice in the matter, and who had committed no such crimes. The basis of this finding is the participation of the organisation in war crimes and crimes against humanity connected with the war; this group declared criminal cannot include, therefore, persons who had ceased to belong to the organisations enumerated in the preceding paragraph prior to 1st September, 1939.

The prosecution has named Die Sturmabteilungen der Nationalsozialistischen Deutschen Arbeiterpartei (commonly known as the SA) as an organisation which should be declared criminal. The SA was founded in 1921 for political purposes. It was organised on military lines. Its members wore their own uniforms and had their own discipline and regulations. After the Nazis had obtained power the SA greatly increased in membership due to the incorporation within it of certain veterans' organisations. In April, 1933, the Stahlheim, an organisation of one and a half million members, was transferred into the SA, with the exception of its members over 45 years of age and some others, pursuant to an agreement between their leader Seldte and Hitler. Another veterans' organisation, the so-called Kyffhauserbund, was transferred in the same manner, together with a number of rural riding organisations.

Until 1933, there is no question but that membership in the SA was voluntary. After 1933 civil servants were under certain political and economic pressure to join the SA. Members of the Stahlheim, the Kyffhauserbund and the rural riding associations were transferred into the SA without their knowledge but the Tribunal is not satisfied that the members in general endeavoured to protest against this transfer or that there was any evidence, except in isolated cases, of the consequences of refusal. The Tribunal therefore finds that membership in the SA was generally voluntary.

By the end of 1933 the SA was composed of four and a half million men. As a result of changes made after 1934, in 1939 the SA numbered one and a half million men.

In the early days of the Nazi movement the storm troopers of the SA acted as the "strong arm of the Party". They took part in the beer hall feuds and were used for street fighting in battles against political opponents. The SA was also used to disseminate Nazi ideology and propaganda and placed particular emphasis on anti-Semitic propaganda, the doctrine of "Lebensraum", the revision of the Versailles Treaty and the return of Germany's colonies.

After the Nazi advent to power, and particularly after the elections of 5th March, 1933, the SA played an important role in establishing a Nazi reign of terror over Germany. The SA was involved in outbreaks of violence against the Jews and was used to arrest political opponents and to guard concentration camps, where they subjected their prisoners to brutal mistreatment.

On 30th June and 1st and 2nd July, 1934, a purge of SA leaders occurred. The protext which was given for this purge, which involved the killing of Roehm, the Chief of Staff of the SA, and many other SA leaders, was the existence of a plot against Hitler. This purge resulted in a great reduction in the influence and power of the SA. After 1934, it rapidly declined in political significance.

After 1934 the SA engaged in certain forms of military or para-military training. The SA continued to engaged in the dissemination of Nazi propaganda. Isolated units of the SA were even involved in the steps leading up to aggressive war and in the commission of war crimes and crimes against humanity. SA units were among the first in the occupation of Austria in March, 1938. The SA supplied many of the men and a large part of the equipment which composed the Sudeten Free Corps of Henlein, although it appears that the corps was under the jurisdiction of SS during its operation in Czechoslovakia.

After the occupation of Poland, the SA group Sudeten was used for transporting prisoners of war. Units of the SA were employed in the guarding of prisoners in Danzig, Posen, Silesia and the Baltic states.

Some SA units were used to blow up synagogues in the Jewish pogrom of the 10th and 11th of November, 1938. Groups of the SA were concerned in the ill-treatment of Jews in the Ghettos of Vilna and Kaunas.

Up until the purge beginning on 30th June, 1934, the SA was a group composed in large part of ruffians and bullies who participated in the Nazi outrages of that period. It has not been shown, however, that these atrocities were part of a specific plan to wage aggressive war, and the Tribunal therefore cannot hold that these activities were criminal under the Charter. After the purge, the SA was reduced to the status of a group of unimportant Nazi hangers-on.

Although in specific instances some units of the SA were used for the commission of war crimes and crimes against humanity, it cannot be said that its members generally participated in or even knew of the criminal acts. For these reasons the Tribunal does not declare the SA to be a criminal organisation within the meaning of Article 9 of the Charter.

∞◇◆◇∞

The prosecution has named as a criminal organisation the Reich Cabinet (Die Reichsregierung) consisting of members of the ordinary cabinet after 30th January, 1933, members of the Council of Ministers for the defence of the Reich and members of the Secret Cabinet Council. The Tribunal is of opinion that no declaration of criminality should be made with respect to the Reich Cabinet for two reasons: (1) because it is not shown that after 1937 it ever really acted as a group or organisation; (2) because the group of persons here charged is so small that members could be conveniently tried in proper cases without resort to a declaration that the Cabinet of which they were members was criminal.

As to the first reason for our decision, it is to be observed that from the time that it can be said that a conspiracy to make aggressive war existed the Reich cabinet did not constitute a governing body, but was merely an aggregation of administrative officers subject to the absolute control of Hitler. Not a single meeting of the Reich Cabinet was held after 1937, but laws were promulgated in the name of one or more of the cabinet members. The Secret Cabinet Council never met at all. A number of the cabinet members were undoubtedly involved in the conspiracy to make aggressive war; but they were involved as individuals, and there is no evidence that the cabinet as a group or organisation took any part in these crimes. It will be remembered that when Hitler disclosed his aims of criminal aggression at the Hoszbach Conference, the disclosure was not made before the cabinet and that the cabinet was not consulted with regard to it, but, on the contrary, that it was made secretly to a small group upon whom Hitler would necessarily rely in carrying on the war. Likewise no cabinet order authorised the invasion of Poland. On the contrary, the defendant Schacht testifies that he sought to stop the invasion by a plea to the Commander-in-Chief of the Army that Hitler's order was in violation of the Constitution because not authorised by the cabinet.

It does appear, however, that various laws authorising acts which were criminal under the Charter were circulated among the members of the Reich Cabinet and issued under its authority signed by the members whose departments were concerned. This does not, however, prove that the Reich Cabinet, after 1937, ever really acted as an organisation.

As to the second reason, it is clear that those members

of the Reich Cabinet who have been guilty of crimes should be brought to trial; and a number of them are now on trial before the Tribunal. It is estimated that there are 48 members of the group, that eight of these are dead and 17 are now on trial, leaving only 23 at the most, as to whom the declaration could have any importance. Any others who are guilty should also be brought to trial; but nothing would be accomplished to expedite or facilitate their trials by declaring the Reich Cabinet to be a criminal organisation. Where an organisation with a large membership is used for such purposes, a declaration obviates the necessity of inquiring as to its criminal character in the later trial of members who are accused of participating through membership in its criminal purposes and thus saves much time and trouble. There is no such advantage in the case of a small group like the Reich Cabinet.

The prosecution has also asked that the General Staff and High Command of the German Armed Forces be declared a criminal organisation. The Tribunal believes that no declaration of criminality should be made with respect to the General Staff and High Command. The number of persons charged, while larger than that of the Reich Cabinet, is still so small that individual trials of these officers would accomplish the purpose here sought better than a declaration such as is requested. But a more compelling reason is that in the opinion of the Tribunal the General Staff and High Command is neither an "organisation" nor a "group" within the meaning of those terms as used in Article 9 of the Charter.

Some comment on the nature of this alleged group is requisite. According to the Indictment and evidence before the Tribunal, it consists of approximately 130 officers, living and dead, who at any time during the period from February, 1938, when Hitler reorganised the Armed Forces, and May, 1945, when Germany surrendered, held certain positions in the military hierarchy. These men were high-ranking officers in the three armed services: OKH—Army, OKM—Navy, and OKL—Air Force. Above them was the over-all armed forces authority, OKW—High Command of the German Armed Forces with Hitler as the Supreme Commander. The Officers in the OKW, including defendant Keitel as Chief of the High Command, were in a sense Hitler's personal staff. In the larger sense they co-ordinated and directed the three services, with particular emphasis the functions of planning and operations.

The individual officers in this alleged group were, at one time of another, in one of four categories: (1) Commanders-in-Chief of one of the three services; (2) Chief of Staff of one of the three services (3) "Oberbefehlshabers", the field commanders-in-chief of one of the three services, which of course comprised by far the largest number of these persons; or (4) an OKW officer, of which there were three, defendant Keitel and Jodl, and the latter's Deputy Chief, Warlimont. This is the meaning of the Indictment in its use of the term "General Staff and High Command".

The Prosecution has here drawn the line. The Prosecution does not indict the next level of the military hierarchy consisting of commanders of army corps, and equivalent ranks in the Navy and Air Force, nor the level below, the division commanders or their equivalent in the other branches. And the staff officers of the four staff commands of OKW, OKH, OKM, and OKL are not included, nor are the trained specialist who were customarily called General Staff officers.

In effect, then, those indicted as members are military leaders of the Reich of the highest rank. No serious effort was made to assert that they composed an "organisation" in the sense of Article 9. The assertion is rather that they were a "group", which is a wider and more embracing term than "organisation".

The Tribunal does not so find. According to the evidence, their planning at staff level, the constant conferences between staff officers and field commanders, their operational technique in the field and at headquarters was much the same as that of the armies, navies and air forces of all other countries. The over-all effort of OKW at co-ordination and direction could be matched by a similar, though not identical form of organisation in other military forces, such as the Anglo-American Combined Chiefs of Staff.

To derive from this pattern of their activities the existence of an association or group does not, in the opinion of the Tribunal, logically follow. On such a theory the top commanders of every other nation are just such an association rather than what they actually are, an aggregation of military men, a number of individuals who happen at a given period of time to hold the high-ranking military positions.

Much of the evidence and the argument has centred around the question of whether membership in these organisations was or was not voluntary; in this case, it seems to the Tribunal to be quite beside the point. For this alleged criminal organisation has one characteristic, a controlling one, which sharply distinguishes it from the other five indicted. When an individual became a member of the

SS for instance, he did so, voluntarily or other wise, but certainly with the knowledge that he was joining something. It the case of the General Staff and High Command, however, he could not know he was joining a group or organisation, for such organisation did not exist except in the charge of the Indictment. He knew only that he had achieved a certain high rank in one of the three services, and could not be conscious of the fact that he was becoming a member of anything so tangible as a "group," as that word is commonly used. His relations with his brother officers in his own branch of the service and his association with those of the other two branches were, in general, like those of other services all over the world.

The Tribunal therefore does not declare the General Staff and High Command to be a criminal organisation.

Although the Tribunal is of the opinion that the term "group" in Article 9 must mean something more than this collection of military officers, it has heard much evidence as to the participation of these officers in planning and waging aggressive war, and in committing war crimes and crimes against humanity. This evidence is, as to many of them, clear and convincing.

They have been responsible in large measure for the miseries and suffering that have fallen on millions of men, women and children. They have been a disgrace to the honourable profession of arms. Without their military guidance the aggressive ambitions of Hitler and his fellow Nazis would have been academic and sterile. Although they were not a group falling within the words of the Charter they were certainly a ruthless military caste. The contemporary German militarism flourished briefly with its recent ally, National Socialism, as well as or better than it had in the generations of the past.

Many of these men have made a mockery of the solder's oath of obedience to military orders. When it suits their defence they say they had to obey; when confronted with Hitler's brutal crimes, which are shown to have been within their general knowledge, they say they disobeyed. The truth is they actively participated in all these crimes, or sat silent and acquiescent, witnessing the commission of crimes on a scale larger and more shocking than the world has ever had the misfortune to know. This must be said.

Where the facts warrant it, these men should be brought to trial so that those among them who are guilty of these crimes should not escape punishment.

The Tribunal will sit to-morrow at 9.30 a.m., and the Tribunal will now adjourn.

(The Tribunal adjourned until 9.30 a.m., 1st October, 1946.)

The PRESIDENT: There is a correction which the Tribunal wishes to make in the judgment pronounced yesterday with reference to the SD.

The Tribunal's attention has been drawn to the fact that the Prosecution expressly excluded honorary informers who were not members of the SS, and members of the Abwehr who were transferred to the SD. In view of that exclusion by the Prosecution, the Tribunal also excludes those persons from the SD which was declared criminal.

Article 26 of the Charter provides that the Judgment of the Tribunal as to the guilt or innocence of any defendant shall give the reasons on which it is based.

The Tribunal will now state those reasons in declaring its Judgment on such guilt or innocence.

GOERING

Goering is indicted on all four counts. The evidence shows that after Hitler he was the most prominent man in the Nazi Régime. He was Commander-in-Chief of the Luftwaffe, Plenipotentiary for the Four Year Plan, and had tremendous influence with Hitler, at least until 1943 when their relationship deteriorated, ending in his arrest in 1945. He testified that Hitler kept him informed of all important military and political problems.

Crimes against Peace

From the moment he joined the Party in 1922 and took command of the street-fighting organisation, the SA, Goering was the adviser, the active agent of Hitler and one of the prime leaders of the Nazi movement. As Hitler's Political deputy he was largely instrumental in bringing the National Socialists to power in 1933, and was charged with consolidating this power and expanding German armed might. He developed the Gestapo, and created the first concentration camps, relinquishing them to Himmler in 1934, conducted the Roehm purge in that year, and engineered the sordid proceedings which resulted in the removal of von Blomberg and von Fritsch from the Army. In 1936 he became Plenipotentiary for the Four Year Plan, and in theory and in practice was the economic dictator of the Reich. Shortly after the Pact of Munich, he announced that he would embark on a five-fold expansion of the Luftwaffe, and speed rearmament with emphasis on offensive weapons.

Goering was one of the five important leaders present

at the Hoszbach Conference of 5th November, 1937, and he attended the other important conferences already discussed in this Judgment. In the Austrian Anschluss, he was indeed the central figure, the ringleader. He said in Court: "I must take 100 per cent. responsibility. . . . I even overruled objections by the Fuehrer and brought everything to its final development." In the seizure of the Sudetenland, he played his rôle as Luftwaffe chief by planning an air offensive which proved unnecessary and his rôle as a politician by lulling the Czechs with false promises of friendship. The night before the invasion of Czechoslovakia and the absorption of Bohemia and Moravia, at a conference with Hitler and President Hacha he threatened to bomb Prague if Hacha did not submit. This threat he admitted in his testimony.

Goering attended the Reich Chancellery meeting of 23rd May, 1939, when Hitler told his military leaders "there is, therefore, no question of sparing Poland," and was present at the Obersalzburg briefing of 22nd August, 1939. And the evidence shows he was active in the diplomatic manœuvres which followed. With Hitler's connivance, he used the Swedish businessman, Dahlerus, as a go-between to the British, as described by Dahlerus to this Tribunal, to try to prevent the British Government from keeping its guarantee to the Poles.

He commanded the Luftwaffe in the attack on Poland and throughout the aggressive wars which followed.

Even if he opposed Hitler's plans against Norway and the Soviet Union, as he alleged, it is clear that he did so only for strategic reasons; once Hitler had decided the issue, he followed him without hesitation. He made it clear in his testimony that these differences were never ideological or legal. He was "in a rage" about the invasion of Norway, but only because he had not received sufficient warning to prepare the Luftwaffe offensive. He admitted he approved of the attack: "My attitude was perfectly positive." He was active in preparing and executing the Yugoslavian and Greek campaigns, and testified that "Plan Marita," the attack on Greece, had been prepared long beforehand. The Soviet Union he regarded as the "most threatening menace to Germany," but said there was no immediate military necessity for the attack. Indeed, his only objection to the war of aggression against the U.S.S.R. was its timing; he wished for strategic reasons to delay until Britain was conquered. He testified: "My point of view was decided by political and military reasons only."

After his own admissions to this Tribunal, from the positions which he held, the conferences he attended, and the public words he uttered, there can remain no doubt that Goering was the moving force for aggressive war second only to Hitler. He was the planner and prime mover in the military and diplomatic preparation for war which Germany pursued.

War Crimes and Crimes against Humanity

The record is filled with Goering's admissions of his complicity in the use of slave labour. "We did use this labour for security reasons so that they would not be active in their own country and would not work against us. On the other hand, they served to help in the economic war." And again: "Workers were forced to come to the Reich. That is something I have not denied." The man who spoke these words was Plenipotentiary for the Four Year Plan charged with the recruitment and allocation of manpower. As Luftwaffe Commander-in-Chief he demanded from Himmler more slave labourers for his underground aircraft factories: "That I requested inmates of concentration camps for the armament of the Luftwaffe is correct and it is to be taken as a matter of course."

As Plenipotentiary, Goering signed a directive concerning the treatment of Polish workers in Germany and implemented it by regulations of the SD, including "special treatment". He issued directives to use Soviet and French prisoners of war in the armament industry; he spoke of seizing Poles and Dutch and making them prisoners of war if necessary, and using them for work. He agrees Russian prisoners of war were used to man anti-aircraft batteries.

As Plenipotentiary, Goering was the active authority in the spoliation of conquered territory. He made plans for the spoliation of Soviet territory long before the war on the Soviet Union. Two months prior to the invasion of the Soviet Union, Hitler gave Goering the over-all direction for the economic administration in the territory. Goering set up an economic staff for this function. As Reichsmarshal of the Greater German Reich, "the orders of the Reichmarshal cover all economic fields, including nutrition and agriculture." His so-called "Green" folder, printed by the Wehrmacht, set up an "Economic Executive Staff, East." This directive contemplated plundering and abandonment of all industry in the food deficit regions and, from the food surplus regions, a diversion of food to German needs. Goering claims its purposes have been misunderstood but admits "that as a matter of course and a matter of duty we would have used Russia for our purposes," when conquered.

And he participated in the conference of 16th July, 1941, when Hitler said the National Socialists had no intention of ever leaving the occupied countries, and that "all necessary measures—shooting, desettling, etc.—" should be taken.

Goering persecuted the Jews, particularly after the November, 1938 riots, and not only in Germany where he raised the billion mark fine as stated elsewhere, but in the

conquered territories as well. His own utterances then and
his testimony now show this interest was primarily economic—how to get their property and how to force them
out of the economic life of Europe. As these countries fell
before the German army, he extended the Reich's anti-
Jewish laws to them; the Reichsgesetzblatt for 1939, 1940,
and 1941 contains several anti-Jewish decrees signed by
Goering. Although their extermination was in Himmler's
hands, Goering was far from disinterested or inactive,
despite his protestations in the witness box. By decree of
31st July, 1941, he directed Himmler and Heydrich to
bring "about a complete solution of the Jewish question in
the German sphere of influence in Europe."

There is nothing to be said in mitigation. For Goering
was often indeed almost always, the moving force, second
only to his leader. He was the leading war aggressor, both
as political and as military leader he was the director of the
slave labour programme and the creator of the oppressive
programme against the Jews and other races, at home and
abroad. All of these crimes he has frankly admitted. On
some specific cases there may be conflict of testimony, but
in terms of the broad outline his own admissions are more
than sufficiently wide to be conclusive of his guilt. His
guilt is unique in its enormity. The record discloses no
excuses for this man.

The tribunal finds the defendant Goering guilty on all
four counts.

Major General Mikitchenko:

HESS

Hess is indicted under all four counts. He joined the Nazi Party in 1920 and participated in the Munich Putsch on 9th November, 1923. He was imprisoned with Hitler in the Landsberg fortress in 1924 and became Hitler's closest personal confidant, a relationship which lasted until Hess's flight to the British Isles. On 21st April, 1933, he was appointed Deputy to the Fuehrer, and on 1st December,

1933, was made Reichs Minister without Portfolio. He was appointed Member of the Secret Cabinet Council on 4th February, 1938, and a member of the Ministerial Council for the Defence of the Reich on 30th August, 1939. In September, 1939, Hess was officially announced by Hitler as successor designate to the Fuehrer after Goering. On 10th May, 1941, he flew from Germany to Scotland.

Crimes against Peace

As Deputy to the Fuehrer, Hess was the top man in the Nazi Party with responsibility for handling all Party matters, and authority to make decisions in Hitler's name on all questions of Party leadership. As Reichs Minister without Portfolio he had the authority to approve all legislation suggested by the different Reichs Ministers before it could be enacted as law. In these positions, Hess was an active supporter of preparations for war. His signature appears on the law of 16th March, 1935, establishing compulsory military service. Throughout the years he supported Hitler's policy of vigorous rearmament in many speeches. He told the people that they must sacrifice for armaments, repeating the phrase, "Guns instead of butter." It is true that between 1933 and 1937 Hess made speeches in which he expressed a desire for peace and advocated international economic co-operation. But nothing which they contained can alter the fact that of all the defendants none knew better than Hess how determined Hitler was to realise his ambitions, how fanatical and violent a man he was, and how little likely he was to refrain from resort to force, if this was the only way in which he could achieve his aims.

Hess was an informed and willing participant in German aggression against Austria, Czechoslovakia and

Poland. he was in touch with the illegal Nazi Party in Austria throughout the entire period between the murder of Dollfuss and the Anschluss, and gave instructions to it during that period. Hess was in Vienna on 12th March, 1938, when the German troops moved in; and on 13th March, 1938, he signed the law for the Reunion of Austria within the German Reich. A law of 10th June, 1939, provided for his participation in the administration of Austria. On 24th July, 1938, he made a speech in commemoration of the unsuccessful putsch by Austrian National Socialists which had been attempted four years before, praising the steps leading up to Anschluss and defending the occupation of Austria by Germany.

In the summer of 1938 Hess was in active touch with Henlein, Chief of the Sudeten German Party in Czechoslovakia. On 27th September, 1938, at the time of the Munich crisis, he arranged with Keitel to carry out the instructions of Hitler to make the machinery of the Nazi Party available for a secret mobilisation. On 14th April, 1939, Hess signed a decree setting up the government of the Sudetenland as an integral part of the Reich; and an ordinance of 10th June, 1939, provided for his participation in the administration of the Sudetenland. On 7th November, 1938, Hess absorbed Henlein's Sudeten Germany Party into the Nazi Party, and made a speech in which he emphasised that Hitler had been prepared to resort to war if this had been necessary to acquire the Sudetenland.

On 27th August, 1939, when the attack on Poland had been temporarily postponed in an attempt to induce Great Britain to abandon its guarantee to Poland, Hess publicly praised Hitler's "magnanimous offer" to Poland, and attacked Poland for agitating for war and England for being responsible for Poland's attitude. After the invasion of Poland Hess signed decrees incorporating Danzig and certain Polish territories into the Reich, and setting up the General Government (Poland).

These specific steps which this defendant took in support of Hitler's plans for aggressive action do not indicate the full extent of his responsibility. Until his flight to England, Hess was Hitler's closest personal confidant. Their relationship was such that Hess must have been informed of Hitler's aggressive plans when they came into existence. And he took action to carry out these plans whenever action was necessary.

With him on his flight to England, Hess carried certain peace proposals which he alleged Hitler was prepared to accept. It is significant to note that this flight took place only ten days after the date on which Hitler fixed 22nd June, 1941, as the time for attacking the Soviet Union. In conversations carried on after his arrival in England Hess wholeheartedly supported all Germany's aggressive actions up to that time, and attempted to justify Germany's action in connection with Austria, Czechoslovakia, Poland, Norway, Denmark, Belgium and the Netherlands. He blamed England and France for the war.

War Crimes and Crimes against Humanity

There is evidence showing the participation of the Party Chancellery, under Hess, in the distribution of orders connected with the commission of war crimes; that Hess may have had knowledge of even if he did not participate in the crimes that were being committed in the East, and proposed laws discriminating against Jews and Poles; and that he signed decrees forcing certain groups of Poles to accept German citizenship. The Tribunal, however, does not find that the evidence sufficiently connects Hess with these crimes to sustain a finding of guilt.

As previously indicated the Tribunal found, after a full medical examination of and report on the condition of this defendant, that he should be tried, without any postponement of his case. Since that time further motions have been made that he should again be examined. These the Tribunal denied, after having had a report from the prison psychologist. That Hess acts in an abnormal manner, suffers from loss of memory, and has mentally deteriorated during this trial, may be true. But there is nothing to show that he does not realise the nature of the charges against him, or is incapable of defending himself. He was ably represented at the trial by counsel, appointed for that purpose by the Tribunal. There is no suggestion that Hess was not completely sane when the acts charged against him were committed.

The Tribunal finds the defendant Hess guilty on Counts One and Two: and not guilty on Counts Three and Four.

RIBBENTROP

Ribbentrop is indicted under all four counts. He joined
the Nazi Party in 1932. By 1933 he had been made
Foreign Policy Adviser to Hitler, and in the same year the
representative of the Nazi Party on Foreign Policy. In 1934
he was appointed Delegate for Disarmament Questions,
and in 1935 Minister Plenipotentiary at Large, a capacity
in which he negotiated the Anglo-German Naval
Agreement in 1935 and the Anti-Comintern Pact in 1936.
On 11th August, 1936, he was appointed Ambassador to

England, On 4th February, 1938, he succeeded von Neurath as Reichsminister for Foreign Affairs as part of the general reshuffle which accompanied the dismissal of von Fritsch and von Blomberg.

Crimes against Peace

Ribbentrop was not present at the Hoszbach Conference held on 5th November, 1937, but on 2nd January, 1938, while still Ambassador to England, he sent a memorandum to Hitler indicating his opinion that a change in the *status quo* in the East in the German sense could only be carried out by force and suggesting methods to prevent England and France from intervening in a European war fought to bring about such a change. When Ribbentrop became Foreign Minister Hitler told him that Germany still had four problems to solve, Austria, Sudetenland, Memel and Danzig, and mentioned the possibility of "some sort of a showdown" or "military settlement" for their solution.

On 12th February, 1938, Ribbentrop attended the conference between Hitler and Schuschnigg at which Hitler, by threats of invasion, forced Schuschnigg to grant a series of concessions designed to strengthen the Nazis in Austria, including the appointment of Seyss-Inquart as Minister of Security and Interior, with control over the Police. Ribbentrop was in London when the occupation of Austria was actually carried out and, on the basis of information supplied him by Goering, informed the British Government that Germany had not presented Austria with an ultimatum, but had intervened in Austria only to prevent civil war. On 13th March, 1938, Ribbentrop signed the law incorporating Austria into the German Reich.

Ribbentrop participated in the aggressive plans against Czechoslovakia. Beginning in March, 1938, he was in close touch with the Sudeten German Party and gave them instructions which had the effect of keeping the Sudeten German question a live issue which might serve as an excuse for the attack which Germany was planning against Czechoslovakia. In August, 1938, he participated in a conference for the purpose of obtaining Hungarian support in the event of a war with Czechoslovakia. After the Munich Pact he continued to bring diplomatic pressure with the object of occupying the remainder of Czechoslovakia. He was instrumental in inducing the Slovaks to proclaim their independence. He was present at the conference of 14th–15th March, 1939, at which Hitler, by threats of invasion, compelled President Hacha to consent to the German occupation of Czechoslovakia. After the German troops had marched in, Ribbentrop signed the law establishing a Protectorate over Bohemia and Moravia.

Ribbentrop played a particularly significant role in the diplomatic activity which led up to the attack on Poland. He participated in a conference held on 12th August, 1939, for the purpose of obtaining Italian support if the attack should lead to a general European war. Ribbentrop discussed the German demands with respect to Danzig and the Polish Corridor with the British Ambassador in the period from 25th August to 30th August, 1939, when he knew that the German plans to attack Poland had merely been temporarily postponed in an attempt to induce the British to abandon their guarantee to the Poles. The way in which he carried out these discussions makes it clear that he did not enter them in good faith in an attempt to reach a settlement of the difficulties between Germany and Poland.

Ribbentrop was advised in advance of the attack on Norway and Denmark and of the attack on the Low Countries, and prepared the official Foreign Office memoranda attempting to justify these aggressive actions.

Ribbentrop attended the conference on 20th January, 1941, at which Hitler and Mussolini discussed the proposed attack on Greece, and the conference in January, 1941, at which Hitler obtained from Antonescu permission for German troops to go through Rumania for this attack. On 25th March, 1941, when Yugoslavia adhered to the Axis Tripartite Pact, Ribbentrop had assured Yugoslavia that Germany would respect its sovereignty and territorial integrity. On 27th March, 1941, he attended the meeting, held after the *coup d'etat* in Yugoslavia, at which plans were made to carry out Hitler's announced intention to destroy Yugoslavia.

Ribbentrop attended a conference in May, 1941 with Hitler and Antonescu relating to Rumanian participation in the attack on the U.S.S.R. He also consulted with Rosenberg in the preliminary planning for the political exploitation of Soviet territories and in July, 1941, after the out-break of war, urged Japan to attack the Soviet Union.

War Crimes and Crimes against Humanity

Ribbentrop participated in a meeting of 6th June, 1944, at which it was agreed to start a programme under which Allied aviators carrying out machine gun attacks on the civilian population should be lynched. In December, 1944 Ribbentrop was informed of the plans to murder one of the French Generals held as a prisoner of war and directed his subordinates to see that the details were worked out in such a way as to prevent its detection by the protecting powers. Ribbentrop is also responsible for war crimes and crimes against humanity because of his activities with respect to occupied countries and Axis satellites. The top German official in both Denmark and Vichy France was a Foreign Office representative, and Ribbentrop is therefore responsible for the general economic and political policies put into effect in the occupation of those countries. He urged the Italians to adopt a ruthless occupation policy in Yugoslavia and Greece.

He played an important part in Hitler's "final solution" of the Jewish question. In September, 1942 he ordered the German diplomatic representatives accredited to various Axis satellites to hasten the deportation of Jews to the East. In June, 1942 the German Ambassador to Vichy requested Laval to turn over 50,000 Jews for deportation to the East. On 25th February, 1943, Ribbentrop protested to Mussolini against Italian slowness in deporting Jews from the Italian occupation zone of France. On 17th April, 1943, he took part in a conference between Hitler and Horthy on the deportation of Jews from Hungary and informed Horthy that the "Jews must either be exterminated or taken to concentration camps." At the same conference Hitler had likened the Jews to "tuberculosis bacilli" and said if they did not work they were to be shot.

Ribbentrop's defence to the charges made against him is that Hitler made all the important decisions and that he was such a great admirer and faithful follower of Hitler that he never questioned Hitler's repeated assertions that he wanted peace or the truth of the reasons that Hitler gave in explaining aggressive action. The Tribunal does not consider this explanation to be true. Ribbentrop participated in all of the Nazi aggressions from the occupation of Austria to the invasion of the Soviet Union. Although he was personally concerned with the diplomatic rather than the military aspect of these actions, his diplomatic efforts were so closely connected with war that he could not have remained unaware of the aggressive nature of Hitler's actions. In the administration of territories over which Germany acquired control by illegal invasion Ribbentrop also assisted in carrying out criminal policies, particularly those involving the extermination of the Jews. There is abundant evidence, moreover, that Ribbentrop was in complete sympathy with all the main tenets of the National Socialist creed, and that his collaboration with Hitler and with other defendants in the commission of crimes against peace, war crimes and crimes against humanity was whole-hearted. It was because Hitler's policy and plans coincided with his own ideas that Ribbentrop served him so willingly to the end.

The Tribunal finds that Ribbentrop is guilty on all four counts.

M. DE VABRES:

KEITEL

Keitel is indicted on all four counts. He was Chief of Staff
to the then Minister of War von Blomberg from 1935 to
4th February, 1938; on that day Hitler took command of
the armed forces, making Keitel Chief of the High
Command of the Armed Forces. Keitel did not have command authority over the three Wehrmacht branches which
enjoyed direct access to the Supreme Commander. OKW
was in effect Hitler's military staff.

Crimes against Peace

Keitel attended the Schuschnigg conference in February, 1938 with two other generals. Their presence, he admitted, was a "military demonstration," but since he had been appointed OKW Chief just one week before he had not known why he had been summoned. Hitler and Keitel then continued to put pressure on Austria with false rumours, broadcasts and troop manœuvres. Keitel made the military and other arrangements and Jodl's diary noted "the effect is quick and strong." When Schuschnigg called his plebiscite, Keitel that night briefed Hitler and his generals, and Hitler issued "Case Otto" which Keitel initialled.

On 21st April, 1938, Hitler and Keitel considered making use of a possible "incident," such as the assassination of the German Minister at Prague, to preface the attack on Czeohoslovakia, Keitel signed many directives and memoranda on "Fall Gruen," including the directive of 30th May, containing Hitler's statement: "It is my unalterable decision to smash Czechoslovakia by military action in the near future." After Munich, Keitel initialed Hitler's directive for the attack on Czechoslovakia, and issued two supplements. The second supplement said the attack should appear to the outside world as "merely an act of pacification and not a warlike undertaking." The OKW Chief attended Hitler's negotiations with Hacha when the latter surrendered.

Keitel was present on 23rd May, 1939, when Hitler announced his decision "to attack Poland at the first suitable opportunity." Already he had signed the directive requiring the Wehrmacht to submit its "Fall Weiss" timetable to OKW by 1st May.

The invasion of Norway and Denmark he discussed on 12th December, 1939, with Hitler, Jodl and Raeder. By directive of 27th January, 1940, the Norway plans were placed under Keitel's "direct and personal guidance." Hitler had said on 23rd May, 1939, he would ignore the neutrality of Belgium and the Netherlands, and Keitel signed orders for these attacks on 15th October, 20th November, and 28th November, 1939. Orders postponing this attack 17 times until Spring, 1940, all were signed by Keitel or Jodl.

Formal planning for attacking Greece and Yugoslavia had begun in November, 1940. On 18th March, 1941, Keitel heard Hitler tell Raeder complete occupation of Greece was a prerequisite to settlement, and also heard Hitler decree on 27th March that the destruction of Yugoslavia should take place with "unmerciful harshness."

Keitel testified that he opposed the invasion of the Soviet Union for military reasons, and also because it would constitute a violation of the non-aggression Pact. Nevertheless he initialed "Case Barbarossa," signed by Hitler on 18th December, 1940, and attended the OKW discussion with Hitler on 3rd February, 1941. Keitel's supplement of 13th March established the relationship between the military and political officers. He issued his timetable for the invasion on 6th June, 1941, and was present at the briefing of 14th June when the generals gave their final reports before attack. He appointed Jodl and Warlimont as OKW representatives to Rosenberg on matters concerning the Eastern Territories. On 16th June he directed all army units to carry out the economic directives issued by Goering in the so-called "Green Folder," for the exploitation of Russian territory, food and raw materials.

War Crimes and Crimes against Humanity

On 4th August, 1942, Keitel issued a directive that paratroopers were to be turned over to the SD. On 18th

October Hitler issued the Commando Order which was carried out in several instances. After the landing in Normandy, Keitel reaffirmed the order, and later extended it to Allied missions fighting with partisans. He admits he did not believe the order was legal but claims he could not stop Hitler from decreeing it.

When, on 8th September, 1941, OKW issued its ruthless regulations for the treatment of Soviet POW's, Canaris wrote to Keitel that under international law the SD should have nothing to do with this matter. On this memorandum in Keitel's handwriting, dated 23rd September and initialled by him, is the statement: "The objections arise from the military concept of chivalrous warfare. This is the destruction of an ideology. Therefore I approve and back the measures." Keitel testified that he really agreed with Canaris and argued with Hitler, but lost. The OKW Chief directed the military authorities to cooperate with the Einsatzstab Rosenberg in looting cultural property in occupied territories.

Lahousen testified that Keitel told him on 12th September, 1939, while aboard Hitler's headquarters train, that the Polish intelligentsia, nobility and Jews were to be liquidated. On 20th October, Hitler told Keitel the intelligentsia would be prevented from forming a ruling class, the standard of living would remain low, and Poland would be used only for labour forces. Keitel does not remember the Lahousen conversation, but admits there was such a policy and that he had protested without effect to Hitler about it.

On 16th September, 1941, Keitel ordered that attacks on soldiers in the East should be met by putting to death 50 to 100 Communists for one German soldier, with the comment that human life was less than nothing in the East. On 1st October he ordered military commanders always to have hostages to execute when German soldiers were attacked. When Terboven, the Reich Commissioner in Norway, wrote Hitler that Keitel's suggestion that workmen's relatives be held responsible for sabotage, could work only if firing squads were authorised, Keitel wrote on this memorand'im in the margin: "Yes, that is the best."

On 12th May, 1941, five weeks before the invasion of the Soviet Union, the OKW urged upon Hitler a directive of the OKH that political commissars be liquidated by the Army. Keitel admitted the directive was passed on to field commanders. And on 13th May Keitel signed an order that civilians suspected of offences against troops should be shot without trial, and that prosecution of German soldiers for offences against civilians was unnecessary. On 27th July all copies of this directive were ordered destroyed without affecting its validity. Four days previously he signed another order that legal punishment was inadequate and troops should use terrorism.

On 7th December, 1941, as already discussed in this opinion, the so-called "Nacht und Nebel" decree, over Keitel's signature, provided that in occupied territories civilians who had been accused of crimes of resistance against the army of occupation would be tried only if a death sentence was likely; otherwise they would be handed to the Gestapo for transportation to Germany.

Keitel directed that Russian POW's be used in German war industry. On 8th September, 1942, he ordered French, Dutch and Belgian citizens to work on the construction of the Atlantic Wall. He was present on 4th January, 1944, when Hitler directed Sauckel to obtain four million new workers from occupied territories.

In the face of these documents Keitel does not deny his connection with these acts. Rather, his defence relies on the fact that he is a soldier, and on the doctrine of "superior orders," prohibited by Article 8 of the Charter as a defence.

There is nothing in mitigation. Superior orders, even to a soldier, cannot be considered in mitigation where crimes as shocking and extensive have been committed consciously, ruthlessly and without military excuse or justification.

The Tribunal finds Keitel guilty on all four counts.

THE PRESIDENT:

KALTENBRUNNER

Kaltenbrunner is indicted under Counts One. Three and Four. He joined the Austrian Nazi Party and the SS in 1932. In 1935 he became leader of the SS in Austria. After the Anschluss he was appointed Austrian State Secretary for Security and when this position was abolished in 1941 he was made Higher SS and Police Leader. On 30th January, 1943, he was appointed Chief of the Security Police and SD and Head of the Reich Security Head Office (RSHA), a position which had been held by Heydrich until his assassination in June, 1942. He held the rank of Obergruppenfuehrer in the SS.

Crimes against Peace

As leader of the SS in Austria Kaltenbrunner was active in the Nazi intrigue against the Schuschnigg Government. On the night of 11th March, 38, after Goering had ordered Austrian National Socialists to seize control of the Austrian Government, 500 Austrian SS men under Kaltenbrunner's command surrounded the Federal Chancellery and a special detachment under the command of his adjutant entered the Federal Chancellery while Seyss-Inquart was negotiating with President

Miklas. But there is no evidence connecting Kaltenbrunner with plans to wage aggressive war on any other front. The Anschluss, although it was an aggressive act, is not charged as an aggressive war, and the evidence against Kaltenbrunner under Count One does not in the opinion of the Tribunal, show his direct participation in any plan to wage such a war.

War Crimes and Crimes against Humanity

When he became Chief of the Security Police and SD and Head of the RSHA on 30th January, 1943, Kaltenbrunner took charge of an organisation which included the main offices of the Gestapo, the SD and the Criminal Police. As Chief of the RSHA, Kaltenbrunner had authority to order protective custody to and release from concentration camps. Orders to this effect were normally sent over his signature. Kaltenbrunner was aware of conditions in concentration camps. He had undoubtedly visited Mauthausen and witnesses testified that he had seen prisoners killed by the various methods of execution, hanging, shooting in the back of the neck and gassing, as part of a demonstration. Kaltenbrunner himself ordered the execution of prisoners in those camps and his office was used to transmit to the camps execution orders which originated in Himmler's office. At the end of the war Kaltenbrunner participated in the arrangements for the evacuation of inmates of concentration camps, and the liquidation of many of them, to prevent them from being liberated by the Allied armies.

During the period in which Kaltenbrunner was Head of the RSHA, it was engaged in a widespread programme of war crimes and crimes against humanity. These crimes included the mistreatment and murder of prisoners of war. Einsatz Kommandos operating under the control of the

Gestapo were engaged in the screening of Soviet prisoners of war. Jews, commissars, and others who were thought to be ideologically hostile to the Nazi system were reported to the RSHA, which had them transferred to a concentration camp and murdered. An RSHA order issued during Kaltenbrunner's régime established the "Bullet Decree," under which certain escaped prisoners of war who were recaptured were taken to Mauthausen and shot. The order for the execution of commando troops was extended by the Gestapo to include parachutists while Kaltenbrunner was Chief of the RHSA. An order signed by Kaltenbrunner instructed the Police not to interfere with attacks on bailed out Allied fliers. In December, 1944, Kaltenbrunner participated in the murder of one of the French Generals held as a prisoner of war.

During the period in which Kaltenbrunner was Head of the RHSA, the Gestapo and SD in occupied territories continued the murder and illtreatment of the population, using methods which included the torture and confinement in concentration camps, usually under orders to which Kaltenbrunner's name was signed.

The Gestapo was responsible for enforcing a rigid labour discipline on the slave labourers and Kaltenbrunner established a series of labour reformatory camps for this purpose. When the SS embarked on a slave labour programme of its own, the Gestapo was used to obtain the needed workers by sending labourers to concentration camps.

The RSHA played a leading part in the "final solution" of the Jewish question by the extermination of the Jews. A special section under the Amt IV of the RSHA was established to supervise this programme. Under its direction approximately six million Jews were murdered, of which two million were killed by Einsatzgruppen and other units of the Security Police. Kaltenbrunner had been informed of the activities of these Einsatzgruppen when he was a Higher SS and Police Leader, and they continued to function after he had become Chief of the RSHA.

The murder of approximately four million Jews in concentration camps has heretofore been described. This part of the programme was also under the supervision of the RSHA when Kaltenbrunner was head of that organisation, and special missions of the RSHA scoured the occupied territories and the various Axis satellites arranging for the deportation of Jews to these extermination institutions. Kaltenbrunner was informed of these activities. A letter which he wrote on 30th June, 1944, described the shipment to Vienna of 12,000 Jews for that purpose, and directed that all who could not work would have to be kept in readiness for "special action," which meant murder. Kaltenbrunner denied his signature to this letter, as he did on a very large number of orders on which his name was stamped or typed, and, in a few instances, written. It is inconceivable that in matters of such importance his signature could have appeared so many times without his authority.

Kaltenbrunner has claimed that when he took office as Chief of the Security Police and SD and as Head of the RSHA he did so pursuant to an understanding with Himmler under which he was to confine his activities to matters involving foreign intelligence, and not to assume overall control over the activities of the RSHA. He claims that the criminal programme had been started before his assumption of office; that he seldom knew what was going on; and that when he was informed he did what he could to stop them. It is true that he showed a special interest in matters involving foreign intelligence. But he exercised control over the activities of the RSHA; was aware of the crimes it was committing, and was an active participant in many of them.

The Tribunal finds that Kaltenbrunner is not guilty on Count One. He is guilty under Counts Three and Four.

Major General NIKITCHENKO:

ROSENBERG

Rosenberg is indicted on all four counts. He joined the Nazi Party in 1919, participated in the Munich Putsch of 9th November, 1923, and tried to keep the illegal Nazi Party together while Hitler was in jail. Recognised as the Party's ideologist, he developed and spread Nazi doctrines in the newspapers "Voelkischer Beobachter" and "N S Monatshefte," which he edited, and in the numerous books he wrote. His book, "Myth of the Twentieth Century," had a circulation of over a million copies.

In 1930, Rosenberg was elected to the Reichstag and he became the Party's representative for Foreign Affairs. In April, 1933, he was made Reichsleiter and head of the Office of Foreign Affairs of the NSDAP (The APA). Hitler, in January, 1934, appointed Rosenberg his Deputy for the Supervision of the Entire Spiritual and Ideological Training of the NSDAP. In January, 1940, he was designated to set up the "Hohe Schule," the Centre of National Socialistic Ideological and Educational Research, and he organised the "Einsatzstab Rosenberg" in connection with this task. He was appointed Reich Minister for the Occupied Eastern Territories on 17th July, 1941.

Crimes Against Peace

As head of the APA, Rosenberg was in charge of an organisation whose agents were active in Nazi intrigue in all parts of the world. His own reports, for example, claim that the APA was largely responsible for Roumania's joining the Axis. As head of the APA, he played an important role in the preparation and planning of the attack on Norway.

Rosenberg, together with Raeder, was one of the originators of the plan for attacking Norway. Rosenberg had become interested in Norway as early as June, 1939, when he conferred with Quisling. Quisling had pointed out the importance of the Norwegian Coast in the event of a conflict between Germany and Great Britain, and stated his fears that Great Britain might be able to obtain Norwegian assistance. As a result of this conference Rosenberg arranged for Quisling to collaborate closely with the National Socialists and to receive political assistance by the Nazis.

When the war broke out Quisling began to express fear of British intervention in Norway. Rosenberg supported this view, and transmitted to Raeder a plan to use Quisling for a coup in Norway. Rosenberg was instrumental in arranging the conferences in December, 1939, between Hitler and Quisling which led to the preparation of the attack on Norway, and at which Hitler promised Quisling financial assistance. After these conferences Hitler assigned to Rosenberg the political exploitation of Norway. Two weeks after Norway was occupied, Hitler told Rosenberg that he had based his decision to attack Norway "on the continuous warnings of Quisling as reported to him by Reichsleiter Rosenberg."

Rosenberg bears a major responsibility for the formulation and execution of occupation policies in the Occupied Eastern Territories. He was informed by Hitler on 2nd April, 1941, of the coming attack against the Soviet Union, and he agreed to help in the capacity of a "Political Adviser." On 20th April, 1941, he was appointed Commissioner for the Central Control of Questions connected with the East-European Region. In preparing the plans for the occupation, he had numerous conferences with Keitel, Raeder, Goering, Funk, Ribbentrop, and other high Reich authorities. In April and May, 1941, he prepared several drafts of instructions concerning the setting up of the administration in the Occupied Eastern Territories. On 20th June, 1941, two days before the attack on the U.S.S.R., he made a speech to his assistants about the problems and policies of occupation. Rosenberg attended Hitler's conference of 16th July, 1941, in the course of which policies of administration and occupation were discussed. On 17th July, 1941, Hitler appointed Rosenberg Reich Minister for the Occupied Eastern Territories, and publicly charged him with responsibility for civil administration.

War Crimes and Crimes against Humanity

Rosenberg is responsible for a system of organised plunder of both public and private property throughout the invaded countries of Europe. Acting under Hitler's orders of January, 1940, to set up the "Hohe Schule," he organised and directed the "Einsatzstab Rosenberg," which plundered museums and libraries, confiscated art treasures and collections and pillaged private houses. His own reports show the extent of the confiscations. In "Action-M" (Moebel), instituted in December, 1941, at Rosenberg's suggestion, 69,619 Jewish homes were plundered in the West, 38,000 of them in Paris alone, and it took 26,984 railroad cars to transport the confiscated furnishings to Germany. As of 14th July, 1944, more than 21,903 art objects, including famous paintings and museum pieces, had been seized by the Einsatzstab in the West.

With his appointment as Reich Minister for Occupied Eastern Territories on 17th July, 1941, Rosenberg became the supreme authority for those areas.

He helped to formulate the policies of Germanisation, exploitation, forced labour, extermination of Jews and opponents of Nazi rule, and he set up the administration which carried them out. He took part in the conference of 16th July, 1941, in which Hitler stated that they were faced with the task of "cutting up the giant cake according to our needs, in order to be able: first, to dominate it, second, to administer it, and third, to exploit it," and he indicated that ruthless action was contemplated. Rosenberg accepted his appointment on the following day.

Rosenberg had knowledge of the brutal treatment and terror to which the Eastern people were subjected. He directed that the Hague Rules of Land Warfare were not applicable in the Occupied Eastern Territories. He had knowledge of and took an active part in stripping the Eastern Territories of raw materials and foodstuffs, which were all sent to Germany. He stated that feeding the German people was first on the list of claims on the East, and that the Soviet people would suffer thereby. His directives provided for the segregation of Jews, ultimately in Ghettos. His subordinates engaged in mass killings of Jews, and his civil administrators in the East considered that cleansing the Eastern Occupied Territories of Jews was necessary. In December, 1941, Rosenberg made the suggestion to Hitler that in a case of shooting 100 hostages, Jews only be used. Rosenberg had knowledge of the deportation of labourers from the East, of the methods of "recruiting" and the transportation horrors, and of the treatment Eastern labourers received in the Reich. He gave his civil administrators quotas of labourers to be sent to the Reich, which had to be met by whatever means necessary. His signature of approval appears on the order of 14th June, 1944, for the "Heu Aktion,' the apprehension of 40,000 to 50,000 youths, aged 10–14, for shipment to the Reich.

Upon occasion Rosenberg objected to the excesses and atrocities committed by his subordinates, notably in the case of Koch, but these excesses continued and he stayed in office until the end.

The Tribunal finds that Rosenberg is guilty on all four counts.

∘⊶⊷∘

MR. BIDDLE:

FRANK

Frank is indicted under Counts One, Three and Four.
Frank joined the Nazi Party in 1927. He became a member of the Reichstag in 1930, the Bavarian State Minister of Justice in March, 1933, and when this position was incorporated into the Reich Government in 1934, Reich Minister without Portfolio. He was made a Reichsleiter of the Nazi Party in charge of Legal Affairs in 1933, and in the same year President of the Academy of German Law. Frank was also given the honorary rank of

Obergruppenfuehrer in the SA. In 1942 Frank became involved in a temporary dispute with Himmler as to the type of legal system which should be in effect in Germany. During the same year he was dismissed as Reichsleiter of the Nazi Party and as President of the Academy of German Law.

Crimes against Peace

The evidence has not satisfied the Tribunal that Frank was sufficiently connected with the common plan to wage aggressive war to allow the Tribunal to convict him on Count One.

War Crimes and Crimes against Humanity

Frank was appointed Chief Civil Administration Officer for occupied Polish territory and, on 12th October, 1939, was made Governor General of the occupied Polish territory. On 3rd October, 1939, he described the policy which he intended to put into effect by stating: "Poland shall be treated like a colony; the Poles will become the slaves of the Greater German World Empire." The evidence establishes that this occupation policy was based on the complete destruction of Poland as a national entity, and a ruthless exploitation of its human and economic resources for the German war effort. All opposition was crushed with the utmost harshness. A reign of terror was instituted, backed by summary police courts which ordered such actions as the public shootings of groups of twenty to two hundred Poles, and the widespread shootings of hostages. The concentration camp system was introduced in the General Government by the establishment of the notorious. Treblinka and Maydanek camps. As early as 6th February, 1940, Frank gave an indication of the extent of this reign of terror by his cynical comment to a newspaper reporter on von Neurath's poster announcing the execution of the Czech students: "If I wished to order that one should hang up posters about every seven Poles shot, there would not be enough forests in Poland with which to make the paper for these posters." On 30th May, 1940, Frank told a police conference that he was taking advantage of the offensive in the West which diverted the attention of the world from Poland to liquidate thousands of Poles who would be likely to resist German domination of Poland, including "the leading representatives of the Polish intelligentsia." Pursuant to these instructions the brutal A.B. action was begun under which the Security Police and SD carried out these exterminations which were only partially subjected to the restraints of legal procedure. On 2nd October, 1943, Frank issued a decree under which any non-Germans hindering German construction in the General Government were to be tried by summary courts of the Security Police and SD and sentenced to death.

The economic demands made on the General Government were far in excess of the needs of the army of occupation, and were out of all proportion to the resources of the country. The food raised in Poland was shipped to Germany on such a wide scale that the rations of the population of the occupied territories were reduced to the starvation level, and epidemics were widespread. Some steps were taken to provide for the feeding of the agricultural workers who were used to raise the crops, but the requirements of the rest of the population were disregarded. It is undoubtedly true, as argued by counsel for the defence, that some suffering in the General Government was inevitable as a result of the ravages of war and the economic confusion resulting therefrom. But the suffering was increased by a planned policy of economic exploitation.

Frank introduced the deportation of slave labourers to Germany in the very early stages of his administration. On 25th January, 1940, he indicated his intention of deporting one million labourers to Germany, suggesting on 10th May, 1940, the use of police raids to meet this quota. On 18th August, 1942, Frank reported that he had already supplied 800,000 workers for the Reich, and expected to be able to supply 140,000 more before the end of the year.

The persecution of the Jews was immediately begun in the General Government. The area originally contained from 2,500,000 to 3,500,000 Jews. They were forced into ghettos, subjected to discriminatory laws, deprived of the food necessary to avoid starvation, and finally systematically and brutally exterminated. On 16th December, 1941, Frank told the Cabinet of the Governor General: "We must annihilate the Jews wherever we find them and wherever it is possible, in order to maintain there the structure of Reich as a whole." By 25th January, 1944, Frank estimated that there were only 100,000 Jews left.

At the beginning of his testimony, Frank stated that he had a feeling of "terrible guilt" for the atrocities committed in the occupied territories. But his defence was largely devoted to an attempt to prove that he was not in fact responsible; that he ordered only the necessary pacification measures; that the excesses were due to the activities of the police which were not under his control; and that he never even knew of the activities of the concentration camps. It has also been argued that the starvation was due to the aftermath of the war and policies carried out under the Four Year Plan; that the forced labour programme was under the direction of Sauckel; and that the extermination of the Jews was by the police and SS under direct orders from Himmler.

It is undoubtedly true that most of the criminal programme charged against Frank was put into effect through the police, that Frank had jurisdictional difficulties with Himmler over the control of the police, and that Hitler resolved many of these disputes in favour of Himmler. It therefore may well be true that some of the crimes committed in the General Government were committed without the knowledge of Frank, and even occasionally despite his opposition. It may also be true that some of the criminal policies put into effect in the General Government did not originate with Frank but were carried out pursuant to orders from Germany. But it is also true that Frank was a willing and knowing participant in the use of terrorism in Poland; in the economic exploitation of Poland in a way which led to the death by starvation of a large number of people; in the deportation to Germany as slave labourers of over a million Poles; and in a programme involving the murder of at least three million Jews.

The Tribunal finds that Frank is not guilty on Count One but guilty under Counts Three and Four.

∞⧉∞

M. DE VABRES:

FRICK

Frick is indicted on all four counts. Recognised as the chief Nazi administrative specialist and bureaucrat, he was appointed Reichminister of the Interior in Hitler's first cabinet. He retained this important position until August, 1943, when he was appointed Reich Protector of Bohemia and Moravia. In connection with his duties at the centre of all internal and domestic administration, he became the Prussian Minister of the Interior, Reich Director of Elections, General Plenipotentiary for the Administration of the Reich, and a member of the Reich

Defence Council, the Ministerial Council for Defence of the Reich, and the "Three Man College." As the several countries incorporated into the Reich were overrun, he was placed at the head of the Central Offices for their incorporation.

Though Frick did not officially join the Nazi Party until 1925, he had previously allied himself with Hitler and the National Socialist cause during the Munich Putsch, while he was an official in the Munich Police Department. Elected to the Reichstag in 1924, he became a Reichsleiter as leader of the National Socialist faction in that body.

Crimes against Peace

An avid Nazi, Frick was largely responsible for bringing the German Nation under the complete control of the NSDAP. After Hitler became Reich Chancellor, the new Minister of the Interior immediately began to incorporate local governments under the sovereignty of the Reich. The numerous laws he drafted, signed, and administered abolished all opposition parties and prepared the way for the Gestapo and their concentration camps to extinguish all individual opposition. He was largely responsible for the legislation which suppressed the Trade Unions, the Church, the Jews. He performed this task with ruthless efficiency.

Before the date of the Austrian aggression Frick was concerned only with domestic administration within the Reich. The evidence does not show that he participated in any of the conferences at which Hitler outlined his aggressive intentions. Consequently the Tribunal takes the view that Frick was not a member of the common plan or conspiracy to wage aggressive war as defined in this Judgment.

Six months after the seizure of Austria, under the

provisions of the Reich Defence Law of 4th September, 1938, Frick became General Plenipotentiary for the Administration of the Reich. He was made responsible for war administration, except the military and economic, in the event of Hitler's proclaiming a state of defence. The Reich Ministries of Justice, Education, Religion, and the Office of Spatial Planning were made subordinate to him. Performing his allotted duties, Frick devised an administrative organisation in accordance with wartime standards. According to his own statement, this was actually put into operation after Germany decided to adopt a policy of war.

Frick signed the law of 13th March, 1938, which united Austria with the Reich, and he was made responsible for its accomplishment. In setting up German administration in Austria, he issued decrees which introduced German law, the Nürnberg Decrees, the Military Service Law, and he provided for police security by Himmler.

He also signed the laws incorporating into the Reich the Sudetenland, Memel, Danzig, the Eastern territories (West Prussia and Posen) and Eupen, Malmedy, and Moresnot. He was placed in charge of the actual incorporation, and of the establishment of German administration over these territories. He signed the law establishing the Protectorate of Bohemia and Moravia.

As the head of the Central Offices for Bohemia and Moravia, the Government General, and Norway, he was charged with obtaining close co-operation between the German officials in these occupied countries and the supreme authorities of the Reich. He supplied German civil servants for the administrations in all occupied territories, advising Rosenberg as to their assignment in the Occupied Eastern Territories. He signed the laws appointing Terboven Reich Commissioner to Norway and Seyss-Inquart to Holland.

War Crimes and Crimes against Humanity

Always rabidly anti-Semitic, Frick drafted, signed, and administered many laws designed to eliminate Jews from German life and economy. His work formed the basis of the Nürnberg Decrees, and he was active in enforcing them. Responsible for prohibiting Jews from following various professions, and for confiscating their property, he signed a final decree in 1943, after the mass destruction of Jews in the East, which placed them "outside the law" and handed them over to the Gestapo. These laws paved the way for the "final solution", and were extended by Frick to the Incorporated Territories and to certain of the Occupied Territories. While he was Reich Protector of Bohemia and Moravia, thousands of Jews were transferred from the Terezin Ghetto in Czechoslovakia to Auschwitz, where they were killed. He issued a decree providing for special penal laws against Jews and Poles in the Government General.

The police officially fell under the jurisdiction of the Reichminister of the Interior. But Frick actually exercised little control over Himmler and police matters. However, he signed the law appointing Himmler Chief of the German Police, as well as the decrees establishing Gestapo jurisdiction over concentration camps and regulating the execution of orders for protective custody. From the many complaints he received, and from the testimony of witnesses, the Tribunal concludes that he knew of atrocities committed in these camps. With knowledge of Himmler's methods, Frick signed decrees authorising him to take necessary security measures in certain of the Incorporated Territories. What these "security measures" turned out to be has already been dealt with.

As the Supreme Reich Authority in Bohemia and Moravia, Frick bears general responsibility for the acts of oppression in that territory after 20th August, 1943, such as terrorism of the population, slave labour, and the deportation of Jews to the concentration camps for extermination. It is true that Frick's duties as Reich Protector were considerably more limited than those of his predecessor, and that he had no legislative and limited personal executive authority in the Protectorate. Nevertheless, Frick knew full well what the Nazi policies of occupation were in Europe, particularly with respect to Jews, at that time, and by accepting the office of Reich Protector he assumed responsibility for carrying out those policies in Bohemia and Moravia.

German citizenship in the occupied countries as well as in the Reich came under his jurisdiction while he was Minister of the Interior. Having created a racial register of persons of German extraction, Frick conferred German citizenship on certain categories of citizens of foreign countries. He is responsible for Germanisation in Austria, Sudetenland, Memel, Danzig, Eastern Territories (West Prussia and Posen), and in the territories of the Eupen, Malmedy, and Moresnot. He forced on the citizens of these territories, German law, German courts, German education, German police security, and compulsory military service.

During the war nursing homes, hospitals, and asylums in which euthanasia was practised as described elsewhere in this Judgment, came under Frick's jurisdiction. He had knowledge that insane, sick and aged people, "useless eaters," were being systematically put to death. Complaints of these murders reached him, but he did nothing to stop them. A report of the Czechoslovak War Crimes Commission estimated that 275,000 mentally deficient and aged people, for whose welfare he was responsible, fell victim to it.

The Tribunal finds that Frick is not guilty on Count One. He is guilty on Counts Two, Three and Four.

∞∞

THE PRESIDENT:

STREICHER

Streicher is indicated on Counts One and Four. One of the earliest members of the Nazi Party, joining in 1921, he took part in the Munich Putsch. From 1925 to 1940 he was Gauleiter of Franconia. Elected to the Reichstag in 1933, he was an honorary general in the SA. His persecution of the Jews was notorious. He was the publisher of "Der Stürmer," an anti-Semitic weekly newspaper, from 1923 to 1945 and was its editor until 1933.

Crimes against Peace

Streicher was a staunch Nazi and supporter of Hitler's main policies. There is no evidence to show that he was ever within Hitler's inner circle of advisers; nor during his career was he closely connected with the formulation of the policies which led to war. He was never present, for example, at any of the important conferences when Hitler explained his decisions to his leaders. Although he was a Gauleiter there is no evidence to prove that he had knowledge of those policies. In the opinion of the Tribunal, the evidence fails to establish his connection with the conspiracy or common plan to wage aggressive war as that conspiracy has been elsewhere defined in this Judgment.

Crimes against Humanity

For his twenty-five years of speaking, writing, and preaching hatred of the Jews, Streicher was widely known as "Jew-Baiter Number One." In his speeches and articles, week after week, month after month, he infected the German mind with the virus of anti-Semitism, and incited the German people to active persecution. Each issue of "Der Stürmer", which reached a circulation of 600,000 in 1935, was filled with such articles, often lewd and disgusting.

Streicher had charge of the Jewish boycott of 1st April, 1933. He advocated the Nürnberg Decrees of 1935. He was responsible for the demolition on 10th August, 1938, of the Synagogue in Nürnberg. And on 10th November, 1938, he spoke publicly in support of the Jewish pogrom which was taking place at that time.

But it was not only in Germany that this defendant advocated his doctrines. As early as 1938 he began to call for the annihilation of the Jewish race. Twenty-three different articles of "Der Stürmer" between 1938 and 1941 were produced in evidence, in which the extermination "root and branch" was preached. Typical of his teachings was a leading article in September, 1938, which termed the Jew a germ and a pest, not a human being, but "a parasite, and enemy, an evil-doer, a disseminator of diseases who must be destroyed in the interest of mankind." Other articles urged that only when world Jewry had been annihilated would the Jewish problem have been solved, and predicted that fifty years hence the Jewish graves "will proclaim that this people of murderers and criminals has after all met its deserved fate." Streicher, in February, 1940, published a letter from one of "Der Stürmer's" readers which compared Jews with swarms of locusts which must be exterminated completely. Such was the poison Streicher injected into the minds of thousands of Germans which caused them to follow the National Socialists policy of Jewish persecution and extermination. A leading article of "Der Stürmer" in May, 1939, shows clearly his aim:

"A punitive expedition must come against the Jews in Russia. A punitive expedition which will provide the same fate for them that every murderer and criminal must expect. Death sentence and execution. The Jews in Russia must be killed. They must be exterminated root and branch."

As the war in the early stages proved successful in acquiring more and more territory for the Reich, Streicher even intensified his efforts to incite the Germans against the Jews. In the record are twenty-six articles from "Der Stürmer", published between August, 1941 and September, 1944, twelve by Streicher's own hand, which demanded annihilation and extermination in unequivocal terms. He wrote and published on 25th December, 1941:

"If the danger of the reproduction of that curse of God in the Jewish blood is to finally come to an end, then there is only one way—the extermination of that people whose father is the devil."
And in February, 1944, his own article stated:

"Whoever does what a Jew does is a scoundrel, a criminal. And he who repeats and wishes to copy him deserves the same fate, annihilation, death."

With knowledge of the extermination of the Jews in the Occupied Eastern Territory, this defendant continued to write and publish his propaganda of death. Testifying in this trial, he vehemently denied any knowledge of mass executions of Jews. But the evidence makes it clear that he continually received current information on the progress of the "final solution". His press photographer was sent to visit the ghettos of the East in the Spring of 1943, the time of the destruction of the Warsaw Ghetto. The Jewish newspaper, "Israelitisches Wochenblatt", which Streicher received and read, carried in each issue accounts of Jewish atrocities in the East, and gave figures on the number of Jews who had been deported and killed. For example, issues appearing in the summer and fall of 1942 reported the death of 72,729 Jews in Warsaw, 17,542 in Lodz, 18,000 in Croatia, 125,000 in Rumania, 14,000 in Latvia, 85,000 in Yugoslavia, 700,000 in all of Poland. In November, 1943. Streicher quoted verbatim an article from the "Israelitisches Wochenblatt" which stated that the Jews had virtually disappeared from Europe, and commented "This is not a Jewish lie." In December, 1942, referring to an article in the "London Times" about the atrocities, aiming at extermination, Streicher said that Hitler had given warning that the second World War would lead to the destruction of Jewry. In January, 1943, he wrote and published an article which said that Hitler's prophecy was being fulfilled, that world Jewry was being extirpated, and that it was wonderful to know that Hitler was freeing the world of its Jewish tormentors.

In the face of the evidence before the Tribunal it is idle for Streicher to suggest that the solution of the Jewish problem which he favoured was strictly limited to the classification of Jews as aliens, and the passing of discriminatory legislation such as the Nürnberg Laws, supplemented if possible by international agreement on the creation of a Jewish State somewhere in the world, to which all Jews should emigrate.

Streicher's incitement to murder and extermination at the time when Jews in the East were being killed under the most horrible conditions clearly constitutes persecution on political and racial grounds in connection with war crimes, as defined by the Charter, and constitutes a crime against humanity.

The Tribunal finds that Streicher is not guilty of Count One, but that he is guilty on Count Four.

FUNK

Funk is indicted under all four counts. Funk, who had previously been a financial journalist, joined the Nazi Party in
1931, and shortly thereafter became one of Hitler's personal economic advisers. On 30th January, 1933, Funk was
made Press Chief in the Reich Government, and on 11th
March, 1933, became Under Secretary in the Ministry of
Propaganda and shortly thereafter a leading figure in the
various Nazi organisations which were used to control the
press, films, music and publishing houses. Funk took office

as Minister of Economics and Plenipotentiary General for War Economy in early 1938 and as President of the Reichsbank in January, 1939. He succeeded Schacht in all three of these positions. He was made a member of the Ministerial Council for the Defence of the Reich on August, 1939, and a member of the Central Planning Board in September, 1943.

Crimes against Peace

Funk became active in the economic field after the Nazi plans to wage aggressive war had been clearly defined. One of his representatives attended a conference on 14th October, 1938, at which Goering announced a gigantic increase in armaments and instructed the Ministry of Economics to increase exports to obtain the necessary exchange. On 28th January, 1939, one of Funk's subordinates sent a memorandum to the OKW on the use of prisoners of war to make up labour deficiencies which would arise in case of mobilisation. On 30th May, 1939, the Under Secretary of the Ministry of Economics attending a meeting at which detailed plans were made for the financing of the war.

On 25th August, 1939, Funk wrote a letter to Hitler expressing his gratitude that he had been able to participate in such world shaking events; that his plans for the "financing of the war," for the control of wage and price conditions and for the strengthening of the Reichsbank had been completed; and that he had inconspicuously transferred into gold all foreign exchange resources available to Germany. On 14th October, 1939, after the war had begun, Funk made a speech in which he stated that the economic and financial departments of Germany working under the Four Year Plan had been engaged in the secret economic preparation for war for over a year.

Funk participated in the economic planning which preceded the attack on the U.S.S.R. His deputy held daily conferences with Rosenberg on the economic problems which would arise in the occupation of Soviet territory. Funk himself participated in planning for the printing of double notes in Germany prior to the attack to serve as occupation currency in the U.S.S.R. After the attack he made a speech in which he described plans he had made for the economic exploitation of the "vast territories of the Soviet Union" which were to be used as a source of raw material for Europe.

Funk was not one of the leading figures in originating the Nazi plans for aggressive war. His activity in the economic sphere was under the supervision of Goering as Plenipotentiary General of the Four Year Plan. He did, however, participate in the economic preparation for certain of the aggressive wars, notably those against Poland and the Soviet Union, but his guilt can be adequately dealt with under Count Two of the Indictment.

War Crimes and Crimes against Humanity

In his capacity as Under Secretary in the Ministry of Propaganda and Vice-Chairman of the Reichs Chamber of Culture, Funk had participated in the early Nazi programme of economic discrimination against the Jews. On 12th November, 1938, after the pogroms of November, he attended a meeting held under the chairmanship of Goering to discuss the solution of the Jewish problem and proposed a decree providing for the banning of Jews from all business activities, which Goering issued the same day under the authority of the Four Year Plan. Funk has testified that he was shocked at the outbreaks of 10th November, but on 15th November, he made a speech describing these outbreaks as a "violent explosion of the disgust of the German people, because of a criminal Jewish attack against the German people," and saying that the elimination of the Jews from economic life followed logically their elimination from political life.

In 1942 Funk entered into an agreement with Himmler under which the Reichsbank was to receive certain gold and jewels and currency from the SS and instructed his subordinates, who were to work out the details, not to ask too many questions. As a result of this agreement the SS sent to the Reichsbank the personal belongings taken from the victims who had been exterminated in the concentration camps. The Reichsbank kept the coins and bank notes and sent the jewels, watches and personal belongings to Berlin Municipal Pawn Shops. The gold from the eyeglasses, and gold teeth and fillings was stored in the Reichsbank vaults. Funk has protested that he did not know that the Reichsbank was receiving articles of this kind. The Tribunal is of the opinion that Funk either knew what was being received or was deliberately closing his eyes to what was being done.

As Minister of Economics and President of the Reichsbank, Funk participated in the economic exploitation of occupied territories. He was President of the Continental Oil Company which was charged with the exploitation of the oil resources of occupied territories in the East. He was responsible for the seizure of the gold reserves of the Czechoslovakian National Bank and for the liquidation of the Yugoslavian National Bank. On 6th June, 1942, Funk's deputy sent a letter to the OKW requesting that funds from the French Occupation Cost Fund be made available for black market purchases. Funk's knowledge of German occupation policies is shown by his presence at the meeting of 8th August, 1942, at which Goering addressed the various German occupation chiefs, told them of the products required from their territories, and added, "It makes no difference to me in this connection if you say that your people will starve."

In the fall of 1943, Funk was a member of the Central Planning Board which determined the total number of labourers needed for German industry, and required Sauckel to produce them, usually by deportation from occupied territories. Funk did not appear to be particularly interested in this aspect of the forced labour programme, and usually sent a deputy to attend the meetings, often SS General Ohlendorf, the former Chief of the SD inside of Germany and the former Commander of Einsatzgruppe D. But Funk was aware that the Board of which he was a member was demanding the importation of slave labourers, and allocating them to the various industries under its control.

As President of the Reichsbank, Funk was also indirectly involved in the utilisation of concentration camp labour. Under his direction the Reichsbank set up a revolving fund of 12,000,000 Reichsmarks to the credit of the SS for the construction of factories to use concentration camp labourers.

In spite of the fact that he occupied important official positions, Funk was never a dominant figure in the various programmes in which he participated. This is a mitigating fact of which the Tribunal takes notice.

The Tribunal finds that Funk is not guilty on Count One but is guilty under Counts Two, Three and Four.

The PRESIDENT: The Court will adjourn for 10 minutes. (A short recess was taken).

Mr. Biddle:

SCHACHT

Schacht is indicted under Counts One and Two of the
Indictment. Schacht served as Commissioner of Currency
and President of the Reichsbank from 1923 to 1930; was
reappointed President of the bank on 17th March, 1933;
Minister of Economics in August, 1934; and
Plenipotentiary General for War Economy in May, 1935.
He resigned from these two positions in November, 1937,
and was appointed Minister without Portfolio. He was
reappointed as President of the Reichsbank for a one-year
term on 16th March, 1937, and for a four-term on 9th

March, 1938, but was dismissed on 20th January, 1939. He was dismissed as Minister without Portfolio on 22nd January, 1943.

Crimes against Peace

Schacht was an active supporter of the Nazi Party before its accession to power on 30th January, 1933, and supported the appointment of Hitler to the post of Chancellor. After that date he played an important rôle in the vigorous rearmament programme which was adopted, using the facilities of the Reichsbank to the fullest extent in the German rearmament effort. The Reichsbank, in its traditional capacity as financial agent for the German Government, floated long-term Government loans, the proceeds of which were used for rearmament. He devised a system under which five-year notes, known as M.E.F.O. bills, guaranteed by the Reichsbank and backed, in effect, by nothing more than its position as a bank of issue, were used to obtain large sums for rearmament from the short-term money market. As Minister of Economics and as Plenipotentiary General for War Economy he was active in organising the German economy for war. He made detailed plans for industrial mobilisation and the coordination of the Army with industry in the event of war. He was particularly concerned with shortages of raw materials and started a scheme of stock-piling, and a system of exchange control designed to prevent Germany's weak foreign exchange position from hindering the acquisition abroad of raw materials needed for rearmament. On 3rd May, 1935, he sent a memorandum to Hitler stating that "the accomplishment of the armament programme with speed and in quantity is the problem of German politics, that everything else therefore should be subordinated to this purpose."

Schacht, by April, 1936, began to lose his influence as the central figure in the German rearmament effort when Goering was appointed Coordinator for Raw Materials and Foreign Exchange. Goering advocated a greatly expanded programme for the production of synthetic raw materials which was opposed by Schacht on the ground that the resulting financial strain might involve inflation. The influence of Schacht suffered further when on 16th October, 1936, Goering was appointed Plenipotentiary for the Four-Year Plan with the task of putting "the entire economy in a state of readiness for war" within four years. Schacht had opposed the announcement of this plan and the appointment of Goering to head it, and it is clear that Hitler's action represented a decision that Schacht's economic policies were too conservative for the drastic rearmament policy which Hitler wanted to put into effect.

After Goering's appointment, Schacht and Goering promptly became embroiled in a series of disputes. Although there was an element of personal controversy running through these disputes. Schacht disagreed with Goering on certain basic policy issues. Schacht, on financial grounds, advocated a retrenchment in the rearmament programme, opposed as uneconomical much of the proposed expansion of production facilities, particularly for synthetics, urged a drastic tightening on government credit and a cautious policy in dealing with Germany's foreign exchange reserves. As a result of this dispute and of a bitter argument in which Hitler accused Schacht of upsetting his plans by his financial methods, Schacht went on leave of absence from the Ministry of Economics on 5th September, 1937, and resigned as Minister of Economics and as Plenipotentiary General for War Economy on 16th November, 1937.

As President of the Reichsbank, Schacht was still involved in disputes. Throughout 1938, the Reichsbank continued to function as the financial agent for the German Government in floating long-term loans to finance armaments. But on 31st March, 1938, Schacht discontinued the practice of floating short-term notes guaranteed by the Reichsbank for armament expenditures. At the end of 1938, in an attempt to regain control of fiscal policy through the Reichsbank, Schacht refused an urgent request of the Reichsminister of Finance for a special credit to pay the salaries of civil servants which were not covered by existing funds. On 2nd January, 1939, Schacht held a conference with Hitler at which he urged him to reduce expenditures for armaments. On 7th January, 1939, Schacht submitted to Hitler a report signed by the Directors of the Reichsbank which urged a drastic curtailment of armament expenditures and a balanced budget as the only method of preventing inflation. On 19th January, Hitler dismissed Schacht as President of the Reichsbank. On 22nd January, 1943, Hitler dismissed Schacht as Reich Minister without Portfolio because of his "whole attitude during the present fateful fight of the German nation." On 23rd July, 1944, Schacht was arrested by the Gestapo and confined in a concentration camp until the end of the war.

It is clear that Schacht was a central figure in Germany's rearmament programme, and the steps which he took, particularly in the early days of the Nazi régime, were responsible for Nazi Germany's rapid rise as a military power. But rearmament of itself is not criminal under the Charter. To be a crime against peace under Article 6 of the Charter it must be shown that Schacht carried out this rearmament as part of the Nazi plans to wage aggressive wars.

Schacht has contended that he participated in the rearmament programme only because he wanted to build up a strong and independent Germany which would carry out a foreign policy which would command respect on an equal basis with other European countries; that when he discovered that the Nazis were rearming for aggressive purposes he attempted to slow down the speed of rearmament; and that after the dismissal of von Fritsch and von Blomberg he participated in plans to get rid of Hitler, first by deposing him and later by assassination

Schacht, as early as 1936, began to advocate a limitation of the rearmament programme for financial reasons. Had the policies advocated by him been put into effect, Germany would not have been prepared for a general European war. Insistence on his policies led to his eventual dismissal from all positions of economic significance in Germany. On the other hand, Schacht, with his intimate knowledge of German finance, was in a peculiarly good position to understand the true significance of Hitler's frantic rearmament, and to realise that the economic policy adopted was consistent only with war as its object.

Moreover Schacht continued to participate in German economic life and even, in a minor way, in some of the early Nazi aggressions. Prior to the occupation of Austria he set a rate of exchange between the mark and the schilling. After the occupation of Austria he arranged for the incorporation of the Austrian National Bank into the Reichsbank and made a violently pro-Nazi speech in which he stated that the Reichsbank would always be Nazi as long as he was connected with it, praised Hitler, defended the occupation of Austria, scoffed at objections to the way it was carried out, and ended with "to our Fuehrer a triple 'Sieg Heil'." He has not contended that this speech did not represent his state of mind at the time. After the occupation of the Sudetenland, he arranged for currency conversion and for the incorporation into the Reichsbank of local Czech banks of issue. On 29th November, 1938, he made a speech in which he pointed with pride to his economic policy which had created the high degree of German armament, and added that this armament had made Germany's foreign policy possible.

Schacht was not involved in the planning of any of the specific wars of aggression charged in Count Two. His participation in the occupation of Austria and the Sudetenland (neither of which are charged as aggressive wars) was on such a limited basis that it does not amount to participation in the common plan charged in Count One. He was clearly not one of the inner circle around Hitler which was most closely involved with this common plan. He was regarded by this group with undisguised hostility. The testimony of Speer shows that Schacht's arrest on 23rd July, 1944, was based as much on Hitler's enmity towards Schacht growing out of his attitude before the war as it was on suspicion of his complicity in the bomb plot. The case against Schacht therefore depends on the inference that Schacht did in fact know of the Nazi aggressive plans.

On this all important question evidence has been given for the prosecution, and a considerable volume of evidence for the defence. The Tribunal has considered the whole of this evidence with great care, and comes to the conclusion that this necessary inference has not been established beyond a reasonable doubt.

The Tribunal finds that Schacht is not guilty on this Indictment, and directs that he shall be discharged by the Marshal, when the Tribunal presently adjourns.

M. DE VABRES:

DOENITZ

Doenitz is indicted on Counts One, Two and Three. In 1935 he took command of the first U-boat flotilla commissioned since 1918, became in 1936 commander of the submarine arm, was made Vice-Admiral in 1940, Admiral in 1942, and on 30th January, 1943, Commander-in-Chief of the German Navy. On 1st May, 1945, he became the Head of State, succeeding Hitler.

Crimes Against Peace

Although Doenitz built and trained the German U-boat arm, the evidence does not show he was privy to the conspiracy to wage aggressive wars or that he prepared and initiated such wars. He was a line officer performing strictly tactical duties. He was not present at the important conferences when plans for aggressive wars were announced, and there is no evidence he was informed about the decisions reached there. Doenitz did, however, wage aggressive war within the meaning of that word as used by the Charter. Submarine warfare which began immediately upon the outbreak of war, was fully co-ordinated with the other branches of the Wehrmacht. It is clear that his U-boats, few in number at the time, were fully prepared to wage war.

It is true that until his appointment in January, 1943, as Commander-in-Chief he was not an "Oberbefehlshaber". But this statement underestimates the importance of Doenitz' position. He was no mere Army or division commander. The U-boat arm was the principal part of the German fleet and Doenitz was its leader. The High Seas fleet made a few minor, if spectacular, raids during the early years of the war but the real damage to the enemy was done almost exclusively by his submarines as the millions of tons of allied and neutral shipping sunk will testify. Doenitz was solely in charge of this warfare. The Naval War Command reserved for itself only the decision as to the number of submarines in each area. In the invasion of Norway, for example, Doenitz made recommendations in October, 1939, as to submarine bases, which he claims were no more than a staff study, and in March, 1940, he made out the operational orders for the supporting U-boats, as discussed elsewhere in this Judgment.

That his importance to the German war effort was so regarded is eloquently proved by Reader's rcommendation of Doenitz as his successor and his appointment by Hitler on 30th January, 1943, as Commander-in-Chief of the Navy. Hitler too knew that submarine warfare was the essential part of Germany's naval warfare.

From January, 1943, Doenitz was consulted almost continuously by Hitler. The evidence was that they conferred on naval problems about 120 times during the course of the war.

As late as April, 1945, when he admits he knew the struggle was hopeless, Doenitz as its Commander-in-Chief urged the Navy to continue its fight. On 1st May, 1945, he became the Head of State and as such ordered the Wehrmacht to continue its war in the East, until capitulation on 9th May, 1945. Doenitz explained that his reason for these orders was to insure that the German civilian population might be evacuated and the Army might make an orderly retreat from the East.

In the view of the Tribunal, the evidence shows that Doenitz was active in waging aggressive war.

War Crimes

Doenitz is charged with waging unrestricted submarine warfare contrary to the Naval Protocol of 1936([11]) to which Germany acceded, and which reaffirmed the rules of submarine warfare laid down in the London Naval Agreement of 1930([12]).

The prosecution has submitted that on 3rd September, 1939, the German U-boat arm began to wage unrestricted submarine warfare upon all merchant ships, whether enemy or neutral, cynically disregarding the Protocol; and that a calculated effort was made throughout the war to disguise this practice by making hypocritical references to international law and supposed violations by the Allies.

Doenitz insists that at all times the Navy remained within the confines of international law and of the Protocol. He testified that when the war began, the guide to submarine warfare was the German Prize Ordinance taken almost literally from the Protocol, that pursuant to the German view, he ordered submarines to attack all merchant ships in convoy, and all that refused to stop or used their radio upon sighting a submarine. When his reports indicated that British merchant ships were being used to give information by wireless, were being armed and were attacking submarines on sight, he ordered his submarines on 17th October, 1939, to attack all enemy merchant ships without warning on the ground that resistance was to be expected. Orders already had been issued on 21st September, 1939, to attack all ships, including neutrals, sailing at night without lights in the English Channel.

On 24th November, 1939, the German Government issued a warning to neutral shipping that, owing to the frequent engagements taking place in the waters around the British Isles and the French Coast between U-boats and Allied merchant ships which were armed and had instructions to use those arms as well as to ram U-boats, the safety of neutral ships in those waters could no longer be taken for granted. On 1st January, 1940, the German U-boat command, acting on the instructions of Hitler, ordered U-boats to attack all Greek merchant ships in the zone surrounding the British Isles which was banned by the United States to its own ships and also merchant ships of every nationality in the limited area of the Bristol Channel. Five days later a further order was given to U-boats to "make immediately unrestricted use of weapons against all ships" in an area of the North Sea, the limits of which were defined. Finally on the 18th January, 1940, U-boats were authorised to sink, without warning, all ships "in those waters near the enemy coasts in which the use of mines can be pretended." Exceptions were to be made in the cases of United States, Italian, Japanese and Soviet ships.

Shortly after the outbreak of war the British Admiralty, in accordance with its Handbook of Instructions of 1938 to the Merchant Navy, armed its merchant vessels, in many cases convoyed them with armed escort, gave orders to send position reports upon sighting submarines, thus integrating merchant vessels into the warning network of naval intelligence. On 1st October, 1939, the British Admiralty announced British merchant ships had been ordered to ram U-boats if possible.

In the actual circumstances of this case, the Tribunal is not prepared to hold Doenitz guilty for his conduct of submarine warfare against British armed merchant ships.

However, the proclamation of operational zones and the sinking of neutral merchant vessels which enter those zones presents a different question. This practice was employed in the War of 1914–18 by Germany and adopted in retaliation by Great Britain. The Washington conference of 1922, the London Naval Agreement of 1930, and the Protocol of 1936, were entered into with full knowledge that such zones had been employed in the First World War. Yet the Protocol made no exception for operational zones. The order of Doenitz to sink neutral ships without warning when found within these zones was, therefore, in the opinion of the Tribunal, violation of the Protocol.

It is also asserted that the German U-boat arm not only did not carry out the warning and rescue provisions of the Protocol but that Doenitz deliberately ordered the killing of survivors of shipwrecked vessels, whether enemy or neutral. The prosecution has introduced much evidence surrounding two orders of Doenitz, War Order No. 154, issued in 1939, and the so-called "Laconia" Order of 1942. The defence argues that these orders and the evidence supporting them do not show such a policy and introduced much evidence to the contrary. The Tribunal is of the opinion that the evidence does not establish with the certainty required that Doenitz deliberately ordered the killing of shipwrecked survivors. The orders were undoubtedly ambiguous, and deserve the strongest censure.

The evidence further shows that the rescue provisions were not carried out and that the defendant ordered that they should not be carried out. The argument of the defence is that the security of the submarine is, as the first rule of the sea, paramount to rescue and that the development of aircraft made rescue impossible. This may be so, but the Protocol is explicit. If the commander cannot rescue, then under its terms he cannot sink a merchant vessel and should allow it to pass harmless before his periscope. The orders, then, prove Doenitz is guilty of a violation of the Protocol.

In view of all the facts proved and in particular of an order of the British Admiralty announced on the 8th May, 1940, according to which all vessels should be sunk at sight in the Skagerrak, and the answers to interrogatories by Admiral Nimitz stating that unrestricted submarine warfare was carried on in the Pacific Ocean by the United States from the first day that nation entered the war, the sentence of Doenitz is not assessed on the ground of his breaches of the international law of submarine warfare.

Doenitz was also charged with responsibility for Hitler's Commando Order of 18th October, 1942. Doenitz admitted he received and knew of the order when he was Flag Officer of U-boats, but disclaimed responsibility. He points out that the order by its express terms excluded men captured in naval warfare, that the

Navy had no territorial commands on land, and that submarine commanders would never encounter commandos.

In one instance, when he was Commander-in-Chief of the Navy, in 1943, the members of an allied motor torpedo boat were captured by German Naval Forces. They were interrogated for intelligence purposes on behalf of the local admiral, and then turned over by his order to the SD and shot. Doenitz said that if they were captured by the Navy their execution was a violation of the commando order, that the execution was not announced in the Wehrmacht communiqué, and that he was never informed of the incident. He pointed out that the admiral in question was not in his chain of command, but was subordinate to the army general in command of the Norway occupation. But Doenitz permitted the order to remain in full force when he became commander-in-chief, and to that extent he is responsible.

In a conference of 11th December, 1944, Doenitz said "12,000 concentration camp prisoners will be employed in the shipyards as additional labour." At this time Doenitz had no jurisdiction over shipyard construction, and claims that this was merely a suggestion at the meeting that the responsible officials do something about the production of ships, that he took no steps to get these workers since it was not a matter for his jurisdiction and that he does not know whether they ever were procured. He admits he knew of concentration camps. A man in his position must necessarily have known that citizens of occupied countries in large numbers were confined in the concentration camps.

In 1945, Hitler requested the opinion of Jodl and Doenitz whether the Geneva Convention should be denounced. The notes of the meeting between the two military leaders on 20th February, 1945, show that Doenitz expressed his view that the disadvantages of such

an action outweighed the advantages. The summary of
Doenitz's attitude shown in the notes taken by an officer,
included the following sentence:

"It would be better to carry out the measures considered
necessary without warning, and at all costs to save face
with the outer world."

The prosecution insisted that "the measures" referred
to meant the Convention should not be denounced, but
should be broken at will. The defence explanation is that
Hitler wanted to break the Convention for two reasons: to
take away from German troops the protection of the
Convention, thus preventing them from continuing to
surrender in large groups to the British and Americans;
and also to permit reprisals against Allied prisoners of war
because of Allied bombing raids. Doenitz claims that what
he meant by "measures" were disciplinary measures against
German troops to prevent them from surrendering, and
that his words had no reference to measures against the
Allies; moreover that this was merely a suggestion, and that
in any event no such measures were ever taken, either
against Allies or Germans. The Tribunal, however, does not
believe this explanation. The Geneva Convention was not,
however, denounced by Germany. The defence has introduced several affidavits to prove that British naval
prisoners of war in camps under Doenitz's jurisdiction
were treated strictly according to the Convention, and the
Tribunal takes this fact into consideration, regarding it as a
mitigating circumstance.

The Tribunal finds Doenitz is not guilty on Count One of
the Indictment and is guilty on Counts Two and Three.

∞◇◇◇∞

THE PRESIDENT:

READER

Reader is indicted on Counts One, Two and Three. In 1928 he became Chief of Naval Command and in 1935 Oberbefehlshaber der Kriegsmarine (OKM); in 1939 Hitler made him Gross-Admiral. He was a member of the Reich Defence Council. On 30th January, 1943, Doenitz replaced him at his own request, and he became Admiral Inspector of the Navy, a nominal title.

Crimes against Peace

In the 15 years he commanded it, Raeder built and directed the German Navy; he accepts full responsibility until retirement in 1943. He admits the Navy violated the Versailles Treaty, insisting it was "a matter of honour for every man" to do so, and alleges that the violations were for the most part minor, and Germany built less than her allowable strength. These violations, as well as those of the Anglo-German Naval Agreement of 1935, have already been discussed elsewhere in this Judgment.

Raeder received the directive of 24th June, 1937, from von Blomberg requiring special preparations for war against Austria. He was one of the five leaders present at the Hoszbach Conference of 5th November, 1937. He claims Hitler merely wished by this conference to spur the Army to faster rearmament, insists he believed the questions of Austria and Czechoslovakia would be settled peacefully, as they were, and points to the new naval treaty with England which had just been signed. He received no orders to speed construction of U-boats, indicating that Hitler was not planning war.

Raeder received directives on "Fall Gruen" and the directives on "Fall Weiss" beginning with that of 3rd April, 1939; the latter directed the Navy to support the Army by intervention from the sea. He was also one of the few chief leaders present at the meeting of 23rd May, 1939. He attended the Obersalzburg briefing of 22nd August, 1939.

The conception of the invasion of Norway first arose in the mind of Raeder and not that of Hitler. Despite Hitler's desire, as shown by his directive of October, 1939, to keep Scandinavia neutral, the Navy examined the advantages of naval bases there as early as October. Admiral Karls originally suggested to Raeder the desirable aspects of bases in Norway. A questionnaire, dated 3rd October,

1939, which sought comments on the desirability of such bases, was circulated within SKL. On 10th October, Raeder discussed the matter with Hitler; his War Diary entry for that day says Hitler intended to give the matter consideration. A few months later Hitler talked to Raeder, Quisling, Keitel and Jodl; OKW began its planning and the Naval War Staff worked with OKW staff officers. Raeder received Keitel's directive for Norway on 27th January, 1940, and the subsequent directive of 1st March, signed by Hitler.

Raeder defends his actions on the ground it was a move to forestall the British. It is not necessary again to discuss this defence, which the Tribunal have heretofore treated in some detail, concluding that Germany's invasion of Norway and Denmark was aggressive war. In a letter to the Navy, Raeder said: "The operations of the Navy in the occupation of Norway will for all time remain the great contribution of the Navy to this war."

Raeder received the directives, including the innumerable postponements, for the attack in the West. In a meeting of 18th March, 1941, with Hitler, he urged the occupation of all Greece. He claims this was only after the British had landed and Hitler had ordered the attack, and points out the Navy had no interest in Greece. He received Hitler's directive on Yugoslavia.

Raeder endeavoured to dissuade Hitler from embarking upon the invasion of the U.S.S.R. In September, 1940, he urged on Hitler an aggressive Mediterranean policy as an alternative to an attack on Russia. On 14th November, 1940, he urged the war against England "as our main enemy" and that submarine and naval air force construction be continued. He voiced "serious objections against the Russian campaign before the defeat of England," according to notes of the German Naval War Staff. He claims his objections were based on the violation of the

Non-Aggression Pact as well as strategy. But once the decision had been made, he gave permission six day before the invasion of the Soviet Union to attack Russian submarines in the Baltic Sea within a specified warning area and defends this action because these submarines were "snooping" on German activities.

It is clear from this evidence that Raeder participated in the planning an waging of aggressive war.

War Crimes

Raeder is charged with war crimes on the high seas. The "Athenia," an unarmed British passenger liner, was sunk on 3rd September, 1939, while outward bound to America. The Germans two months later charged that Mr. Churchill deliberately sank the "Athenia" to encourage American hostility to Germany. In fact, it was sunk by the German U-boat 30. Raede claims that an inexperienced U-boat commander sank it in mistake for an armed merchant cruiser, that this was not known until the U-30 returned several weeks after the German denial and that Hitler then directed the Navy and Foreign Office to continue denying it. Raeder denied knowledge of the propaganda campaign attacking Mr. Churchill.

The most serious charge against Raeder is that he carried out unrestricted submarine warfare, including sinking of unarmed merchant ships, of neutrals non-rescue and machine-gunning of survivors, contrary to the London Protoco of 1936. The Tribunal makes the same finding on Raeder on this charge as it did as to Doenitz, which has already been announced, up until 30th January, 1943, when Raeder retired.

The Commando Order of the 18th October, 1942, which expressly did not apply to naval warfare, was transmitted by the Naval War Staff to the lower naval commanders with the direction it should be distributed orally by flotilla leaders and section commanders to their subordinates. Two commandos were put to death by the Navy, and not by the SD, at Bordeaux on the 10th December, 1942, the comment of the Naval War Staff was that this was "in accordance with the Fuehrer's special order, but is nevertheless something new in international law, since the soldiers were in uniform." Raeder admits he passed the order down through the chain of command, and he did not object to Hitler.

The Tribunal finds that Raeder is guilty on Counts One, Two, and Three.

GENERAL NIKITCHENKO:

VON SCHIRACH

Von Schirach is indicted under Counts One and Four. He joined the Nazi Party and the SA in 1925. In 1929 he became the Leader of the National Socialist Students Union. In 1931 he was made Reichs Youth Leader of the Nazi Party with control over all Nazi youth organisations including the Hitler Jugend. In 1933, after the Nazis had obtained control of the Government, von Schirach was made Leader of Youth in the German Reich, originally a position within the Ministry of the Interior, but, after 1st December, 1936, an office in the Reich Cabinet. In 1940, von Schirach resigned as head of the Hitler Jugend and Leader of Youth in the German Reich, but retained his position as Reichsleiter with control over Youth Education. In 1940 he was appointed Gauleiter of Vienna, Reichs Governor of Vienna, and Reichs Defence Commissioner for that territory.

Crimes against Peace

After the Nazis had come to power von Schirach, utilising both physical violence and official pressure, either drove out of existence or took over all youth groups which competed with the Hitler Jugend. A Hitler decree of 1st December, 1936, incorporated all German youth within the Hitler Jugend. By the time formal conscription was introduced in 1940, 97 per cent. of those eligible were already members.

Von Schirach used the Hitler Jugend to educate German Youth "in the spirit of National Socialism" and subjected them to an intensive programme of Nazi propaganda. He established the Hitler Jugend as a source of replacements for the Nazi Party formations. In October, 1938, he entered into an agreement with Himmler under which members of the Hitler Jugend who met SS standards would be considered as the primary source of replacements for the SS.

Von Schirach also used the Hitler Jugend for pre-military training. Special units were set up whose primary purpose was training specialists for the various branches of the service. On 11th August, 1939, he entered into an agreement with Keitel under which the Hitler Jugend agreed to carry out its pre-military activities under standards laid down by the Wehrmacht and the Wehrmacht agreed to train 30,000 Hitler Jugend instructors each year. The Hitler Jugend placed particular emphasis on the mil-

itary spirit and its training programme stressed the importance of return of the colonies, the necessity for
Lebensraum and the noble destiny of German youth to
die for Hitler.

Despite the warlike nature of the activities of the
Hitler Jugend, however, it does not appear that von
Schirach was involved in the development of Hitler's plan
for territorial expansion by means of aggressive war, or
that he participated in the planning or preparation of any
of the wars of aggression.

Crimes against Humanity

In July, 1940, von Schirach was appointed Gauleiter of
Vienna. At the same time he was appointed Reichs
Governor for Vienna and Reichs Defence Commissioner
originally for Military District 17, including the Gaus of
Vienna, Upper Danube and Lower Danube and, after 17th
November, 1942, for the Gau of Vienna alone. As Reichs
Defence Commissioner, he had control of the civilian war
economy. As Reichs Governor he was head of the municipal administration of the city of Vienna, and, under the
supervision of the Minister of the Interior, in charge of the
governmental administration of the Reich in Vienna.

Von Schirach is not charged with the commission of
war crimes in Vienna, only with the commission of crimes
against humanity. As has already been seen, Austria was
occupied pursuant to a common plan of aggression. Its
occupation is, therefore, a "crime within the jurisdiction of
the Tribunal," as that term is used in Article 6 (*c*) of the
Charter. As a result, "murder, extermination, enslavement,
deportation and other inhumane acts" and "persecutions
on political, racial or religious grounds" in connection
with this occupation constitute a crime against humanity
under that Article.

As Gauleiter of Vienna, von Schirach came under the Sauckel decree dated 6th April, 1942, making the Gauleiters Sauckel's plenipotentiaries for manpower with authority to supervise the utilisation and treatment of manpower within their Gaus. Sauckel's directives provided that the forced labourers were to be fed, sheltered and treated so as to exploit them to the highest possible degree at the lowest possible expense.

When von Schirach became Gauleiter of Vienna the deportation of the Jews had already been begun, and only 60,000 out of Vienna's original 190,000 Jews remained. On 2nd October, 1940, he attended a conference at Hitler's office and told Frank that he had 50,000 Jews in Vienna which the General Government would have to take over from him. On 3rd December, 1940, von Schirach received a letter from Lammers stating that after the receipt of the reports made by von Schirach, Hitler had decided to deport the 60,000 Jews still remaining in Vienna to the General Government because of the housing shortage in Vienna. The deporation of the Jews from Vienna was then begun and continued until the early fall of 1942. On 15th September, 1942, von Schirach made a speech in which he defended his action in having driven "tens of thousands upon tens of thousands of Jews into the Ghetto of the East" as "contributing to European culture."

While the Jews were being deported from Vienna reports, addressed to him in his official capacity, were received in von Schirach's office from the office of the Chief of the Security Police and SD which contained a description of the activities of Einsatzgruppen in exterminating Jews. Many of these reports were initialled by one of von Schirach's principal deputies. On 30th June, 1944, von Schirach's office also received a letter from Kaltenbrunner informing him that a shipment of 12,000 Jews was on its way to Vienna for essential war work and that all those who were incapable of work would have to be kept in readiness for "special action."

The Tribunal finds that von Schirach, while he did not originate the policy of deporting Jews from Vienna, participated in this deportation after he had become Gauleiter of Vienna. He knew that the best the Jews could hope for was a miserable existence in the Ghettoes of the East. Bulletins describing the Jewish extermination were in his office.

While Gauleiter of Vienna, von Schirach continued to function as Reichsleiter for Youth Education and in this capacity he was informed of the Hitler Jugend's participation in the plan put into effect in the fall of 1944 under which 50,000 young people between the ages of 10 and 20 were evacuated into Germany from areas recaptured by the Soviet forces and used as apprentices in German industry and as auxiliaries in units of the German armed forces. In the summer of 1942, von Schirach telegraphed Bormann urging that a bombing attack on an English cultural town be carried out in retaliation for the assassination of Heydrich which, he claimed, had been planned by the British.

The Tribunal finds that von Schirach is not guilty on Count One. He is guilty under Count Four.

~~~ ⊰⊱ ~~~

Mr. Biddle:

SAUCKEL

Sauckel is indicted under all four counts. Sauckel joined
the Nazi Party in 1923, and became Gauleiter of
Thuringia in 1927. He was a member of the Thuringian
legislature from 1927 to 1933, was appointed
Reichsstatthalter for Thuringia in 1932, and Thuringian
Minister of the Interior and Head of the Thuringian State
Ministry in May, 1933. He became a member of the

Reichstag in 1933. He held the formal rank of Obergruppenfuehrer in both the SA and the SS.

Crimes against Peace

The evidence has not satisfied the Tribunal that Sauckel was sufficiently connected with the common plan to wage aggressive war or sufficiently involved in the planning or waging of the aggressive wars to allow the Tribunal to convict him on Counts One and Two.

War Crime and Crimes against Humanity

On 21st March, 1942, Hitler appointed Sauckel Plenipotentiary General for the Utilisation of Labour, with authority to put under uniform control "the utilisation of all available manpower, including that of workers recruited abroad and of prisoners of war". Sauckel was instructed to operate within the fabric of the Four Year Plan, and on 27th March, 1942, Goering issued a decree as Commissioner for the Four Year Plan transferring his manpower sections to Sauckel. On 30th September, 1942, Hitler gave Sauckel authority to appoint Commissioners in the various occupied territories, and "to take all necessary measures for the enforcement" of the decree of 21st March, 1942.

Under the authority which he obtained by these decrees, Sauckel set up a programme for the mobilisation of the labour resources available to the Reich. One of the important parts of this mobilisation was the systematic exploitation, by force, of the labour resources of the occupied territories. Shortly after Sauckel had taken office, he had the governing authorities in the various occupied territories issue decrees, establishing compulsory labour service in Germany. Under the authority of these decrees

Sauckel's Commissioners, backed up by the police authorities of the occupied territories, obtained and sent to
Germany the labourers which were necessary to fill the
quotas given them by Sauckel. He described so-called
"voluntary" recruiting by Janates "a whole batch of male
and female agents just as was done in the olden times for
shanghaiing". That real voluntary recruiting was the
exception rather than the rule is shown by Sauckel's statement on 1st March, 1944, that "out of five million foreign
workers who arrived in Germany not even 200,000 came
voluntarily". Although he now claims that the statement is
not true, the circumstances under which it was made, as
well as the evidence presented before the Tribunal, leave
no doubt that it was substantially accurate.

The manner in which the unfortunate slave labourers
were collected and transported to Germany, and what
happened to them after they arrived, has already been
described. Sauckel argues that he is not responsible for
these excesses in the administration of the programme. He
says that the total number of workers to be obtained was
set by the demands from agriculture and from industry;
that obtaining the workers was the responsibility of the
occupation authorities, transporting them to Germany
that of the German railways, and taking care of them in
Germany that of the Ministries of Labour and Agriculture,
the German Labour Front and the various industries
involved. He testifies that insofar as he had any authority
he was constantly urging humane treatment.

There is no doubt, however, that Sauckel had over-all
responsibility for the slave labour programme. At the time
of the events in question he did not fail to assert control
over the fields which he now claims were the sole responsibility of others. His regulations provided that his
Commissioners should have authority for obtaining
labour, and he was constantly in the field supervising the

steps which were being taken. He was aware of ruthless methods being taken to obtain labourers, and vigorously supported them on the ground that they were necessary to fill the quotas.

Sauckel's regulations also provided that he had responsibility for transporting the labourers to Germany, allocating them to employers and taking care of them, and that the other agencies involved in these processes were subordinate to him. He was informed of the bad conditions which existed. It does not appear that he advocated brutality for its own sake, or was an advocate of any programme such as Himmler's plan for extermination through work. His attitude was thus expressed in a regulation:

"All the men must be fed, sheltered and treated in such a way as to exploit them to the highest possible extent at the lowest conceivable degree of expenditure."
The evidence shows that Sauckel was in charge of a programme which involved deportation for slave labour of more than 5,000,000 human beings, many of them under terrible conditions of cruelty and suffering.

The Tribunal finds that Sauckel is not guilty on Counts One and Two. He is guilty under Counts Three and Four.

M. De Vabres:

JODL

Jodl is indicted on all four counts. From 1935 to 1938 he was chief of the National Defence Section in the High Command. After a year in command of troops in August, 1939, he returned to become Chief of the Operations Staff of the High Command of the Armed Forces. Although his immediate superior was defendant Keitel, he reported directly to Hitler on operational matters. In the strict military sense, Jodl was the actual planner of the war and responsible in large measure for the strategy and conduct of operations.

Jodl defends himself on the ground he was a soldier sworn to obedience, and not a politician; and that his staff and planning work left him no time for other matters. He said that when he signed or initialled orders, memoranda and letters, he did so for Hitler and often in the absence of Keitel. Though he claims that as a soldier he had to obey Hitler, he says that he often tried to obstruct certain measures by delay, which occasionally proved successful as when he resisted Hitler's demand that a directive be issued to lynch allied "terror fliers."

Crimes against Peace

Entries in Jodl's diary of 13th and 14th February, 1938, show Hitler instructed both him and Keitel to keep up military pressure against Austria begun at the Schuschnigg conference by simulating military measures, and that these achieved their purpose. When Hitler decided "not to tolerate" Schuschnigg's plebiscite, Jodl brought to the conference the "old draft," the existing staff plan. His diary for 10th March shows Hitler then ordered the preparation of "Case Otto", and the directive was initialled by Jodl. Jodl issued supplementary instructions on 11th March, and initialled Hitler's order for the invasion on the same date.

In planning the attack on Czechoslovakia, Jodl was very active according to the Schmundt Notes. He initialled items 14, 17, 24, 36 and 37 in the Notes. Jodl admits he agreed with OKH that the "incident" to provide German intervention must occur at the latest by 2 p.m. on X-1 Day, the day before the attack, and said it must occur at a fixed time in good flying weather. Jodl conferred with the propaganda experts on "imminent common tasks" such as German violations of international law, exploitation of them by the enemy and refutations by the Germans, which "task" Jodl considered "particularly important."

After Munich, Jodl wrote:

"Czechoslovakia as a power is out . . . The genius of the Fuehrer and his determination not to shun even a World War have again won the victory without the use of force. The hope remains that the incredulous, the weak and the doubtful people have been converted and will remain that way."

Shortly after the Sudeten occupation, Jodl went to a post command and did not become Chief of the Operations Staff in OKW until the end of August, 1939.

Jodl discussed the Norway invasion with Hitler, Keitel and Raeder on 12th December, 1939; his diary is replete with late entries on his activities in preparing this attack. Jodl explains his comment that Hitler was still looking for an "excuse" to movement that he was waiting for reliable intelligence on the British plans, and defends the invasion as a necessary move to forestall them. His testimony shows that from October, 1939. Hitler planned to attack the West through Belgium, but was doubtful about invading Holland until the middle of November. On 8th February, 1940, Jodl, his Deputy Warlimont, and Jeschonnek, the air forces planner, discussed among themselves the "new idea" of attacking Norway, Denmark and Holland, but guaranteeing the neutrality of Belgium. Many of the 17 orders postponing the attack in the West for various reasons including weather conditions, until May, 1940, were signed by Jodl.

He was active in the planning against Greece and Yugoslavia. The Hitler order of 11th January, 1941, to intervene in Albania was initialled by Jodl. On 20th January, four months before the attack, Hitler told a conference of German and Italian generals in Jodl's presence that German troop concentrations in Roumania were to be used against Greece. Jodl was present on 18th March when Hitler told Raeder all Greece must be occupied before any settlement could be reached. On 27th March when Hitler told the German High Command that the destruction of Yugoslavia should be accomplished with "unmerciful harshness," and the decision was taken to bomb Belgrade without a declaration of war, Jodl was also there.

Jodl testified that Hitler feared an attack by Russia and so attacked first. This preparation began almost a year before the invasion. Jodl told Warlimont as early as 29th July, 1940, to prepare the plans since Hitler had decided to attack; and Hitler later told Warlimont he had planned to attack in August, 1940, but postponed it for military reasons. He initialled Hitler's directive of 12th November, 1940, according to which preparations verbally ordered should be continued and also initialled "Case Barbarossa" on 18th December. On 3rd February, 1941, Hitler, Jodl and Keitel discussed the invasion, and he was present on 14th June when final reports on "Case Barbarossa" were made.

War Crimes and Crimes against Humanity

On 18th October, 1942, Hitler issued the Commando Order and a day later a supplementary explanation to commanding officers only. The covering memorandum was signed by Jodl. Early drafts of the order were made by Jodl's staff, with his knowledge. Jodl testified he was strongly opposed on moral and legal grounds, but could not refuse to pass it on. He insists he tried to mitigate its harshness in practice by not informing Hitler when it was not carried out. He initialled the OKW memorandum of 25th June, 1944, reaffirming the Order after the Normandy landings.

A plan to eliminate Soviet commissars was in the

directive for "Case Barbarossa". The decision whether they should be killed without trial was to be made by an officer. A draft contains Jodl's handwriting suggesting this should be handled as retaliation, and he testified this was his attempt to get around it.

When in 1945 Hitler considered denouncing the Geneva Convention, Jodl argued the disadvantages outweighed the advantages. On 21st February, he told Hitler adherence to the Convention would not interfere with the conduct of the war, giving as an example the sinking of a British hospital ship as a reprisal and calling it a mistake. He said he did so because it was the only attitude Hitler would consider, that moral or legal arguments had no effect and argues he thus prevented Hitler from denouncing the Convention.

There is little evidence that Jodl was actively connected with the slave labour programme, and he must have concentrated on his strategic planning function. But in his speech of 7th November, 1943, to the Gauleiters he said it was necessary to act "with remorseless vigour and resolution" in Denmark, France and the Low Countries to compel work on the Atlantic Wall.

By teletype of 28th October, 1944, Jodl ordered the evacuation of all persons in Northern Norway and the burning of their houses so they could not help the Russians. Jodl says he was against this, but Hitler ordered it and it was not fully carried out. A document of the Norwegian Government says such an evacuation did take place in Northern Norway and 30,000 houses were damaged. On 7th October, 1941, Jodl signed an order that Hitler would not accept an offer of surrender of Leningrad or Moscow, but on the contrary he insisted that they be completely destroyed. He says this was done because the Germans were afraid those cities would be mined by the Russians as was Kiev. No surrender was ever offered.

His defence, in brief, is the doctrine of "superior orders", prohibited by Article 8 of the Charter as a defence. There is nothing in mitigation. Participation in such crimes as these has never been required of any soldier and he cannot now shield himself behind a mythical requirement of soldierly obedience at all costs as his excuse for commission of these crimes.

The Tribunal finds that Jodl is guilty on all four counts.

∞◦❀◦∞

VON PAPEN

Von Papen is indicted under Counts One and Two. He was appointed Chancellor of the Reich on 1st June, 1932, and was succeeded by von Schleicher on 2nd December, 1932. He was made Vice Chancellor in the Hitler Cabinet on 30th January, 1933, and on 13th November, 1933, Plenipotentiary for the Saar. On 26th July, 1934, he was appointed Minister to Vienna, and was recalled on 4th February, 1938. On 29th April, 1939, he was appointed Ambassador to Turkey. He returned to Germany when

Turkey broke off diplomatic relations with Germany in August, 1944.

Crimes against Peace

Von Papen was active in 1932 and 1933 in helping Hitler to form the Coalition Cabinet and aided in his appointment as Chancellor on 30th January, 1933. As Vice Chancellor in that Cabinet he participated in the Nazi consolidation of control in 1933. On 16th June, 1934, however, von Papen made a speech at Marburg which contained a denunciation of the Nazi attempts to suppress the free press and the church, of the existence of a reign of terror, and of "150 per cent Nazis" who were mistaking "brutality for vitality". On 30th June, 1934, in the wave of violence which accompanied the so-called Roehm Purge, von Papen was taken into custody by the SS, his office force was arrested, and two of his associates, including the man who had helped him work on the Marburg speech, were murdered. Von Papen was released on 3rd July, 1934.

Notwithstanding the murder of his associates, von Papen accepted the position of Minister to Austria on 26th July, 1934, the day after Dollfuss had been assassinated. His appointment was announced in a letter from Hitler which instructed him to direct relations between the two countries "into normal and friendly channels" and assured him of Hitler's complete and unlimited confidence". As Minister to Austria, von Papen was active in trying to strengthen the position of the Nazi Party in Austria for the purpose of bringing about Anschluss. In early 1935 he attended a meeting in Berlin at which the policy was laid down to avoid everything which would give the appearance of German intervention in the internal affairs of Austria. Yet he arranged for 200,000 marks a month to be transmitted to "the persecuted National Socialist sufferers in Austria". On 17th May, 1935, he reported to Hitler the results of a conference with Captain Leopold, the Leader of the Austrian Nazis, and urged Hitler to make a statement recognising the national independence of Austria, and predicting that the result might be to help the formation of a coalition between Schuschnigg's Christian Socialists and the Austrian Nazis against Starhemberg. On 27th July, 1935, von Papen reported to Hitler that the union of Austria and Germany could not be brought about by external pressure but only by the strength of the National Socialist Movement. He urged that the Austrian Nazi Party change its character as a centralised Reich German Party and become a rallying point for all National Germans.

Von Papen was involved in occasional Nazi political demonstrations, supported Nazi propaganda activities and submitted detailed reports on the activities of the Nazi Party, and routine reports relating to Austrian military defences. His Austrian policy resulted in the agreement of 11th July, 1936, which nominally restored relations between Germany and Austria to "normal and friendly form", but which had a secret supplement providing for an amnesty for Austrian Nazis, the lifting of censorship on Nazi papers, the resumption of political activities by Nazis and the appointment of men friendly to the Nazis in the Schuschnigg Cabinet.

After the signing of this agreement von Papen offered to resign but his resignation was not accepted. Thereafter he proceeded to bring continued pressure on the Austrian Government to bring Nazis into the Schuschnigg Cabinet and to get them important positions in the Fatherland Front, Austria's single legal party. On 1st September, 1936, von Papen wrote Hitler advising him that anti-Nazis in the Austrian Ministry of Security were holding up the infiltration of the Nazis into the Austrian Government and recommended bringing "slowly intensified pressure directed at changing the régime".

On 4th February, 1938, von Papen was notified of his recall as Minister to Austria, at the same time that von Fritsch, von Blomberg and von Neurath were removed from their positions. He informed Hitler that he regretted his recall because he had been trying since November, 1937, to induce Schuschnigg to hold a conference with Hitler and Schuschnigg had indicated his willingness to do so. Acting under Hitler's instructions, von Papen then returned to Austria and arranged the conference which was held at Berchtesgaden on 12th February, 1938. Von Papen accompanied Schuschnigg to that conference, and at its conclusion advised Schuschnigg to comply with Hitler's demands. On 10th March, 1938, Hitler ordered von Papen to return to Berlin. Von Papen was in the Chancellery on 11th March when the occupation of Austria was ordered. No evidence has been offered showing that von Papen was in favour of the decision to occupy Austria by force, and he has testified that he urged Hitler not to take this step.

After the annexation of Austria von Papen retired into private life and there is no evidence that he took any part in politics. He accepted the position of Ambassador to Turkey in April, 1939 but no evidence had been offered concerning his activities in that position implicating him in crimes.

The evidence leaves no doubt that von Papen's primary purpose as Minister to Austria was to undermine the Schuschnigg régime and strengthen the Austrian Nazis for the purpose of bringing about Anschluss. To carry through this plan he engaged in both intrigue and bullying. But the Charter does not make criminal such offences against political morality, however bad these may be. Under the Charter von Papen can be held guilty only if he was a

party to the planning of aggressive war. There is no showing that he was a party to the plans under which the
occupation of Austria was a step in the direction of further
aggressive action, or even that he participated in plans to
occupy Austria by aggressive war if necessary. But it is not
established beyond a reasonable doubt that this was the
purpose of his activity, and therefore the Tribunal cannot
hold that he was a party to the common plan charged in
Count One or participated in the planning of the aggressive wars charged under Count Two.

The Tribunal finds that von Papen is not guilty under this
Indictment, and directs that he shall be discharged by the
Marshal, when the Tribunal presently adjourns.

MAJOR GENERAL NIKITCHENKO:

SEYSS-INQUART

Seyss-Inquart is indicted under all Four Counts. Seyss-Inquart, an Austrian attorney, was appointed State Councillor in Austria in May, 1937, as a result of German pressure. He had been associated with the Austrian Nazi Party since 1931, but had often had difficulties with that Party and did not actually join the Nazi Party until 13th March, 1938. He was appointed Austrian Minister of Security and Interior with control over the police pursuant to one of the conditions which Hitler had imposed on Schuschnigg in the Berchtesgaden conference of 12th February, 1938.

Activities in Austria

Seyss-Inquart participated in the last stages of the Nazi intrigue which preceded the German occupation of Austria, and was made Chancellor of Austria as a result of German threats of invasion.

On 12th March, 1938, Seyss-Inquart met Hitler at Linz and made a speech welcoming the German forces and advocating the reunion of Germany and Austria. On 13th March, he obtained the passage of a law providing that Austria should become a province of Germany and succeeded Miklas as President of Austria when Miklas resigned rather than sign the law. Seyss-Inquart's title was changed to Reichs Governor of Austria on 15th March, 1938, and on the same day he was given the title of a General in the SS. He was made a Reichs Minister without Portfolio on 1st May, 1939.

On 11th March, 1939, he visited the Slovakian Cabinet in Bratislava and induced them to declare their independence in a way which fitted in closely with Hitler's offensive against the independence of Czechoslovakia.

As Reichs Governor of Austria, Seyss-Inquart instituted a programme of confiscating Jewish property. Under his régime Jews were forced to emigrate, were sent to concentration camps and were subject to pogroms. At the end of his régime he co-operated with the Security Police and SD in the deportation of Jews from Austria to the East. While he was Governor of Austria, political opponents of the Nazis were sent to concentration camps by the Gestapo, mistreated and often killed.

Criminal Activities in Poland and the Netherlands

In September, 1939, Seyss-Inquart was appointed Chief of Civil Administration of South Poland. On 12th October, 1939, Seyss-Inquart was made Deputy Governor General of the General Government of Poland under Frank. On 18th May, 1940, Seyss-Inquart was appointed Reichs Commissioner for occupied Netherlands. In these positions he assumed responsibility for governing territory which had been occupied by aggressive wars and the administration of which was of vital importance in the aggressive war being waged by Germany.

As Deputy Governor General of the General Government of Poland, Seyss-Inquart was a supporter of the harsh occupation policies which were put in effect. In November, 1939, while on an inspection tour through the General Government, Seyss-Inquart stated that Poland was to be so administered as to exploit its economic resources for the benefit of Germany. Seyss-Inquart also advocated the persecution of Jews and was informed of the beginning of the AB action which involved the murder of many Polish intellectuals.

As Reichs Commissioner for Occupied Netherlands. Seyss-Inquart was ruthless in applying terrorism to suppress all opposition to the German occupation, a programme which he described as "annihilating" his opponents. In collaboration with the local Hitler SS and Police Leaders he was involved in the shooting of hostages for offences against the occupation authorities and sending to concentration camps all suspected opponents of occupation policies including priests and educators. Many of the Dutch police were forced to participate in these programmes by threats of reprisal against their families. Dutch courts were also forced to participate in this programme, but when they indicated their reluctance to give sentences of imprisonment because so many prisoners were in fact killed, a greater emphasis was placed on the use of summary police courts.

Seyss-Inquart carried out the economic administration of the Netherlands without regard for rules of the Hague Convention which he described as obsolete. Instead, a policy was adopted for the maximum utilisation of economic potential of the Netherlands, and executed with small regard for its effect on the inhabitants. There was widespread pillage of public and private property which was given colour of legality by Seyss-Inquart's regulations, and assisted by manipulations of the financial institutions of the Netherlands under his control.

As Reichs Commissioner for the Netherlands, Seyss-Inquart immediately began sending forced labourers to Germany. Up until 1942, labour service in Germany was theoretically voluntary, but was actually coerced by strong economic and governmental pressure. In 1942, Seyss-Inquart formally decreed compulsory labour service, and utilised the services of the Security Police and SD to prevent evasion of his order. During the occupation over 500,000 people were sent from the Netherlands to the Reich as labourers and only a very small proportion were actually volunteers.

One of Seyss-Inquart's first steps as Reich Commissioner of the Netherlands was to put into effect a series of laws imposing economic discriminations against the Jews. This was followed by decrees requiring their registration. decress compelling them to reside in Ghettoes and to wear the Star of David, sporadic arrests and detention in concentration camps, and finally, at the suggestion of Heydrich, the mass deportation of almost 120,000 of Holland's 140,000 Jews to Auschwitz and the "final solution." Seyss-Inquart admits knowing that they were going to Auschwitz but claims that he heard from people who had been to Auschwitz that the Jews were comparatively well off there, and that he thought that they were being held there for resettlement after the war. In light of the evidence and on account of his official position it is impossible to believe this claim.

Seyss-Inquart contends that he was not responsible for many of the crimes committed in the occupation of the Netherlands because they were either ordered from the Reich, committed by the Army, over which he had no control, or by the German Higher SS and Police Leader, who, he claims, reported directly to Himmler. It is true that some of the excesses were the responsibility of the Army, and that the Higher SS and Police Leader, although he was at the disposal of Seyss-Inquart, could always report directly to Himmler. It is also true that in certain cases Seyss-Inquart opposed the extreme measures used by these other agencies, as when he was largely successful in preventing the Army from carrying out a scorched earth policy, and urged the Higher SS and Police Leaders to reduce the number of hostages to be shot. But the fact remains that Seyss-Inquart was a knowing and voluntary participant in war crimes and crimes against humanity which were committed in the occupation of the Netherlands.

The Tribunal finds that Seyss-Inquart is guilty under Counts Two, Three and Four. Seyss-Inquart is not guilty on Count One.

MR. BIDDLE:

SPEER

Speer is indicted under all Four Counts. Speer joined the Nazi Party in 1932. In 1934 he was made Hitler's architect and became a close personal confidant. Shortly thereafter he was made a Department Head in the German Labour Front and the official in charge of Capital Construction on the staff of the Deputy to the Fuehrer, positions which he held through 1941. On 15th February, 1942, after the death of Fritz Todt, Speer was appointed Chief of the Organisation Todt and Reich Minister for Armaments and

Munitions (after 2nd September, 1943, for Armaments and War Production). The positions were supplemented by his appointments in March and April, 1942, as General Plenipotentiary for Armaments and as a member of the Central Planning Board, both within the Four year Plan. Speer was a member of the Reichstag from 1941 until the end of the war.

Crimes Against Peace

The Tribunal is of opinion that Speer's activities do not amount to initiating, planning, or preparing wars of aggression, or of conspiring to that end. He became the head of the armament industry well after all of the wars had been commenced and were under way. His activities in charge of German Armament Production were in aid of the war effort in the same way that other productive enterprises aid in the waging of war; but the Tribunal is not prepared to find that such activities involve engaging in the common plan to wage aggressive war as charged under Count I or waging aggressive war as charged under Count II.

War Crimes and Crimes Against Humanity

The evidence introduced against Speer under Counts Three and Four relates entirely to his participation in the slave labour programme. Speer himself had no direct administrative responsibility for this programme. Although he had advocated the appointment of a General Plenipotentiary for the Utilisation of Labour because he wanted one central authority with whom he could deal on labour matters, he did not obtain administrative control over Sauckel. Sauckel was appointed directly by Hitler, under the decree of 21st March, 1942, which provided that he should be directly responsible to Goering, as Plenipotentiary of the Four-Year Plan.

As Reich Minister for Armaments and Munitions and General Plenipotentiary for Armaments under the Four-Year Plan, Speer had extensive authority over production. His original authority was over construction and production of arms for the OKH. This was progressively expanded to include naval armaments, civilian production and finally, on 1st August, 1944, air armament. As the dominant member of the Central Planning Board, which had supreme authority for the scheduling of German production and the allocation and development of raw materials, Speer took the position that the Board had authority to instruct Sauckel to provide labourers for industries under its control and succeeded in sustaining this position over the objection of Sauckel. The practice was developed under which Speer transmitted to Sauckel an estimate of the total number of workers needed. Sauckel obtained the labour and allocated it to the various industries in accordance with instructions supplied by Speer.

Speer knew when he made his demands on Sauckel that they would be supplied by foreign labourers serving under compulsion. He participated in conferences involving the extension of the slave labour programme for the purpose of satisfying his demands. He was present at a conference held during 10th August and 12th August, 1942, with Hitler and Sauckel at which it was agreed that Sauckel should bring labourers by force from occupied territories where this was necessary to satisfy the labour needs of the industries under Speer's control. Speer also attended a conference in Hitler's headquarters on 4th January, 1944, at which the decision was made that Sauckel should obtain "at least 4 million new workers from occupied territories" in order to satisfy the demands for labour made by Speer, although Sauckel indicated that he could do this only with help from Himmler.

Sauckel continually informed Speer and his representatives that foreign labourers were being obtained by force. At a meeting on 1st March, 1944, Speer's deputy questioned Sauckel very closely about his failure to live up to the obligation to supply four million workers from occupied territories. In some cases Speer demanded labourers from specific foreign countries. Thus, at the conference 10th–12th August, 1942, Sauckel was instructed to supply Speer with "a further million Russian labourers for the German armament industry up to and including October, 1942." At a meeting of the Central Planning Board on 22nd April, 1943, Speer discussed plans to obtain Russian labourers for use in the coal mines, and flatly vetoed the suggestion that this labour deficit should be made up by German labour.

Speer has argued that he advocated the reorganisation of the labour programme to place a greater emphasis on utilisation of German labour in war production in Germany and on the use of labour in occupied countries in local production of consumer goods formerly produced in Germany. Speer took steps in this direction by establishing the so-called "blocked industries" in the occupied territories which were used to produce goods to be shipped to Germany. Employees of these industries were immune from deportation to Germany as slave labourers and any worker who had been ordered to go to Germany could avoid deportation if he went to work for a blocked industry. This system, although somewhat less inhumane than deportation to Germany, was still illegal. The system of blocked industries played only a small part in the over-all slave labour programme knowing the way in which it was actually being administered. In an official sense, he was its principal beneficiary and he constantly urged its extension.

Speer was also directly involved in the utilisation of forced labour as Chief of the Organisation Todt. The Organisation Todt functioned principally in the occupied areas on such projects as the Atlantic Wall and the construction of military highways, and Speer has admitted that he relied on compulsory service to keep it adequately staffed. He also used concentration camp labour in the industries under his control. He originally arranged to tap this source of labour for use in small out of the way factories; and later, fearful of Himmler's jurisdictional ambitions, attempted to use as few concentration camp workers as possible.

Speer was also involved in the use of prisoners of war in armament industries but contends that he only utilised Soviet prisoners of war in industries covered by the Geneva Convention.

Speer's position was such that he was not directly concerned with the cruelty in the administration of the slave labour programme, although he was aware of its existence. For example, at meetings of the Central Planning Board he was informed that his demands for labour were so large as to necessitate violent methods in recruiting. At a meeting of the Central Planning Board on 30th October, 1942, Speer voiced his opinion that many slave labourers who claimed to be sick were malingerers and stated: "There is nothing to be said against SS and Police taking drastic steps and putting those known as slackers into concentration camps." Speer, however, insisted that the slave labourers be given adequate food and working conditions so that they could work efficiently.

In mitigation it must be recognised that Speer's establishment of blocked industries did keep many labourers in their homes and that in the closing stages of the war he was one of the few men who had the courage to tell Hitler that the war was lost and to take steps to prevent the senseless destruction of production facilities, both in occupied territories and in Germany. He carried out his opposition to Hitler's scorched earth programme in some of the Western countries and in Germany by deliberately sabotaging it at considerable personal risk.

The Tribunal finds that Speer is not guilty on Counts One and Two, but is guilty under Counts Three and Four.

M.DE VABRES:

VON NEURATH

Von Neurath is indicted under all Four Counts. He is a professional diplomat who served as German Ambassador to Great Britain from 1930 to 1932. On 2nd June, 1932, he was appointed Minister of Foreign Affairs in the von Papen cabinet, a position which he held under the cabinets of von Schleicher and Hitler. Von Neurath resigned as Minister of Foreign Affairs on 4th February, 1938, and was made Reichs Minister without Portfolio, President of the Secret Cabinet Council and a member of the Reich Defence Council. On 18th March, 1939, he was appointed Reich Protector for Bohemia and Moravia, and served in this capacity until 27th September, 1941. He held the formal rank of Obergruppenfuehrer in the SS.

Crimes Against Peace

As Minister of Foreign Affairs, von Neurath advised Hitler in connection with the withdrawal from the Disarmament Conference and the League of Nations on 14th October, 1933; the institution of rearmament; the passage on 16th March, 1935, of the law for universal military service; and the passage on 21st May, 1935, of the secret Reich Defence Law. He was a key figure in the negotiation of the Naval Accord entered into between Germany and England on 18th June, 1935. Von Neurath played an important part in Hitler's decision to reoccupy the Rhineland on 7th March, 1936, and predicted that the occupation could be carried through without any reprisals from the French. On 18th May, 1936, he told the American Ambassador to France that it was the policy of the German Government to do nothing in foreign affairs until "the Rhineland had been digested" and that as soon as the fortifications in the Rhineland had been constructed and the countries of Central Europe realised that France could not enter Germany at will, "all those countries will begin to feel very differently about their foreign policies and a new constellation will develop."

Von Neurath took part in the Hoszbach conference of 5th November, 1937. He has testified that he was so shocked by Hitler's statements that he had a heart attack. Shortly thereafter, he offered to resign, and his resignation was accepted on 4th February, 1938, at the same time that von Fritsch and von Blomberg were dismissed. Yet with knowledge of Hitler's aggressive plans he retained a formal relationship with the Nazi régime as Reichs Minister without Portfolio, President of the Secret Cabinet Council and a member of the Reichs Defence Council. He took charge of the Foreign Office at the time of the occupation of Austria, assured the British Ambassador that this had not been caused by a German ultimatum, and informed the Czechoslovakian Minister that Germany intended to abide by its arbitration convention with Czechoslovakia. Von Neurath participated in the last phase of the negotiations preceding the Munich Pact but contends that he entered these discussions only to urge Hitler to make every effort to settle the issues by peaceful means.

Criminal Activities in Czechoslovakia

Von Neurath was appointed Reichs Protector for Bohemia and Moravia on 18th March, 1939. Bohemia and Moravia were occupied by military force. Hacha's consent, obtained as it was by duress, cannot be considered as justifying the occupation. Hitler's decree of 16th March, 1939, establishing the Protectorate, stated that this new territory should "belong henceforth to the territory of the German Reich", an assumption that the Republic of Czechoslovakia no longer existed. But it also went on the theory that Bohemia and Moravia retained their sovereignty subject only to the interests of Germany as expressed by the Protectorate. Therefore even if the doctrine of subjugation should be considered to be applicable to territory occupied by aggressive action, the Tribunal does not believe that this Proclamation amounted to an incorporation which was sufficient to bring the doctrine into effect. The occupation of Bohemia and Moravia must therefore be considered a military occupation covered by the rules of warfare. Although Czechoslovakia was not a party to the Hague Convention of 1907, the rules of land warfare expressed in this Convention are declaratory of existing international law and hence are applicable.

As Reichs Protector, von Neurath instituted an administration in Bohemia and Moravia similar to that in effect in Germany. The free press, political parties and trade unions were abolished. All groups which might serve as opposition were outlawed. Czechoslovakian industry was worked into the structure of German war production, and exploited for the German war effort. Nazi anti-Semitic policies and laws were also introduced. Jews were barred from leading positions in Government and business.

In August, 1939, von Neurath issued a proclamation warning against any acts of sabotage and stating that "the responsibility for all acts of sabotage is attributed not only to individual perpetrators but to the entire Czech population." When the war broke out on 1st September, 1939, 8,000 prominent Czechs were arrested by the Security Police in Bohemia and Moravia and put into protective custody. Many of this group died in concentration camps as a result of mistreatment.

In October and November, 1939, Czechoslovakian students held a series of demonstrations. As a result, on Hitler's orders, all universities were closed, 1,200 students imprisoned, and the nine leaders of the demonstration shot by Security Police and SD. Von Neurath testified that he was not informed of this action in advance, but it was announced by proclamation over his signature posted on placards throughout the Protectorate, which he claims, however, was done without his authority.

On 31st August, 1940, von Neurath transmitted to Lammers a memorandum which he had prepared dealing with the future of the Protectorate, and a memorandum with his approval prepared by Carl Herman Frank on the same subject. Both dealt with the question of Germanisation and proposed that the majority of the Czechs might be assimilated racially into the German nation. Both advocated the elimination of the

Czechoslovakian intelligentsia and other groups which might resist Germanisation, von Neurath's by expulsion, Frank's by expulsion or "special treatment."

Von Neurath has argued that the actual enforcement of the repressive measures was carried out by the Security Police and SD who were under the control of his State Secretary, Carl Herman Frank, who was appointed at the suggestion of Himmler and who, as a Higher SS and Police Leader, reported directly to Himmler. Von Neurath further argues that anti-Semitic measures and those resulting in economic exploitation were put into effect in the Protectorate as the result of policies decided upon in the Reich. However this may be, he served as the chief German official in the Protectorate when the administration of this territory played an important rôle in the wars of aggression which Germany was waging in the East knowing that war crimes and crimes against humanity were being committed under his authority.

In mitigation it must be remembered that von Neurath did intervene with the Security Police and SD for the release of many of the Czechoslovaks who were arrested on 1st September, 1939, and for the release of students arrested later in the fall. On 23rd September, 1941, he was summoned before Hitler and told that he was not being harsh enough and that Heydrich was being sent to the Protectorate to combat the Czechoslovakian resistance groups. Von Neurath attempted to dissuade Hitler from sending Heydrich, but in vain, and when he was not successful offered to resign. When his resignation was not accepted he went on leave, on 27th September, 1941, and refused to act as Protector after that date. His resignation was formally accepted in August, 1943.

The Tribunal finds that von Neurath is guilty under all four Counts.

FRITZSCHE

Fritzsche is indicted on Counts One, Three and Four. He was best known as a radio commentator, discussing once a week the events of the day on his own programme, "Hans Fritzsche Speaks." He began broadcasting in September, 1932; in the same year he was made the head of the Wireless News Service, a Reich Government agency. When on 1st May, 1933, this agency was incorporated by the National Socialists into their Reich Ministry of Popular Enlightenment and Propaganda, Fritzsche became a member of the Nazi Party and went to that Ministry. In December, 1938, he became head of the Home Press Division of the Ministry; in October, 1942, he was promoted to the rank of Ministerial Director. After serving briefly on the Eastern Front in a propaganda company, he was, in November, 1942, made head of the Radio Division of the Propaganda Ministry and Plenipotentiary for the Political Organisation of the Greater German Radio.

Crimes Against Peace

As head of the Home Press Division, Fritzsche supervised the German press of 2,300 daily newspapers. In pursuance of this function he held daily press conferences to deliver the directives of the Propaganda Ministry to these papers. He was, however, subordinate to Dietrich, the Reich Press Chief, who was in turn a subordinate of Goebbels. It was Dietrich who received the directives to the press of Goebbels and other Reich Ministers, and prepared them as instructions, which he then handed to Fritzsche for the press.

From time to time, the "Daily Paroles of the Reich Press Chief" as these instructions were labelled, directed the press to present to the people certain themes, such as the leadership principle, the Jewish problem, the problem of living space, or other standard Nazi ideas. A vigorous propaganda campaign was carried out before each major act of aggression. While Fritzsche headed the Home Press Division, he instructed the press how the actions or wars against Bohemia and Moravia, Poland, Yugoslavia, and the Soviet Union should be dealt with. Fritzsche had no control of the formulation of these propaganda policies. He was merely a conduit to the press of the instructions handed him by Dietrich. In February, 1939, and before the absorption of Bohemia and Moravia, for instance, he received Dietrich's order to bring to the attention of the press Slovakia's efforts for independence, and the anti-Germanic policies and politics of the existing Prague Government. This order to Dietrich originated in the Foreign Office.

The Radio Division of which Fritzsche became the head in November, 1942, was one of the twelve divisions of the Propaganda Ministry. In the beginning Dietrich and other heads of divisions exerted influence over the policies to be followed by Radio. Towards the end of the war, however, Fritzsche became the sole authority within the Ministry for radio activities. In this capacity he formulated and issued daily radio "paroles" to all Reich Propaganda Offices, according to the general political policies of the Nazi régime, subject to the directives of the Radio-Political Division of the Foreign Office, and the personal supervision of Goebbels.

Fritzsche, with other officials of the Propaganda Ministry, was present at Goebbels' daily staff conferences. Here they were instructed in the news and propaganda policies of the day. After 1943 Fritzsche himself occasionally held these conferences, but only when Goebbels and his State Secretaries were absent. And even then his only function was to transmit the Goebbels' directives relayed to him by telephone.

This is the summary of Fritzsche's positions and influence in the Third Reich. Never did he achieve sufficient stature to attend the planning conferences which led to aggressive war; indeed according to his own uncontradicted testimony he never even had a conversation with Hitler. Nor is there any showing that he was informed of the decisions taken at these conferences. He activities cannot be said to be those which fall within the definition of the common plan to wage aggressive war as already set forth in this Judgment.

War Crimes and Crimes against Humanity

The prosecution has asserted that Fritzsche incited and encouraged the commission of war crimes, by deliberately falsifying news to arouse in the German people those passions which led them to the commission of atrocities under Counts Three and Four. His position and official duties were not sufficiently important, however, to infer that he took part in originating or formulating propaganda campaigns.

Excerpts in evidence from his speeches show definite anti-Semitism on his part. He broadcast, for example, that the war had been caused by Jews and said their fate had turned out "as unpleasant as the Fuehrer predicted." But these speeches did not urge persecution or extermination of Jews. There is no evidence that he was aware of their extermination in the East. The evidence moreover shows that he twice attempted to have publication of the anti-Semitic "Der Stürmer" suppressed, though unsuccessfully.

In these broadcasts Fritzsche sometimes spread false news, but it was not proved he knew it to be false. For example he reported that no German U-boat was in the vicinity of the "Athenia" when it was sunk. This information was untrue; but Fritzsche, having received it from the German Navy, had no reason to believe it was untrue.

It appears that Fritzsche sometimes made strong statements of a propagandistic nature in his broadcasts. But the Tribunal is not prepared to hold that they were intended to incite the German people to commit atrocities on conquered peoples, and he cannot be held to have been a participant in the crimes charged. His aim was rather to arouse popular sentiment in support of Hitler and the German war effort.

The Tribunal finds that Fritzsche is not guilty under this Indictment, and directs that he shall be discharged by the Marshal when the Tribunal presently adjourns.

BORMANN

Bormann is indicted on Counts One, Three, and Four. He joined the National Socialist Party in 1925, was a member of the Staff of the Supreme Command of the SA from 1928 to 1930, was in charge of the Aid Fund of the Party, and was Reichsleiter from 1933 to 1945. From 1933 to 1941 he was Chief of Staff in the Office of the Fuehrer's Deputy and, after the flight of Hess to England, became Head of the Party Chancellery on 12th May, 1941. On 12th April, 1943, he became Secretary to the Fuehrer. He was political and organisational head of the Volkssturm and a General in the SS.

Crimes Against Peace

Bormann, in the beginning a minor Nazi, but then steadily rose to a position of power and, particularly in the closing days, of great influence over Hitler. He was active in the Party's rise to power and even more so in the consolidation of that power. He devoted much of his time to the persecution of the churches and of the Jews within Germany.

The evidence does not show that Bormann knew of Hitler's plans to prepare, initiate or wage aggressive wars. He attended none of the important conferences when Hitler revealed piece by piece these plans for aggression. Nor can knowledge be conclusively inferred from the positions he held. It was only when he became Head of the Party Chancellery in 1941, and later in 1943 secretary to the Fuehrer when he attended many of Hitler's conferences, that his positions gave him the necessary access. Under the view stated elsewhere which the Tribunal has taken of the conspiracy to wage aggressive war, there is not sufficient evidence to bring Bormann within the scope of Count One.

War Crimes and Crimes Against Humanity

By decree of 29th May, 1941, Bormann took over the offices and powers held by Hess; by the decree of 24th January, 1942, these powers were extended to give him control over all laws and directives issued by Hitler. He was thus responsible for laws and orders issued thereafter. On 1st December, 1942, all Gaus became Reich Defence districts, and the Party Gauleiters responsible to Bormann were appointed Reich Defence Commissioners. In effect, this made them the administrators of the entire civilian war effort. This was so not only in Germany, but also in those territories which were incorporated into the Reich from the absorbed and conquered territories.

Through this mechanism Bormann controlled the ruthless exploitations of the subjected populace. His order of 12th August, 1942, placed all party agencies at the disposal of Himmler's programme for forced resettlement and denationalisation of persons in the occupied countries. Three weeks after the invasion of Russia, he attended the conference of 16th July, 1941, at Hitler's field quarters with Goering, Rosenberg and Keitel; Bormann's report shows that there were discussed and developed detailed plans of enslavement and annihilation of the population of these territories. And on 8th May, 1942, he conferred with Hitler and Rosenberg on the forced resettlement of Dutch personnel in Latvia, the extermination programme in Russia, and the economic exploitation of the Eastern Territories. He was interested in the confiscation of art and other properties in the East. His letter of 11th January, 1944, called for the creation of a large-scale organisation to withdraw commodities from the occupied territories for the bombed-out German populace.

Bormann was extremely active in the persecution of the Jews, not only in Germany but also in the absorbed and conquered countries. He took part in the discussions which led to the removal of 60,000 Jews from Vienna to Poland in co-operation with the SS and the Gestapo. He signed the decree of 31st May, 1941, extending the Nürnberg Laws to the annexed Eastern Territories. In an order of 9th October, 1942, he declared that the permanent elimination of Jews in Greater German territory could no longer be solved by emigration, but only by applying "ruthless force" in the special camps in the East.

On 1st July, 1943, he signed an ordinance withdrawing Jews from the protection of the law courts and placing them under the exclusive jurisdiction of Himmler's Gestapo.

Bormann was prominent in the slave labour programme. The Party Leaders supervised slave labour matters in the respective Gaus, including employment, conditions of work, feeding and housing. By his circular of 5th May, 1943, to the Leadership Corps, distributed down to the level of Ortsgruppenleiters, he issued directions regulating the treatment of foreign workers, pointing out they were subject to SS control on security problems, and ordered the previous mistreatment to cease. A report of 4th September, 1942, relating to the transfer of 500,000 female domestic workers from the East to Germany showed that control was to be exercised by Sauckel, Himmler and Bormann. Sauckel by decree of 8th September, directed the Kreisleiters to supervise the distribution and assignment of these female labourers.

Bormann also issued a series of orders to the Party Leaders dealing with the treatment of prisoners of war. On 5th November, 1941, he prohibited decent burials for Russian prisoners of war. On 25th November, 1943, he directed Gauleiters to report cases of lenient treatment of prisoners of war. And on 13th September, 1944, he ordered liaison between the Kreisleiters with the camp commandants in determining the use to be made of prisoners of war for forced labour. On 29th January, 1943, he transmitted to his leaders OKW instructions allowing the use of firearms, and corporal punishment on recalcitrant prisoners of war, contrary to the Rules of Land Warfare. On 30th September, 1944, he signed a decree taking from the OKW jurisdiction over prisoners of war and handing them over to Himmler and the SS.

Bormann is responsible for the lynching of Allied

airmen. On 30th May, 1944, he prohibited any police action or criminal proceedings against persons who had taken part in the lynching of Allied fliers. This was accompanied by a Goebbels' propaganda campaign inciting the German people to take action of this nature and the conference of 6th June, 1944, where regulations for the application of lynching were discussed.

His counsel, who has laboured under difficulties, was unable to refute this evidence. In the face of these documents which bear Bormann's signature it is difficult to see how he could do so even were the defendant present. Counsel has argued that Bormann is dead and that the Tribunal should not avail itself of Article 12 of the Charter which gives it the right to take proceedings *in absentia*. But the evidence of death is not conclusive, and the Tribunal, as previously stated, determined to try him *in absentia*. If Bormann is not dead and is later apprehended, the Control Council for Germany may, under Article 29 of the Charter, consider any facts in mitigation, and alter or reduce his sentence, if deemed proper.

The Tribunal finds that Bormann is not guilty on Count One, but is guilty on Counts Three and Four.

THE PRESIDENT: Before pronouncing sentence on any of the defendants, and while all of the defendants are present, the Tribunal takes the occasion to advise them that any applications for clemency of the Control Council must be lodged with the General Secretary of this Tribunal within four days from to-day.

The Tribunal will now adjourn and will sit again at ten minutes to three.

(A recess was taken until 2.50 p.m.)

2.50 p.m.

The PRESIDENT: In accordance with Article 27 of the Charter, the International Military Tribunal will now pronounce the sentences on the defendants convicted on this Indictment.

Defendant Hermann Wilhelm Goering, on the counts of the Indictment on which you have been convicted, the International Military Tribunal sentences you to death by hanging.

Defendant Rudolf Hess, on the counts of the Indictment on which you have been convicted, the Tribunal sentences you to imprisonment for life.

Defendant Joachim von Ribbentrop, on the counts of the Indictment on which you have been convicted, the Tribunal sentences you to death by hanging.

Defendant Wilhelm Keitel, on the counts of the Indictment on which you have been convicted, the Tribunal sentences you to death by hanging.

Defendant Ernst Kaltenbrunner, on the counts of the Indictment on which you have been convicted, the Tribunal sentences you to death by hanging.

Defendant Alfred Rosenberg, on the counts of the Indictment on which you have been convicted, the Tribunal sentences you to death by hanging.

Defendant Hans Frank, on the counts of the Indictment on which you have been convicted, the Tribunal sentences you to death by hanging.

Defendant Wilhelm Frick, on the counts of the Indictment on which you have been convicted, the Tribunal sentences you to death by hanging.

Defendant Julius Streicher, on the count of the Indictment on which you have been convicted, The Tribunal sentences you to death by hanging.

Defendant Walther Funk, on the counts of the

Indictment on which you have been convicted, the Tribunal sentences you to imprisonment for life.

Defendant Karl Doenitz, on the counts of the Indictment on which you have been convicted, the Tribunal sentences you to ten years imprisonment.

Defendant Erich Raeder, on the counts of the Indictment on which you have been convicted, the Tribunal sentences you to imprisonment for life.

Defendant Baldur von Schirach, on the counts of the Indictment on which you have been convicted, the Tribunal sentences you to twenty years imprisonment.

Defendant Fritz Sauckel, on the counts of the Indictment on which you have been convicted, the Tribunal sentences you to death by hanging.

Defendant Alfred Jodl, on the counts of the Indictment on which you have been convicted, the Tribunal sentences you to death by hanging.

Defendant Arthur Seyss-Inquart, on the counts of the Indictment on which you have been convicted, the Tribunal sentences you to death by hanging.

Defendant Albert Speer, on the counts of the Indictment on which you have been convicted, the Tribunal sentences you to twenty years imprisonment.

Defendant Konstantin von Neurath, on the counts of the Indictment on which you have been convicted, the Tribunal sentences you to fifteen years imprisonment.

The Tribunal sentences the Defendant Martin Bormann, on the counts of the Indictment on which he has been convicted, to death by hanging.

I have an announcement to make. The Soviet Member of the International Military Tribunal desires to record his dissent from the decisions in the cases of the Defendants Schacht, von Papen, and Fritzsche. He is of the opinion that they should have been convicted and not acquitted.

He also dissents from the decisions in respect of the Reichs Cabinet, the General Staff and High Command, being of the opinion that they should have been declared to be criminal organisations.

He also dissents from the decision in the case of the sentence on the Defendant Hess, and is of the opinion that the sentence should have been death, and not life imprisonment.

This dissenting opinion will be put into writing and annexed to the judgment and will be published as soon as possible.

(The Tribunal adjourned.)

DISSENTING OPINION of the Soviet Member of the International Military Tribunal, Major General Jurisprudence I. T. Nikitchenko on the Judgment concerning defendants Schacht, von Papen, Fritzsche and Hess and the accused organisations Reichscabinet, General Staff, and OKW.

The Tribunal decided:

(a) to acquit the defendants Hjalmar Schacht, Franz von Papen and Hans Fritzsche;

(b) to sentence the defendant Rudolf Hess to life imprisonment;

(c) not to declare criminal the following organisations: the Reichscabinet, General Staff and OKW.

In this respect I cannot agree with the decision adopted by the Tribunal as it does not correspond to the facts of the case and is based on incorrect conclusions.

1. The unfounded acquittal of defendant Schacht

The evidence, submitted to the Tribunal in the case of Schacht, confirms the following facts:

(a) Schacht established contact with Goering in December, 1930, and with Hitler at the beginning of 1931. He subsequently established contact between the leadership of the Nazi Party and the foremost representatives of the German industrial and financial circles. This, in particular, is confirmed by the testimony of Witness Severing.

(b) In July, 1932, Schacht, demanded that Papen resign his post as Reich Chancellor in favour of Hitler. This fact is confirmed by Papen's testimony at the preliminary interrogation and by Schacht's own testimony in Court.

(c) In November, 1932, Schacht collected signatures of German industrialists, urging them to come out for Hitler's appointment as Reich Chancellor. On 12th November, 1932, Schacht wrote to Hitler:

"I have no doubt that the way we are directing the course of events can only lead to your appointment as Reich Chancellor. We are trying to secure a large number of signatures among the industrial circles to ensure your appointment to this post."

(d) In February, 1933, Schacht organised the financing of the pre-election campaign conducted by the Nazi Party, and demanded at the conference of Hitler and Goering with the industrialists, that the latter provide three million marks (D—203). Schacht admitted in Court that he had pointed out the necessity for providing the Nazi leaders with this sum (Transcript, Afternoon Session, 3rd May, 1946), while the defendant Funk and the former member of the management of "I.G. Farbenindustrie" Schnitzler, who were present at this conference, both confirmed that it was Schacht who was the Initiator of the financing of the pre-election campaign.

(*e*) Utilising his prestige Schacht also repeatedly admitted in his public statements that he asked for the support in the elections of both the Nazi Party and of Hitler.

On 2nd August, 1932, Schacht wrote to Hitler:

"No matter where my activities lead me in the near future, even if some day you see me imprisoned in a fortress, you can always depend on me as your loyal aide." *Thus, Schacht consciously and deliberately supported the Nazi Party and actively aided in the seizure of power in Germany by the Fascists*. Even prior to his appointment as Plenipotentiary for War Economy, and immediately after the seizure of power by the Nazis, Schacht led in planning and developing the German armaments, as follows:

(*a*) On 17th March, 1933, Schacht was appointed President of the Reichsbank, and as he himself stated in a speech before his Reichsbank colleagues on 21st March, 1938, the Reichsbank under his management was "none other than a national socialist institution".

(*b*) In August, 1934, Schacht was appointed Reich Minister of Economy. His Ministry "was given the task of carrying out the economic preparation for war". A special decree granted Schacht in his capacity of Reich Minister of Economy, unlimited authority in the field of economy.

(*c*) Making use of these powers in 1934, Schacht launched upon the execution of the "new programme" developed by him , and, as Schacht himself noted in his

speech of 29th November, 1938, this organisation played a
tremendous part in the course of Germany's rearmament.

(*d*) For the purpose of the most effective execution of
this "new programme" Schacht used the property and
means of those political enemies of the Nazi Régime, who
either became the victims of terror or were forced to emigrate (Schacht's note to Hitler of 3rd May, 1939)

Schacht used swindler's tactics and coercion "in an
effort to acquire raw material and foreign currency for
armaments".

(*e*) During the very first day of his association with
Reichsbank, Schacht issued a series of decrees, which in
the long run helped realise the broad programme of the
financing of armaments, developed by him, and with the
aid of which, as he testified, he "had found the way to
finance the rearmament programme".

In his speech in Leipzig on 1st March, 1935, Schacht,
while summing up his preceding economic and financial
activities, announced ". . . everything that I say and do has
the Fuehrer's full agreement and I shall not do or say anything which is not approved by the Fuehrer".

Having become the Plenipotentiary General for War
Economy, Schacht unified under himself the leadership of
the entire Germany economy and through his efforts the
establishment of the Hitlerite war machine was accomplished.

(*a*) The secret law of 21st May, 1935, which appointed
Schacht the Plenipotentiary General for War Economy,
states as follows: "The task of the Plenipotentiary General
for War Economy is to place all the economic resources in
the service of warfare." "The Plenipotentiary General for
War Economy within the framework of his functions is
given the right to issue legal orders, deviating from the
existing laws." "He is the responsible head for financing
wars through the Reich Ministry and the Reichsbank."

(*b*) Schacht financed German armaments through the MEFO system of promissory notes, which was a swindling venture on a national scale that has no precedent, and the success of which was dependent upon the realisation of the aggressive plans of the Hitlerites. It was because of this that Schacht set 1942 as the date when the MEFO notes were to mature, and he pointed out in his speech of 29th November, 1938, the relation between "the daring credit policy" of the Reichsbank and the aims of the Hitlerite foreign policy.

(*c*) Having made full use of his plenary powers, Schacht carefully developed and carried out a broad programme of economic mobilisation which allowed the Hitlerite leaders to wage war at any time considered most favourable. In particular, from the report of Schacht's deputy, Wohltat, "the preparation for mobilisation carried out by the Plenipotentiary for War Economy" shows that Schacht provided to the last detail for the system of exploitation of the German economy in war time, all the way from the utilisation of industrial enterprises, of raw material resources and manpower down to the distribution of 80,000,000 ration cards. It is significant that this report was drawn up a month after Hitler's statement at the conference of 5th November, 1937, at which Hitler set forth this concrete plan of aggression

Summarising his past activity, Schacht wrote in January, 1937: "I worked out the preparation for war in accordance with the principle that the plan of our war economy must be built in peace time in such a way that there will be no necessity for any reorganisation in case of war". Schacht confirmed his statement in Court

Schacht consciously and deliberately prepared Germany for war.

(*d*) The former Minister of War, von Blomberg, testified that: "Schacht was fully cognisant of the plans for development and increase of the German armed forces, since he was constantly informed . . . of all the financing necessary for the development of the German armed forces".

On 31st August, 1936, von Blomberg informed Schacht that: "The establishment of all the Air Force units must be completed by 1st April, 1937, and therefore large expenditures must be entailed in 1936 . . ."

In the Spring of 1937, Schacht participated in the military exercises in Godesberg.

(*e*) In his memorandum to Hitler on 3rd May, 1935, entitled the "Financing of Rearmament", Schacht wrote: "A speedy fulfilment of the programme for rearmament on a mass scale is the basis of German policy, and, therefore, everything else must be subordinate to this task; the completion of this task, the achievement of this purpose must meet no obstacles . . ."

In his speech on 29th November, 1938, Schacht announced the Reichsbank's policy made possible for Germany to create an "unsurpassed machine, and, in turn, this war machine made possible the realisation of the aims of our policy".

One must exclude the supposition that Schacht was not informed as to what purposes these weapons were to serve since he could not but take into consideration their unprecedented scale and an obvious preference for offensive types of weapons, heavy tanks, bombers, and so on. Besides, Schacht knew perfectly well that not a single country intended to wage war on Germany nor had it any reasons to do so.

(*a*) Schacht utilised the military might growing under his direction to back Germany's territorial demands which grew in proportion to the increase in armaments.

Schacht testified in court that "at first he confined himself (in his demands) to the colonies which had once

belonged to Germany." (Transcript, Morning Session, 3rd
May, 1946.)

In September, 1934, during his talk with the
American Ambassador Dodd, Schacht pointed out that he
"desired annexation if possible without war, but through
war, if the U.S. would stay out of it".

In 1935, Schacht announced to the American Consul
Fuller: "Colonies are essential to Germany. If it is possible,
we shall acquire them through negotiations; if not, we shall
seize them."

Schacht admitted in Court that military pressure put
upon Czechoslovakia was "in some measure the result and
the fruit of his labour".

(*b*) Schacht personally participated in the plunder of
private and State property of the countries which became
victims of Hitlerite aggressions.

The minutes of the conference of the Military-
Economic Staff on 11th March, 1938, in which Schacht
participated, state that those present were given Hitler's
latest directives about the invasion of Austria. Further, the
minutes state that: "After this, at the suggestion of Schacht,
it was decided that . . . all the financial accounting will be
made in Reichsmarks at the rate of exchange: 2 shillings
for one Reichsmark".

Schacht admitted in court that he personally was in
charge of the seizure of the Czechoslovak National Bank
after the occupation of Czechoslovakia.

(*c*) At the beginning of 1940, Schacht offered Hitler
his services for negotiations with the United States of
America in regard to the discontinuance of aid to England
and he informed Goering of his offer.

(*d*) Schacht considered it his duty to greet and con-
gratulate Hitler publicly after the signing of armistice with
France, although Schacht, better than anyone else, understood the usurpatory nature of the armistice.

(*e*) In his letter to Funk on 17th October, 1941, Schacht suggested a more effective exploitation of occupied territory. In this case, too, Schacht acted on his own initiative.

Schacht also participated in the persecution of the Jews:

(*a*) He testified in court that he "continued the policy of the persecution of the Jews as a matter of principle" (Transcript, Afternoon Session, 2nd May, 1946) although, he stated, "to a certain extent" it was a matter of conscience which, however, "was not serious enough to bring about a break" between him and the Nazis.

(*b*) In his capacity of Minister of Economy, Schacht signed a series of decrees, in accordance with which the property of the Jews in Germany was subject to plunder with impunity. Schacht confirmed in Court the fact that he had signed a series of anti-semitic decrees.

As to the reasons for Schacht's resignation from the post of the Minister of Economy and the Plenipotentiary General for War Economy in November, 1937, and also from the post of the President of the Reichsbank on 20th November, 1939, and finally from the post of the Minister without Portfolio in January, 1943, the evidence submitted establishes the following:

(*a*) The reason is not Schacht's disagreement with the economic preparation for aggressive wars.

Three weeks before leaving the Ministry of Economy and the post of Plenipotentiary General for War Economy, Schacht wrote to Goering: ". . . I also don't consider that my opinion can differ from yours on economic policy . . ."

In his reply Goering states: ". . . You promised me your support and collaboration . . . You have repeated this promise many times, even after differences of opinion began to creep up between us."

Schacht testified in Court that Goering and he "differed in matters of procedure".

In the preliminary examination Goering testified that Schacht's leaving the Reichsbank "had no relation to the programme of rearmament".

The vice-president of the Reichsbank, Puhl, confirmed that Schacht's resignation from the Reichsbank can be explained by "his desire to extricate himself from a dangerous situation" which developed as the result of Schacht's own crooked financial operations.

(*b*) The reason is not Schacht's disapproval of mass terror conducted by the Hitlerites.

The witness for the Defence, Gesevius, testified that he constantly informed Schacht of the criminal actions of the Gestapo, created by Goering, and that nevertheless, right up to the end of 1936, Schacht looked for "Goering's support".

In his letter to von Blomberg on 24th December, 1935, Schacht suggested that Gestapo apply "more cautious methods" since the open terror of the Gestapo "hinders the objectives of rearmament".

On 30th January, 1937, Schacht was awarded a golden Party insignia by Hitler. (EC—393, US—643.) As stated in an official German publication, "he was able to be of greater help to the Party than if he were actually a member of the Party".

Only in 1943, having understood earlier than many other Germans, the inevitability of the failure of the Hitlerite régime, did Schacht establish contact with the opposition circles, however, doing nothing to help depose this régime. Therefore, it was not by chance that having found out these connections of Schacht, Hitler still spared Schacht's life.

It is thus indisputably established that:

(1) Schacht actively assisted in the seizure of power by the Nazis;

(2) During a period of 12 years Schacht closely collaborated with Hitler;

(3) Schacht provided the economic and financial basis for the creation of the Hitlerite military machine;

(4) Schacht prepared Germany's economy for the waging of aggressive wars;

(5) Schacht participated in the persecution of Jews and in the plunder of territories occupied by the Germans.

Therefore, Schacht's leading part in the preparation and execution of the common criminal plan is proved.

The decision to acquit Schacht is in obvious contradiction with the evidence in possession of the Tribunal.

II. The Unfounded Acquittal of defendant von Papen

The verdict does not dispute the fact that von Papen prepared the way for Hitler's appointment to the post of the Reichskanzler and that he actively helped Nazis in their seizure of power.

In a speech of the 2nd of November, 1933, von Papen said the following on the subject:

"Then and there, on becoming the Reichskanzler (this was in 1932) I spoke in favour of the young and fighting movement for freedom; just as on the 30th of January I was chosen by Fate to surrender power into the hands of our Kanzler and Fuehrer, so to-day I must tell the German people and all those who have maintained their trust in me: merciful God blessed Germany by granting her in these days of deep sorrow a Fuehrer like this."

It was von Papen who revoked Bruening's order dissolving the SS and the SA, thus allowing the Nazis to realise their programme of mass terror.

Again it was the defendant who, by the application of

brute force, did away with the Social Democrat Government of Braun and Severing.

On the 4th of January, 1933, Papen had a conference with Hitler, Hess, and Himmler.

Papen participated in the purge of the State machinery of all personnel considered unreliable from the Nazi point of view; *on the 21st of March, 1933, he signed a decree creating special political tribunals*; he had also signed an order granting amnesty to criminals whose crimes were committed in the course of the "national revolution"; he participated in drafting the text of the order "insuring party and state unity"; and so on.

Subsequently Papen faithfully served the Hitler régime.

During the Putsch of 1934, *Papen ordered his subordinate Tschirschky to appear in the Gestapo*, knowing full well what awaited him there. Tschirschky as is well known, was executed while Papen helped to keep the bloody murder secret from public opinion.

Defendant played a tremendous rôle in helping Nazis to take possession of Austria.

Three weeks after the assassination of Dollfuss, on the 26th of July, 1934, Hitler told Papen that he was being appointed Minister to Vienna, specially noting in a letter: "You have been and continue to be in possession of my full and unlimited trust."

In this connection it is impossible to ignore the testimony of the American Ambassador Messerschmidt who quoted Papen as saying that "the seizure of Austria is only the first step" and that he, von Papen is in Austria for the purpose of "further weakening the Austrian Government."

Defendant was Hitler's chief adviser in effecting plans for the seizure of Austria. It was he who proposed several tactical manœuvres, to quiet the vigilance of world opinion on the one hand, and allow Germany to conclude her war preparations, on the other.

This follows indisputably from Papen's statement to the Austrian Minister Berger-Waldeneck , from the Report of Gauleiter Reuner of 6th July, 1939), from Papen's Report to Hitler of 26th August, 1936 , from Papen's Report to Hitler of 1st September, 1936, and from a series of other documents which had been submitted in evidence.

Papen played this game until the issuance of the order for alerting the German Armed Forces for moving into Austria. (US—69.) He participated in arranging the conference between Hitler and Schuschnigg of 12th February, 1938. (US—69.)

It was Papen who in a letter to Hitler emphatically recommended that financial aid be given the Nazi organisation in Austria known as the "Freedom Union", specifically for "its fight against the Jewry."

Indisputable appears the fact of the Nazi seizure of Austria and of Papen's participation in this act of aggression. After the occupation of Austria, Hitler rewarded von Papen with the golden insignia of the Nazi Party.

Neither is it possible to ignore von Papen's rôle as *agent provocateur* when in his capacity of diplomat he was the German Ambassador to Turkey— whenever evaluation of his activity there is made.

The post of Ambassador to Turkey was at the time of considerable importance in helping the Nazis realise their aggressive plans.

The official Nazi biographer wrote about von Papen as follows:

"Shortly after (the occupation of Austria) the Fuehrer had need of von Papen's services again and on 18th April, 1939, he therefore, appointed him German Ambassador in Ankara".

It should also be noted that for his Turkish activities, Hitler rewarded von Papen with the Knight's Cross for his "military services".

Thus evidence submitted establishes beyond doubt that:

1. Von Papen actively aided the Nazis in their seizure of power.
2. Von Papen used both his efforts and his connections to solidify and strengthen the Hitlerian terroristic régime in Germany.
3. Von Papen actively participated in the Nazi aggression against Austria culminating in its occupation.
4. Von Papen faithfully served Hitler up to the very end aiding the Nazi plans of aggression both with his ability and his diplomatic skill.

It therefore follows that defendant von Papen bears considerable responsibility for the crimes of the Hitlerite régime.

For these reasons I cannot consent to the acquittal of defendant von Papen.

III. The Unfounded Acquittal of defendant Fritzsche

The acquittal of defendant Hans Fritzsche follows from the reasoning that Fritzsche, allegedly, had not reached in Germany the official position making him responsible for the criminal actions of the Hitler régime and that his own personal activity in this respect cannot be considered criminal. The verdict characterises him as a secondary figure carrying out the directives of Goebbels and Ribbentrop, and of the Reich Press Director Dietrich.

The verdict does not take into consideration or mention the fact that it was Fritzsche who until 1942 was the Director *de facto* of the Reich Press and that, according to himself, subsequent to 1942, he became the "Commander-in-Chief of the German radio."

For the correct definition of the rôle of defendant Hans Fritzsche it is necessary, firstly, to keep clearly in mind the importance attached by Hitler and his closest associates (as Goering, for example) to propaganda in general and to radio propaganda in particular. This was considered one of the most important and essential factors in the success of conducting an aggressive war.

The Germany of Hitler, propaganda was invariably a factor in preparing and conducting acts of aggression and in training the German populace to accept obediently the criminal enterprises of German fascism.

The aims of these enterprises were served by a huge and well centralised propaganda machinery. With the help of the police controls and of a system of censorship it was possible to do away altogether with the freedom of the press and of speech.

The basic method of the Nazi propagandistic activity lay in the false presentation of facts. This is stated quite frankly in Hitler's "Mein Kampf"; "With the help of a skilful and continuous application of propaganda it is possible to make the people conceive even of heaven as hell and also make them consider heavenly the most miserly existence."

The dissemination of provocative lies and the systematic deception of public opinion were as necessary to the Hitlerites for the realisation of their plans as were the production of armaments and the drafting of military plans. Without propaganda, founded on the total eclipse of the freedom of press and of speech, it would not have been possible for German Fascism to realise its aggressive intentions, to lay the groundwork and then to put to practice the war crimes and the crimes against humanity.

In the propaganda system of the Hitler State it was the

daily press and the radio that were the most important weapons.

In his court testimony, defendant Goering named three factors as essential in the successful conduct of modern war according to the Nazi concept, namely, (1) the military operations of the armed forces, (2) economic warfare, (3) propaganda. With reference to the latter he said: "*Propaganda has tremendous value, particularly propaganda carried by means of radio* ... Germany has learned this through experience better than anyone else".

With such concepts in ascendance it is impossible to suppose that the supreme rulers of the Reich would appoint to the post of Director of Radio Propaganda who supervised radio activity of all the broadcasting companies and directed their propagandistic content—a man they considered a secondary figure.

The point of view of the verdict contradicts both the evidence submitted and the actual state of affairs.

Beginning with 1942, and into 1945, Fritzsche was not only Chief of the Radio Department of the Reich Ministry of Propaganda but also "Plenipotentiary for the Political Organisation of Radio in Greater Germany". This circumstance is fully proven by the sworn affidavit of Fritzsche himself. It thus follows that not at all was Fritzsche merely "one of the twelve departmental chiefs in the Ministry of Propaganda" who acquired responsibility for all radio propaganda only toward the end of the war, as the verdict asserts.

Fritzsche was the Political Director of the German radio up and into 1945. i.e., up to the moment of German defeat and capitulation. For this reason it is Fritzsche who bears responsibility for the false and provocative broadcasts of the German radio during the years of the war.

As chief of the Press Section inside Germany it was also Fritzsche who was responsible for the activity of the

German daily press consisting of 2,300 newspapers. It was Fritzsche who created and perfected the Information Section winning from the Reich Government for the purpose an increase in the subsidy granted the newspapers from 400,000 to 4,000,000 marks. Subsequently Fritzsche participated energetically in the development of the propaganda campaigns preparatory to the acts of aggression against Czechoslovakia and Poland. A similar active propaganda campaign was conducted by the Defendant prior to the attack on Yugoslavia as he himself admitted on oath in court. (Transcript, Morning Session, 23rd January, 1946.)

Fritzsche was informed of the plan to attack the Soviet Union and was put "au courant" the military intentions at a conference with Rosenberg.

Fritzsche headed the German press campaign falsifying reports of Germany's aggressive war against France, England, Norway, the Soviet Union, the U.S.A., and the other States.

The assertion that Fritzsche was not informed of the war crimes and the crimes against humanity then being perpetrated by the Hitlerities in the occupied regions does not agree with the facts. From Fritzsche's testimony in court it is obvious that already in May, 1942, while in the Propaganda Section of the 6th Army, he was aware of Hitler's decree ordering execution for all Soviet political workers and Soviet intellectuals, the so-called "Commissar Decree". It is also established that already at the beginning of hostilities Fritzsche was fully aware of the fact that the Nazis were carrying out their decision to do away with all Jews in Europe. For instance, when commenting on Hitler's statement that "among results of the war there will be the annihilation of the Jewish race in Europe" (p. 248 of the transcript), Fritzsche stated that: "As the Further predicted it will occur in the event of war in Europe, the fate of the European Jewry turned out to be quite sad." (P.

3231 of the transcript.) It is further established that the defendant systematically preached the anti-social theory of race hatred and characterised peoples inhabiting countries victimised by aggression as 'subhumans".

When the fate of Nazi Germany became clear, Fritzsche came out with energetic support of the defendant Martin Bormann and of other fanatical Hitler adherents who organised the undercover fascist association, the so-called "Werewolf."

On the 7th of April, 1945, for example, in his last radio address, Fritzsche agitated for all the civilian population of Germany to take active part in the activities of this terroristic Nazi underground organisation.

He said: "Let no one be surprised to find the civilian population, wearing civilian clothes, still continuing the fight in the regions already occupied and even after occupation has taken place. We shall call this phenomenon "Werewolf" since it will have arisen without any preliminary planning and without a definite organisation, out of the very instinct of life."

In his radio addresses Fritzsche welcomes the German use of the new terror weapons in conducting the war, specifically the use of the "V" rockets. On receiving a plan for the introduction of bacterial warfare he immediately forwarded it to the OKW for acceptance.

I consider Fritzsche's responsibility fully proven. His activity had a most basic relation to the preparation and the conduct of aggressive warfare as well as to the other crimes of the Hitler régime.

IV. Concerning the Sentence of the Defendant Rudolf Hess.

The Judgment of the Tribunal correctly and adequately portrays the outstanding position which Rudolf Hess occupied in the leadership of the Nazi party and State. He was indeed Hitler's closest personal confident and his authority was exceedingly great. In this connection it is sufficient to quote Hitler's decree appointing Hess as his deputy: "I hereby appoint Hess as my deputy and give him full power to make decisions in my name on all questions of Party Leadership.

But the authority of Hess was not only confined to questions of Party leadership.

The official NSDAP publication "Party Year Book for 1941", which was admitted as USA Exhibit No. 255, PS— 3163, states that: . . . "In addition to the duties of Party leadership, the Deputy of the Fuehrer has far-reaching powers in the field of the State. These are first: participation in national and State legislation, including the preparation of Fuehrer's order. The Deputy of the Fuehrer in this way validates the conception of the Party . . . . second, Approval of the Deputy of the Fuehrer of proposed appointments for official and labour service leaders. Three, securing the influence of the Party over the self-government of the municipal units.".

Hess was an active supporter of Hitler's aggressive policy. The crimes against peace committed by him are dealt with in sufficient detail in the Judgment. The mission undertaken by Hess in flying to England should be considered as the last of these crimes, as it was undertaken in the hope of facilitating the realisation of aggression against the Soviet Union by temporarily restraining England from fighting.

The failure of this mission led to Hess's isolation and he took no direct part in the planning and commission of subsequent crimes of the Hitler régime. There can be no doubt, however, that Hess did everything possible for the preparation of these crimes.

Hess, together with Himmler, occupied the rôle of

creator of the SS police organisations of German fascism which afterwards committed the most ruthless crimes against humanity. The defendant clearly pointed out the "special tasks" which faced the SS formations on occupied territories.

When the Waffen SS were being formed Hess issued a special order through the Party Chancellery which made aiding the conscription of Party members into these organisations by all means compulsory for Party organs. He outlined the tasks set before the Waffen—SS as follows:

"The units of the Waffen—SS composed of National Socialists are more suitable than other armed units for the specific tasks to be solved in the occupied Eastern territories due to the intensive training in regard to questions of race and nationality."

As early as 1934 the defendant initiated a proposal that the so-called SD under the Reichsfuehrer SS (Security Service) be given extraordinary powers and thus become the leading force in Nazi Germany.

On the 9th of June, 1934, Hess issued a decree in accordance with which the "Security Service of the Reichsfuehrer SS" was declared to be the "sole political news and defence service of the Party".

Thus the defendant played a direct part in the creation and consolidation of the system of special police organs which were being prepared for the commission of crimes on occupied territories.

We find Hess to have always been an advocate of the man-hating "master race" theory. In a speech made on the 16th January, 1937, while speaking of the education of the German nation, Hess pointed out:

"Thus, they are being educated to put Germans above the subjects of a foreign nation, regardless of their positions or their origin."

Hess signed the so-called "Law for the Protection of Blood and Honour" on the 15th September, 1935. The body of this law states that "the Fuehrer's deputy is authorised to issue all necessary decrees and directives" for the practical realisation of the "Nuremberg decrees."

On the 14th of November, 1935, Hess issued an ordinance under the Reich citizenship law in accordance with which the Jews were denied the right to vote at elections or hold public office.

On the 20th of May, 1938, a decree signed by Hess extended the Nuremberg laws to Austria.

On 12th October, 1939, Hess signed a decree creating the administration of Polish occupied territories . Article 2 of this decree gave the defendant Frank the power of dictator.

There is sufficiently convincing evidence showing that this defendant did not limit himself to this general directive which introduced into the occupied Polish territories a régime of unbridled terror. As is shown in the letter of the Reichsminister of Justice to the Chief of the Reichs Chancellery dated 17th April, 1941, Hess was the initiator in the formation of special "penal laws" for Poles and Jews in occupied Eastern territories. The rôle of this defendant in the drawing up of these "laws" is characterised by the Minister of Justice in the following words:

"In accordance with the opinion of the Fuehrer's deputy I started from the point of view that the Pole is less susceptible to the infliction of ordinary punishment. . . . Under these new kinds of punishment, prisoners are to be lodged outside prisons in camps and are to be forced to do heavy and heaviest labour. . . . The introduction of corporal punishment which the Deputy of the Fuehrer has brought up for discussion has not been included in the draft. I can not agree to this type of punishment. . . . The procedure for enforcing prosecution has been abrogated, for it seemed intolerable that Poles or Jews should be able to instigate a public indictment. Poles and Jews have also been deprived of the right to prosecute in their own names or join the public prosecution in an action.... From the very beginning it was intended to intensify special treatment in case of need: When this necessity became actual a supplementary decree was issued to which the Fuehrer's deputy refers to in his letter ...."

Thus, there can be no doubt that Hess together with the other major war criminals is guilty of crimes against humanity.

Taking into consideration that among political leaders of Hitlerite Germany Hess was third in significance and played a decisive rôle in the crimes of the Nazi régime. I consider the only justified sentence in his case can be—death.

V. Incorrect Judgment With Regard to the Reich Cabinet

The Prosecution has posed before the Tribunal the question of declaring the Reich Cabinet a criminal organisation. The verdict rejects the claim of the Prosecution, unfoundedly refusing to declare the Hitler Government a criminal organisation.

With such a decision I cannot agree.

The Tribunal considers it proven that the Hitlerites have committed innumerable and monstrous crimes.

The Tribunal also considers it proven that these crimes, were as a rule committed intentionally and on an organised scale, according to previously prepared plans and directives. ("Plan Barbarossa", "Night and Fog", "Bullet", etc.)

The Tribunal has declared several of the Nazi mass

organisations criminal, the organisations founded for the realisation and putting to practice the plans of the Hitler Government.

In view of this it appears particularly untenable and rationally incorrect to refuse to declare the Reich Cabinet, the directing organ of the State with a direct and active rôle in the working out of the criminal enterprises, a criminal organisation. The members of this directing staff had great power, each headed an appropriate government agency, each participated in preparing and realising the Nazi programme.

In confirmation it is deemed proper to cite several facts:

1. Immediately after the Nazi ascent to power—on the 24th of March, 1933—there was a law passed entitled "The Law of Defence of the People and the State" whereby the Reich Cabinet, besides the Reichstag, received the right of issuing new legislature.

On the 26th May, 1933, the Reich Government issued a decree ordering the confiscation of the property of all Communist organisations and on the 14th of June, the same year, it also confiscated the property of the Social Democrat organisations. On the 1st December, 1933, the Reich Government issued the law "Ensuring Party and State Unity".

Following through its programme of liquidating democratic institutions, in 1934, the Government passed a law of the "Reconstruction of the Reich" whereby democratic elections were abolished for both central and local representative bodies. The Reichstag thereby became an institution without functional meaning.

By the law of 7th April, 1933, and others, all Reich government employees, including judges, ever noted for any anti-Nazi tendencies or ever having belonged to left-ish organisations, as well as all Jews, were to be removed from the government service and substituted by Nazis. In accordance with the "Basic Positions of the German Law on Government Employees" of the 26th January, 1937, "the inner harmony of the official and the Nazi party is a necessary presupposition of his appointment to his post . . . government employees must be the executors of the will of the National Socialist State, directed by the NSDAP".

On the 1st May, 1934, there was created the Ministry of Education instructed to train students in the spirit of militarism, of racial hatred, and in terms of reality thoroughly falsified by Nazi ideology.

Free trade unions were abolished, their property confiscated, and the majority of the leaders jailed.

To suppress even a semblance of resistance the Government created the Gestapo and the concentration camps. Without any trial or even a concrete charge hundreds of thousands of persons were arrested and then done away with merely on a suspicion of an anti-Nazi tendency.

There were issued the so-called Nuremburg Laws against the Jews. Hess and Frick, both members of the Reich Government, implemented these by additional decrees.

It was the activity of the Reich Cabinet that brought on the war which took millions of human lives and caused inestimable damage in property and in suffering borne by the many nations.

On the 4th February, 1938, Hitler organised the Secret Council of Ministers defining its activity as follows: "To aid me by advice on problems of foreign policies I am creating this Secret Council". ("Reichsgesetzblatt" for 1938, Part I, p. 112, PS—2031.) The foreign policy of the Hitler Government was the policy of aggression. For this reason the members of the Secret Council should be held responsible for this policy. There were attempts in court to represent the Secret Council as a fictitious organisation, never actually functioning. This however, is an inadmissible position. It is sufficient to recall Rosenberg's letter to Hitler where the former insistently tried to be appointed member of the Secret Council of Ministers—to appreciate fully the significance of the Council.

Even more important practically in conducting aggressive warfare was the Reich Defence Council headed by Goering. The following were members of the Defence Council, as is well known: Hess, Frick, Funk, Keitel, Raeder, Lammers.

Goering characterised the function of the Defence Council and its rôle in war preparations as follows, during the Court Session of 23rd June, 1939: "The Defence Council of the Reich *was the deciding Reich organ on all questions concerning preparation for war*"

At the same time Goering emphasised the fact that "the meetings of the Defence Council always took place for the purpose of making the most important decisions". From the minutes of these meetings, submitted as evidence by the Prosecution, it is quite clear that the Council made very important decisions indeed. The minutes also show that other Cabinet ministers sometimes took part in the meetings of the Council for the Defence alongside the members of the Council when war enterprises and war preparedness were discussed.

For example, the following Cabinet ministers took part in the meeting of 23rd June, 1939: of Labour, of Food and Agriculture, of Finance, of Communications and a number of others, while the minutes of the meeting were sent to all the members of the Cabinet.

The verdict of the Tribunal justly points out certain peculiarities of the Hitler Government as the directing organ of the State, namely: the absence of regular Cabinet meetings, the occasional issuance of laws by the individual ministers having unusual independence of action, the

tremendous personal power of Hitler himself. These peculiarities do not refute but on the contrary further confirm
the conclusion that the Hitler Government is not an ordinary rank-of-the-file Cabinet but a criminal organisation.

Certainly Hitler had an unusual measure of personal
power but this in no way frees of responsibility the members of his Cabinet who were his convinced followers and
the actual executors of his programme until and when the
day of reckoning arrived.

I consider that there is every reason to declare the
Hitler Government a criminal organisation.

VI. Incorrect Judgment with Regard to the General Staff and the OKW.

The verdict incorrectly rejects the accusation of criminal
activity directed against the General Staff and the OKW.

The rejection of the accusation of criminal activity of
the General Staff and of the OKW contradicts both the
actual situation and the evidence submitted in the course
of the trial.

It has been established beyond doubt that the leadership corps of the Armed Forces of Nazi Germany together
with the SS-Party machine, represented the most important agency in the preparing and realising the Nazi
aggressive and man-hating programme. This was constantly and forcefully reiterated by the Hitlerites
themselves in their official bulletins meant for the officer
personnel of the armed forces. In the Nazi Party Bulletin
called "Politics and the Officer in the III Reich" it is quite
clearly stated that the Nazi régime is founded on "two pil-
lars: the Party and the Armed Forces. Both are forms of
expression of the same philosophy of life", "the tasks
before the Party and the Armed Forces are in an organic
relationship to each other and each bears the same respon-

sibility ... both these agencies depend on each other's success or failure".

This organic interrelationship between the Nazi Party and the SS on the one hand and the Nazi Armed Forces on the other hand, was particularly evident among the upper circles of military hierarchy which the Indictment groups together under the concept of criminal organisation—that is, among the members of the General Staff and the OKW.

The very selection of members of the Supreme Command of the Army in Nazi Germany was based on the criteria of their loyalty to the régime and their readiness not only to pursue aggressive militaristic policies but also to fulfil such special directives as related to treatment meted out to prisoners-of-war and to the civilian populations of occupied territories.

The leaders of the German Armed Forces were not merely officers who reached certain levels of the military hierarchy. They represented, first of all, a closely-knit group which was entrusted with the most secret plans of the Nazi leadership. Evidence submitted to the Tribunal has fully confirmed the contention that the military leaders of Germany justified this trust completely and that they were the convinced followers and ardent executors of Hitler's plans.

It is not accidental that at the head of the Air Force stood the "second man" of the Nazi Reich, namely Goering; that the Commander-in-Chief of the Navy was Doenitz, subsequently designated by Hitler to be the latter's successor; that the command of the Ground Forces was concentrated in the hands of Keitel who signed the major part of the decrees concerning the execution of the prisoners-of-war and the civilians in occupied territories.

Thus the comparisons made with the organisation of the Supreme Commands in Allied countries cannot be considered valid. In a democratic country, not one self-respecting military expert would agree to prepare plans for mass reprisals and merciless killings of prisoners-of-war side by side with plans of the purely military and strategic character.

Meanwhile it is precisely such matters that occupied the Supreme Command of the General Staff and of the OKW in Nazi Germany. The commission by them of the heaviest crimes against peace, of the war crimes, and of the crimes against humanity is not denied but is particularly emphasised in the verdict of the Tribunal. And yet the commission of these crimes has not brought the logical conclusion.

The verdict states:

"They have been a disgrace to the honourable profession of arms. Without their military guidance the aggressive ambitions of Hitler and his fellow Nazis would have been academic and sterile . . ."
And subsequently:

"Many of these men have made a mockery of the soldier's oath of obedience to military orders. When it suits their defence they say they had to obey; when confronted with Hitler's brutal crimes, which are shown to have been within their general knowledge, they say they disobeyed. The truth is they actively participated in all these crimes, or sat silent and acquiescent, witnessing the commission of crimes on a scale larger and more shocking than the world ever had the misfortune to know . . . This must be said."

All these assertions in the verdict are correct and are based on numerous and reliable depositions. The only thing that remains incomprehensible is the reasoning which does not recognise as criminal that "hundreds of higher ranking officers" who caused the world and their own country so much sorrow, the reasons backing the decision not to declare the organisation criminal.

The verdict advances the following reasons for the decision, reasons quite contradictory to the facts:

(*a*) That the crimes were committed by representatives of the General Staff and of the OKW as private individuals and not as members of a criminal conspiracy.

(*b*) That the General Staff and the OKW were merely weapons in the hands of the conspirators and interpreters or executors of the conspirators' will.

Numerous evidence disputes such conclusions.

1. *The leading representative of the General Staff and of the OKW, along with a small circle of the higher Hitlerite officials, were called upon by the conspirators to participate in the development and the realisation of the plans of aggression, not as passive functionaries, but as active participants in the conspiracy against peace and humanity.*

Without their advice and active co-operation, Hitler could not have solved these problems.

In the majority of cases their opinion was decisive. It is impossible to imagine how the aggressive plans of Hitler's Germany could have been realised had it not been for the full support given him by the leading staff members of the Armed Forces.

Least of all did Hitler conceal his criminal plans and motivation from the leaders of the Supreme Command.

For instance, while preparing for the attack on Poland, as early as 29th May, 1939, at a conference with the high military commanders of the new Reich Chancellery, he stated:

"For us the matter consists of the expansion of 'Lebensraum' to the East."

"Thus the question of sparing Poland cannot be considered, and, instead, we have to consider the decision to attack Poland at the first opportunity."

Long before the seizure of Czechoslovakia, in a directive of 30th May, 1938, Hitler, addressing the representatives of the Supreme Command cynically stated:

"From the military and political point of view, the most favourable time is a lightning attack on the basis of some incident, by which Germany will have been strongly provoked and which will morally justify the military measures to at least part of the world opinion."

Prior to the invasion of Yugoslavia, in a directive dated 27th March, 1941, addressing the representatives of the High Command, Hitler wrote:

"Even if Yugoslavia declares its loyalty, it must be considered an enemy and must, therefore, be smashed as soon as possible."

While preparing for the invasion of the U.S.S.R., Hitler invited the representatives of the General Staff and the OKW to help him work out the related plans and directives not at all as simply the military experts.

In the instructions to apply propaganda in the region "Barbarossa," issued by the OKW in June, 1941, it is pointed out that:

"For the time we should not have propaganda directed at the dismemberment of the Soviet Union."

As early as 13th May, 1941, OKW ordered the troops to use any terrorist measures against the civilian populations of the temporarily occupied regions of the Soviet Union.

Here a special stipulation read: "To confirm only such sentences as are in accordance with the political intentions of the Leadership."

2. *OKW and the General Staff issued the most brutal decrees and orders for relentless measures against the unarmed peaceful population and the prisoners of war.*

In the "decree of special liability to punishment in the region Barbarossa" while preparing for the attack upon the Soviet Union, the OKW abolished beforehand the jurisdiction of the military courts, granting the right of repressions over the peaceful population to individual officers and soldiers.

It is particularly stated there that:

"Crimes of hostile civilians are excluded from the jurisdiction of the courts martial . . . .", "Suspected elements must be immediately delivered to the officer. The latter will decide whether they should be shot . . . .", "it is absolutely forbidden to hold suspects for the purpose of bringing them to trial." There are also provisions for "the most extreme measures, and, in particular, 'Measures for mass violence', if circumstances do not permit the rapid detection of the guilty."

In the same decree of the OKW the guarantee of impunity was assured in advance to the military criminals from the service personnel of the German Army. It states there as follows: "The bringing of suits of actions, committed by officials of the Army and by the service personnel against hostile civilians is not obligatory even in the cases where such actions at the same time constitute military crimes or offences . . . .".

In the course of the war the High Command consistently followed this policy, increasing its terroristic actions with regard to prisoners of war and the peaceful populations of occupied countries.

The OKW directive of 16th September, 1941, states:

"It is important to realise that human life in the countries to which this refers, means nothing, and that intimidating action is possible only through the application of unusual brutality".

Addressing the commanders of the Army groups on 23rd July, 1941, the OKW simply briefed them as follows: "It is not in the demand for additional security detachments, but in the application of appropriate draconic measures that the commanding officers must use to keep order in the regions under their jurisdiction."

The OKW directive of 16th December, 1941, states:

"The troops . . . have the right and are obliged to apply . . . any measures whatsoever *also against women and children* if this contributes to success . . . ."

Among the most brutal OKW directives concerning the treatment of prisoners of war one must consider the order entitled "Night and Fog". The reasons for resorting to capital punishment for prisoners of war were offences, which according to international conventions, generally should not carry any punishment; for example, escape from the camp.

The order states:

"Penalty for such offences, consisting of loss of freedom and even a life sentence is a sign of weakness. Only death sentences or measures which entail ignorance of the fate of the guilty by local population will achieve real effectiveness."

In the course of the present trial a great deal of evidence of application of this order has been submitted. One example of this kind of crime is the murder of 50 officer-pilots. The fact that this crime was inspired by the High Command cannot be doubted.

OKW also issued an order for the destruction of the "Commando" units. The original order was submitted to the Court. According to this order, officers and soldiers of the "Commando" units had to be shot, except in cases when they were to be questioned, after which they were shot in any case.

This order was unswervingly carried out by the commanding officers of Army units. In June, 1944, Rundstedt, the Commander-in-Chief of the German troops in the West, reported that Hitler's order in regard to "the treatment of the Commando groups of the enemy is still being carried out".

3. *The High Command, along with the SS and the Police, is guilty of the most brutal police actions in the occupied regions.*

The instructions relating to special regions, issued by OKW on 13th March, 1941, contemplated the necessity of synchronising the activities in occupied territories between the Army Command and the Reichsfuehrer of the SS. As is seen from the testimony of the chief of the 3d Department of RSHA and who was concurrently chief of the Einsatzgruppe "D", Otto Ohlendorf, and of the chief of the VI Department of RSHA, Walter Schellenberg, in accordance with OKW instructions there was an agreement made between the general staff and the RSHA about the organisation of special "operational groups" of the Security Police and SD—"Einsatzgruppen" assigned to the appropriate army detachments.

Crimes committed by the Einsatzgruppen on the territory of the temporarily occupied regions are countless. The Einsatzgruppen were acting in close contact with the commanding officers of the appropriate army groups.

The following excerpt from the report of Einsatzgruppe "A" is extremely characteristic as evidence:

". . . among our functions is the establishment of personal liaison with the commanding officer both at the front and in the rear. It must be pointed out that the relations with the army were of the best, in some cases very close, almost hearty, as, for instance, the commander of the tank group, Colonel-General Hoppner".

4. *The representatives of the High Command acted in all the echelons of the army as members of a criminal group.*

In spite of the violation of international law and of the customs of war, the directives of the OKW and of the General Staff and the command of individual army units were applied in life and were augmented by even more brutal orders issued as implementation to these directives.

In this connection it is characteristic to note the directive of Field Marshal von Reichenau, Army group commander, addressed to his soldiers: "The soldier in the eastern territories is not only a warrior skilled in the art of warfare but a bearer of a merciless national ideology." And elsewhere, calling for the extermination of the Jews. Reichenau wrote: "Thus the soldier must be in full cognisance of the necessity for harsh and just revenge on those sub-humans, the Jews".

As another example the order of Field Marshal von Mannstein addressed to his soldiers can be referred to. On the basis of the "political aims of the war" the Field Marshal cynically appealed to his soldiers to wage the war in violation of the "recognised laws of warfare in Europe".

Thus, in the course of the hearing of evidence it has been proved beyond all doubt that the General Staff and the Supreme Command of the Hitlerite Army comprised a highly dangerous criminal organisation.

I consider it my duty as a Judge to draw up my dissenting opinion concerning those important questions in which I disagree with the decision adopted by the members of the Tribunal.

Soviet Member I.M.T.,
Major General Jurisprudence,
I. T. NIKITCHENKO.

Other titles in the series

John Profumo and Christine Keeler, 1963

"The story must start with Stephen Ward, aged fifty. The son of a clergymen, by profession he was an osteopath ... his skill was very considerable and he included among his patients many well-known people ... Yet at the same time he was utterly immoral."

The Backdrop

The beginning of the '60s saw the publication of 'Lady Chatterley's Lover' and the dawn of sexual and social liberation as traditional morals began to be questioned and in some instances swept away.

The Book

In spite of the spiralling spate of recent political falls from grace, The Profumo Affair remains the biggest scandal ever to hit British politics. The Minister of War was found to be having an affair with a call girl who had associations with a Russian Naval Officer at the height of the Cold War. There are questions of cover-up, lies told to Parliament, bribery and stories sold to the newspapers. Lord Denning's superbly written report into the scandal describes with astonishment and fascinated revulsion the extraordinary sexual behaviour of the ruling classes. Orgies, naked bathing, sado-masochistic gatherings of the great and good and ministers and judges cavorting in masks are all uncovered.

ISBN 0 11 702402 3

The Loss of the Titanic, 1912

"From 'Mesabe' to 'Titanic' and all east bound ships. Ice report in Latitude 42N to 41.25N; Longitude 49 to 50.30W. Saw much Heavy Pack Ice and a great number of Large Icebergs. Also Field Ice. Weather good. Clear."

The Backdrop

The watchwords were 'bigger, better, faster, more luxurious' as builders of ocean-going vessels strove to outdo each other as they raced to capitalise on a new golden age of travel.

The Book

The story of the sinking of the Titanic, as told by the official enquiry, reveals some remarkable facts which have been lost in popular re-tellings of the story. A ship of the same line, only a few miles away from the Titanic as she sank, should have been able to rescue passengers, so why did this not happen? Readers of this fascinating report will discover that many such questions remain unanswered and that the full story of a tragedy which has entered into popular mythology has by no means been told.

ISBN 0 11 702403 1

Tragedy at Bethnal Green, 1943

"Immediately the alert was sounded a large number of people left their houses in the utmost haste for shelter. A great many were running. Two cinemas at least in the near vicinity disgorged a large number of people and at least three omnibuses set down their passengers outside the shelter."

The Backdrop

The beleaguered East End of London had born much of the brunt of the Blitz but, in 1943, four years into WW2, it seemed that the worst of the bombing was over.

The Book

The new unfinished tube station at Bethnal Green was one of the largest air raid shelters in London. After a warning siren sounded on March 3, 1943, there was a rush to the shelter. By 8.20pm, a matter of minutes after the alarm had sounded, 174 people lay dead, crushed trying to get into the tube station's booking hall. At the official enquiry, questions were asked about the behaviour of certain officials and whether the accident could have been prevented.

ISBN 0 11 702404 X

The Judgement of Nuremberg, 1946

"Efficient and enduring intimidation can only be achieved either by Capital Punishment or by measures by which the relatives of the criminal and the population do not know the fate of the criminal. This aim is achieved when the criminal is transferred to Germany."

The Backdrop

WW2 is over, there is a climate of jubilation and optimism as the Allies look to rebuilding Europe for the future but the perpetrators of Nazi War Crimes have yet to be reckoned with, and the full extent of their atrocities is as yet widely unknown.

The Book

Today, we have lived with the full knowledge of the extent of Nazi atrocities for over half a century and yet they still retain their power to shock. Imagine what it was like as they were being revealed in the full extent of their horror for the first time. In this book the Judges at the Nuremberg Trials take it in turn to describe the indictments handed down to the defendants and their crimes. The entire history, purpose and method of the Nazi party since its foundation in 1918 is revealed and described in chilling detail.

ISBN 0 11 702406 6

The Boer War: Ladysmith and Mafeking, 1900

"4th February – From General Sir. Redfers Buller to Field-Marshall Lord Roberts … I have today received your letter of 26 January. White keeps a stiff upper lip, but some of those under him are desponding. He calculates he has now 7000 effectives. They are eating their horses and have very little else. He expects to be attacked in force this week … "

The Backdrop

The Boer War is often regarded as one of the first truly modern wars, as the British Army, using traditional tactics, came close to being defeated by a Boer force which deployed what was almost a guerrilla strategy in punishing terrain.

The Book

Within weeks of the outbreak of fighting in South Africa, two sections of the British Army were besieged at Ladysmith and Mafeking. Split into two parts, the book begins with despatches describing the losses at Spion Kop on the way to rescue the garrison at Ladysmith, followed by the army report as the siege was lifted. In the second part is Lord Baden Powell's account of the siege of Mafeking and how the soldiers and civilians coped with the hardship and waited for relief to arrive.

ISBN 0 11 702408 2

The British Invasion Tibet: Colonel Younghusband, 1904

"On the 13th January I paid ceremonial visit to the Tibetans at Guru, six miles further down the valley in order that by informal discussion might assure myself of their real attitude. There were present at the interview three monks and one general from Lhasa ... these monks were low-bred persons, insolent, rude and intensely hostile; the generals, on the other hand, were polite and well-bred."

The Backdrop

At the turn of the century, the British Empire was at its height, with its army in the forefront of the mission to bring what it saw as the tremendous civilising benefits of the British way of life to what it regarded as nations still languishing in the dark ages.

The Book

In 1901, a British Missionary Force under the leadership of Colonel Francis Younghusband crossed over the border from British India and invaded Tibet. Younghusband insisted on the presence of the Dalai Lama at meetings to give tribute to the British and their empire. The Dalai Lama merely replied that he must withdraw. Unable to tolerate such an insolent attitude, Younghusband marched forward and inflicted considerable defeats on the Tibetans in several onesided battles.

ISBN 0 11 702409 0

War 1914: Punishing the Serbs

" ... I said that this would make it easier for others such as Russia to counsel moderation in Belgrade. In fact, the more Austria could keep her demand within reasonable limits, and the stronger the justification she could produce for making any demands, the more chance there would be for smoothing things over. I hated the idea of a war between any of the Great Powers, and that any of them should be dragged into a war by Serbia would be detestable."

The Backdrop

In Europe before WW1, diplomacy between the Embassies was practised with a considered restraint and politeness which provided an ironic contrast to the momentous events transforming Europe forever.

The Book

Dealing with the fortnight leading up to the outbreak of the First World War, and mirroring recent events in Serbia to an astonishing extent. Some argued for immediate and decisive military action to punish Serbia for the murder of the Archduke Franz Ferdinand. Others pleaded that a war should not be fought over Serbia. The powers involved are by turn angry, conciliatory and, finally, warlike. Events take their course and history is changed.

ISBN 0 11 702410 4

War 1939: Dealing with Adolf Hitler

The Backdrop

As he presided over the rebuilding of a Germany shattered and
humiliated after WW1, opinion as to Hitler and his intentions
was divided and the question of whether his ultimate aim was
military aggression by no means certain.

The Book

Sir Arthur Henderson, the British ambassador in Berlin in 1939
describes here, in his report to Parliament, the failure of his
mission and the outbreak of war. He tells of his attempts to deal
with both Hitler and von Ribbentrop to maintain peace and
gives an account of the changes in German foreign policy
regarding Poland.

ISBN 0 11 702411 2

The Strange Story of Adolph Beck

*"He said he was Lord Winton de Willoughby. He asked why
I lived alone in a flat. I said I had an income and wished to do
so ... Two or three hours after he had gone I missed some tigers' claws
and the teeth of an animal mounted in silver with my monogram."*

The Backdrop

The foggy streets of Edwardian London were alive with cads,
swindlers and ladies of dubious reputation and all manner of
lowlife who fed on human frailty.

The Book

In 1895, Adolph Beck was arrested and convicted of the crimes
of deception and larceny. Using the alias Lord Winton de
Willoughby, he had entered into the apartments of several ladies,
some of whom preferred, for obvious reasons, not to give their
names. The ladies gave evidence, as did a handwriting expert, and
Mr Beck was imprisoned. But an utterly bizarre sequence of
events culminated in a judge who declared that, since he could
himself determine perfectly whether the accused is of the criminal classes, juries should never be allowed to decide the outcome
of a trial. The account given here is of one of the strangest true
stories in the entire British legal history.

ISBN 0 11 702414 7

Rillington Place

The Backdrop

The serial killer, or mass-murderer, is often seen as a creation of modern society but quiet killers, drawing no attention to themselves in the teeming streets of the metropolis, have been responsible for some of the most notorious crimes of the 20th century.

The Book

In 1949, Timothy Evans was hung for the self-confessed murder of his wife and daughter at 10 Rillington Place, Notting Hill but their bodies could not be found. Two years later, a couple moved into the same ground floor flat, vacated by a man named Christie. They discovered bodies in cupboards, Christie's wife under the floorboards and Evans wife and daughter in the garden shed. Christie was convicted of mass murder and hung. At two subsequent enquiries, it was suggested that Evans may not have been a murderer. So, why did he confess?

ISBN 0 11 702417 1

Wilfrid Blunt's Egyptian Garden : Fox-hunting in Cairo

"Cairo. July 23, 1901 — On Sunday morning a fox-hunt was taking place near Cairo, in the desert, the hounds following a scent crossed the boundary-wall of Mr. Wilfrid Blunt's property, and two of the field, being British officers, who were acting as whips, went in to turn them back. Mr. Blunt's watchmen surrounded them, and, although they explained their intention, treated them with considerable violence."

The Backdrop

In the days of Empire, the British way of life was carried on with a blithe disregard for local peculiarities and this went hand in hand with a sometimes benevolent, sometimes despotic, belief in the innate inferiority of those under its thumb.

The Book

In 1900, the Imperial British Army occupied Egypt and, in order to provide sport for the officers who were kicking their heels, a pack of hounds was shipped out from England to hunt the Egyptian fox. Unfortunately, the desert provides poor cover and, one day, the pack, followed in hot pursuit by the officers, found itself in the garden of the rich and eccentric poet Wilfrid Scarwen Blunt. Attempting to protect the absent Mr. Blunt's property, his servants tried to prevent the hunt and were promptly arrested. Mr. Blunt objected to the officer's behaviour, both to the government and the press and the matter became quite a scandal.

ISBN 0 11 702416 3

Wilfrid Blunt's Egyptian Garden: Fox-hunting in Cairo

"Cairo. July 23, 1901 – On Sunday morning a fox-hunt was taking place near Cairo, in the desert, the hounds following a scent crossed the boundary-wall of Mr. Wilfrid Blunt's property, and two of the field, being British officers, who were acting as whips, went in to turn them back. Mr. Blunt's watchmen surrounded them, and, although they explained their intention, treated them with considerable violence."

The Backdrop

In the days of Empire, the British way of life was carried on with a blithe disregard for local peculiarities and this went hand in hand with a sometimes benevolent, sometimes despotic, belief in the innate inferiority of those under its thumb.

The Book

In 1900, the Imperial British Army occupied Egypt and, in order to provide sport for the officers who were kicking their heels, a pack of hounds was shipped out from England to hunt the Egyptian fox. Unfortunately, the desert provides poor cover and, one day, the pack, followed in hot pursuit by the officers, found itself in the garden of the rich and eccentric poet Wilfrid Scarwen Blunt. Attempting to protect the absent Mr. Blunt's property, his servants tried to prevent the hunt and were promptly arrested. Mr. Blunt objected to the officer's behaviour, both to the government and the press and the matter became quite a scandal.

ISBN 0 11 702416 3